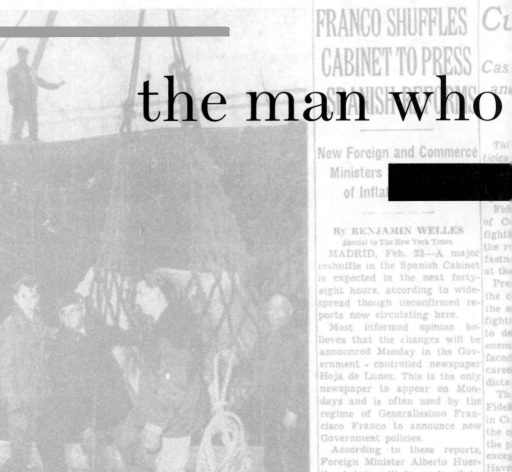

the man who

FRANCO SHUFFLES CABINET TO PRESS

New Foreign and Commerce
Ministers ▮▮▮▮▮▮▮▮
of Infla▮▮▮▮▮▮

By BENJAMIN WELLES
Special to The New York Times.

MADRID, Feb. 23—A major
reshuffle in the Spanish Cabinet
is expected in the next forty-
eight hours, according to widespread though unconfirmed reports now circulating here.

Most informed opinion be-
lieves that the changes will be
announced Monday in the Government - controlled newspaper
Hoja de Lunes. This is the only
newspaper to appear on Mon-
days and is often used by the
regime of Generalissimo Francisco Franco to announce new
Government policies.

According to these reports,
Foreign Minister Alberto Huer-
tin Artajo will be replaced by
Fernando Ma▮▮ ▮▮

Cu

Cas
an

Thi
ticles

Fid
of C
fighti
the r
fastn
at the

Pre
the c
the a
fighti
to de
enem
faced
caree
dicta

Th
Fidel
in Cu
the d
the p
excep
Havs

invented fidel

UBA, CASTRO, AND HERBERT L. MATTHEWS OF *THE NEW YORK TIMES*

Anthony DePalma

PublicAffairs

New York

Published in the United States by PublicAffairs™, a member of the
Perseus Books Group.

Book Design by Janet Tingey

Library of Congress Cataloging-in-Publication Data
DePalma, Anthony.
The man who invented Fidel : Castro, Cuba, and Herbert L.
    Matthews of the New York Times / Anthony DePalma
p. cm.
Includes bibliographical references and index.
ISBN–13: 978–1–58648–332–6
ISBN–10: 1–58648–332–3
1. Matthews, Herbert Lionel, 1900-1977. 2. Journalists—United
    States—Biography. 3. Castro, Fidel, 1926-. I. Title.
PN4874.M4836D47 2006
070.92—dc22
[B]
2005056493

First Edition

10 9 8 7 6 5 4 3 2 1

For Miriam
My treasure and my truth

And in Memory of
My Cherished Mother
Phyllis DePalma

"When the fakers are all dead they will read Matthews in the schools to find out what really happened."

—Ernest Hemingway

"The great enemy of the truth is very often not the lie—deliberate, contrived, and dishonest—but the myth—persistent, persuasive, and unrealistic."

—John F. Kennedy

"Our ideas are our weapons"

—Propaganda billboard in Cuba

CONTENTS

A lifetime of tracking down the truth had taught Herbert Lionel Matthews that there are no lies as powerful as myths, no truths more fragile than those no one wants to hear. It was myth, he believed, that had nearly ruined his forty-five-year career as editorial writer, reporter, and correspondent—one of the most influential yet controversial foreign correspondents of the twentieth century. And he blamed unpopular truths for making his life hell.

Now, in the winter of 1967, in a drafty villa on the French Riviera, huddled against the December breezes and the hoary demons of his past, Matthews was determined to tame those myths and unshackle those rejected truths. He sifted through the files he had brought with him when he retired from *The New York Times* a few months earlier, searching for evidence to prove he had been right all along. Then one day he stumbled across a long-lost scrap of paper that he had nearly forgotten about since he'd brought it back from the dead.

Matthews had figured the paper was gone for good. But there it was, tucked inside a dusty folder of photographs from Cuba that he hadn't looked through for years. Matthews couldn't remember the last time he had seen the paper, but he did recall the first time as though it were tattooed on the back of his faded brown eyes. Over a lifetime of extraordinary memories, spanning dozens of countries around the globe, nothing stood above the three hours he had spent in the rugged Sierra Maestra of southeastern Cuba while a boyish Fidel Castro whispered into his war-weary ears his hopes and dreams for a Cuba that never came to be. Knowing there would be doubters, Matthews had asked Castro to sign his interview notes. With a blue ink pen, Castro scrawled out his signature with self-confidence and precision, starting with an orthodox capital F, and capping it with a bold flourish, like the tail of a kite, that might have gotten his hands slapped in the Catholic schools he had attended as a boy. Then he put the date, February 17, 1957.

In those cha-cha days of the Cold War, when America flexed its military muscles around the globe and contented Americans lived like they had little to worry about but car payments and Communists, Matthews had journeyed into the almost impenetrable Cuban mountains and emerged with a sensational page-one, worldwide exclusive for *The New York Times:* Fidel Castro, widely thought to have been killed months before, was alive and well and destined to bring revolution to Cuba. His signature, ripped from Matthews's notes, was printed beneath a photograph of Castro emerging from the forest with a telescopic rifle and a face full of innocence. The interview at Castro's Sierra hideout became a turning point in the history of Cuba and, eventually, the United States, because it marked the beginning of Castro's rise to power. It made heroes of both Matthews and Castro, at least for a while. Then, as Castro embraced communism, and American enthusiasm for the youthful, bearded rebel faded, the historic encounter came to be seen as a fool's errand, or worse. Either Castro had manipulated a gullible Matthews, or a sympathetic Matthews had taken the rebel's side. For years following that fleeting encounter in the Sierra, Matthews tried to explain his side of the story. Hardly anyone believed him, not even those he most expected to understand.

When Matthews retired from the *Times*, there was no big send-off for him, no party, no champagne, no long-winded speeches or falsely congratulatory slaps on the back. He refused to have any of it, telling colleagues that celebrating his retirement would be like attending his own funeral. A common enough sentiment, perhaps, but in Matthews's case it was more complicated because it was his own reputation that had nearly died, the victim of savage criticism from outside the paper, as well as from within. He had few friends left in the newsroom. When it was time to go, he just turned out the lights of his office on the tenth floor of the newspaper's Times Square headquarters and walked out, passing quietly through the revolving brass doors in the lobby without looking back.

He took off for a friend's apartment in Cap d'Antibes on the French Riviera. During the 1950s, when Matthews thought of himself as being at the top of his game, the Cap d'Antibes had been considered one of the most seductively attractive places on earth, a mecca for movie stars and the wealthy, who loved to lounge there under gentle breezes and the admiring eyes of others. But now the old resort had started to fall out of fashion, as he had too. Painfully thin and frail looking, with sullen, suspicious eyes, he spent much of his time there indoors, out of the off-season sun, sorting through the voluminous files he had brought with him as he worked on a biography of Castro that he hoped would set the record straight about Castro and about himself.

The scrap of paper with Castro's signature was the key to understanding how his entire life had been turned upside down. And it was more than that. It represented the volatility of truth, and the imperfect nature of journalism. The signature was Matthews's proof that he had seen Castro and had talked to him about the revolution. That at least was certain, an indisputable fact. But if Matthews's portrait of Castro had turned out to be wrong, was it because he did not get it right in the first place, or because Castro's complex character had metamorphosed over time? Which had been the real Fidel Castro in 1957—the young man who had embraced democracy before signing Matthews's notes, or the Communist demagogue who has raged against *Yanqui* imperialists for five decades?

He had done what he had always believed a newspaperman is supposed to do—be present where and when important things happen. He boasted that he had never reported anything he did not believe to be true. But the truth can hurt, and the Cold War paranoia of those days had distorted the very notion of truth. The 1950s were a critical time for journalism. Television was becoming more powerful as Edward R. Murrow went head to head with Senator Joseph McCarthy over his ruinous witch hunt for Communists. And the traditional news media were starting to abandon the patriotic sympathies of World War II for a more skeptical relationship with government. Matthews, who became a print superstar just as newspapers were falling beneath television's shadow, ended up being blamed for helping bring Communists to the Western Hemisphere. He was accused of being anti-American. Even worse, when his own newspaper thought he was too close to the story, it prohibited him from reporting on the subject he knew better than any newspaperman in North America. Despite the ban, Matthews kept drifting back to the Cuba story. He agreed with some of his few supporters, who pointed out that blaming him for what happened in Cuba made no more sense than blaming a meteorologist for the storm he forecast. Yet that is what he felt had happened, and it made him more determined than ever to dispel the myths, look behind the legends, and tell the truth.

And where exactly does the myth end, and truth begin? That was the question I started out with several years ago when I began to look at Castro's earliest days as a rebel. For me, investigating Herbert Matthews's story became a personal exploration of the very nature of truth.

Early in 2001, an editor at the *Times* asked me to write Castro's advance obituary, an assignment that I welcomed because of my personal interest in Latin America, where I had worked as a foreign correspondent for the *Times*, and my fascination with troublesome, intriguing Cuba, birthplace of my wife, Miriam, and where she lived until just after the revolution. I, like most journalists, had heard the apocryphal tale about Matthews's failure long before, and I knew that an obituary of Castro in the *Times* would have to lay out that controversial event in detail. But something about it bothered me. The popular story had Castro marching his men in circles around Matthews to fool him into thinking he had a much larger army, and from that simple ruse Castro had built his revolution. I didn't buy it. I had seen a similar attempt at guerrilla theater in 1994 in the jungle of Chiapas, Mexico. A masked rebel leader who called himself Subcommandante Marcos was putting on a political show that he had named the Democratic National Convention just before the fractious 1994 presidential election. Thousands of leftist sympathizers from around the world sat on crude benches made of tree limbs in an amphitheater that Marcos's Indian followers had carved into the side of a mountain. At one point in the show, Marcos tried to impress the crowd by ordering his soldiers to march in front of the stage. Even with martial music blaring and the huge crowd pressing in, I easily recognized the same battered .22 rifle stock carried by an Indian soldier as soon as he came around the stage a second time. The green bandanna sticking out of another soldier's back pocket confirmed the chicanery. Marcos's attempt to deceive the crowd was so crude that it was hard for me to believe that any but the most naive would ever fall for such a trick.

And the more I learned about Matthews, the less I could accept the notion that he had been tricked in the same way. I read his books, starting with the Castro biography he wrote in Antibes, and looked through every article he published about Cuba, starting with the Sierra interview. I found them to be far more powerful and much less professional than I expected. They burned with raw passion that sometimes crystallized into an unmistakable bias toward Castro. I tried to pry the truth from the myth that had formed over Castro and the revolution, and my curiosity turned to doubt. Some parts of Matthews's past suggested he was an ideologue, a Socialist sympathizer not above using his position to further a cause. But he was also scrupulously honest about his writing, and self-critical about his reporting, admitting mistakes of fact but insisting that he never wrote anything that he did not believe to be true at the time he wrote it. That contradiction raised questions about the nature of the truth itself. If the truth that is reported turns out later to be something else, was it truth in the first place? And if, as it seemed, those early accounts influenced American policy decisions about dealing with Cuba and Castro, was Matthews to blame?

Shortly after I completed Castro's obituary, terrorists attacked New York City and Washington, D.C. Many things changed in the months and years that followed, and at times it seemed that truth itself had been redefined. I came to realize that the difficulties Matthews had gone through were similar to those in the air at the dawn of the twenty-first century. The Cold War of Matthews's time was like the war on terror in our time—both unconventional confrontations representing a clash of ideas, without fixed fronts or conventional military strategies. Both brewed suspicion and painted dissenters as the enemy—the McCarthyism of the 1950s has been reborn as the obsession of the age of terrorism. Matthews suspected, but never fully grasped, the extent to which Cold War hysteria distorted American foreign policy. A veteran correspondent who had covered the Italian invasion of Ethiopia, the Spanish Civil War, and all of World War II with energy and bravery, Matthews was no stranger to weapons or war. His newspaper clips showed that he was a keen observer, a facile writer, and a perceptive reporter, one whom Ernest Hemingway once described as "brave as a badger." As my research continued, I found it more difficult to imagine such a man being duped by Castro. The question then became even more complex, for if he had not been fooled by Castro, did he take sides early in the Cuban story and deliberately distort the truth?

As the war on terror turned into the war in Iraq, and weapons of mass destruction could not be found, newspapers, especially the *Times*, came under attack. First it was a young reporter named

Jayson Blair who had deliberately deceived his readers and editors. That was, the *Times* said, a "low point in the 152-year history of the newspaper." Then, two years later, one of the paper's star reporters, Judith Miller, got caught up in the investigation of a White House leak that raised new questions about her misleading pre-war stories on weapons of mass destruction in Iraq. She came in for furious criticism over her reliance on a questionable Iraqi source, Ahmed Chalabi, and on Bush administration officials who had apparently tried to manipulate her as they made a case for war. "If your sources are wrong, you are wrong," Miller said, an eerie echo of Matthews's reporting on Castro a half century earlier. During the hand-wringing and self-flagellation that followed both incidents, Matthews's name was often mentioned, along with that of another controversial *Times* correspondent, Walter Duranty. Editors at the *Times* distanced themselves from Duranty's work in the Soviet Union, and from the Pulitzer Prize he won in 1932 for stories that were overly sympathetic to Stalin's regime. The editors forced Blair to resign, then publicly criticized Miller before she was forced to resign. But when it came to Matthews and his reporting on Cuba, they were silent.

Finding out whether Matthews deserved to be included in the same category as Duranty and Blair, and later Miller, was one of my goals as I was drawn deeper into his life. Before he left the *Times*, Matthews acknowledged that he was, indeed, the man who had invented Fidel. And he was proud of it, believing that his act of creation enabled him, more than any other journalist, to be on the front line of the truth. As someone interested in the history of U.S. relations with Latin America, I needed to know what role, if any, Matthews had played in turning a nation that by all rights should have been our neighbor into one of our fiercest and most dangerous enemies. I found myself in a peculiar situation regarding Matthews, whom I never knew. My first byline in the *Times* appeared a year after he died in 1977. But as I was preparing the obituary that would announce Castro's death, I needed to understand how Matthews had resurrected Castro from the dead. I needed to know whether Matthews had fallen into the trap of believing that there was no truth but the version of it that he, him-self, had grasped. Until he died, Matthews was firmly convinced that history would rescue him and his reputation, little realizing that half a century later his interview with Castro would remain as controversial as ever, a singular moment of Cold War paranoia that survives as though sealed in a bottle that has been bobbing in a sea of rhetoric and recrimination ever since.

No matter what Matthews wrote later on about Castro or about his own life, the story always came back to those days in early 1957 when only he knew with certainty whether Castro had managed to survive the bumbling episode that he called his invasion of Cuba.

CHAPTER 1

could anything be madder?

Saturday, December 1, 1956
Off the southeast coast of Cuba

They listened.

Smothered by the darkness of that winter night, they listened, and as they strained to hear the voice it grew fainter.

"Aquí! Aquí! Aquí!"

The waters were as black as the night was dense, a perfect blanket that absorbed every scrap of light and deflected every sound. For a week, the eighty-two men jammed aboard the battered sixty-one-foot wooden pleasure boat had held their tongues, speaking in tones no bolder than a whisper so they could slip unnoticed past the patrols set up by Fulgencio Batista, the Cuban dictator they had vowed to overthrow. Now, drenched with panic, they damned the night and the sea that had taken one of them.

"Here!" The voice was fading, like footsteps down a city street.

Only the men who were closest knew that it was Roberto Roque who had climbed to the slippery top of the captain's cabin searching for a glimmer of light. By their calculations, the Cabo Cruz lighthouse, on the heavily forested tip of Oriente Province, about 500 miles east of Havana, should have been blinking on the horizon. Holding onto a crossbar attached to the boat's antenna, he had leaned forward, straining for a glimpse of anything up ahead to give the men hope that they were nearing land. But there was nothing.

It was a sign of the improbable nature of their mission that they seemed unable to find their way home. After all, Cuba is by far the largest island in the Caribbean, with 2,319 miles of coastline and several mountain ranges, including the rugged Sierra Maestra in Oriente with Pico Turquino towering above everything. The island is smeared across the aquamarine waters of the Caribbean like the smoke from a campfire, billowing directly toward the intimidating shores of the United States. And like fire, it is hot and ethereal, from sultry Santiago de Cuba in the east, to sophisticated Havana in the west. In between are farms, beaches, railroads, factories, museums, opera houses, elegantly dressed women, and slick, dark-haired businessmen, an entire, exotic, magical world unto itself. And they couldn't find it.

Roque started to lower himself onto the mass of arms and legs tangled like rope on the deck just as a wave rocked the old boat. He lost his grip.

"Stop the engines," someone shouted. All the men who could get up peered over the side, but it was like staring into a mine shaft.

"Here!"

The Dominican pilot, Pichirilo Mejías, pulled hard on the wheel to bring the old ship around, navigating entirely on hope. He kept circling, circling, but it was useless. How could they find a man's head bobbing like a coconut in the water when they couldn't even locate the jagged coast of Cuba? The men were tired, and hungry, and sick of the sea that had tortured them for the last seven days as they crossed the Gulf from Tuxpan, Mexico, to the waters off the southeastern coast of their bewitching homeland. They were already despairingly behind schedule. They had listened on their scratchy shipboard radio as the insurrection they were supposed to have launched began without them in Santiago de Cuba and quickly died out. While their comrades were being arrested or murdered, they remained two days out to sea.

"Here!"

Roque's voice had almost faded completely and several of the men began to panic. Everything was going wrong, and they had not yet fired a single shot. They all had vowed to give everything, including their lives. That's what they had trained for under the old Spanish colonel in Mexico who drilled them in handling a rifle and marching for days without complaining. That's what they were prepared for as they loaded their arms and ammunition aboard the worm-eaten yacht that its former American owner had affectionately christened the *Granma*. And that's what they had focused on as they hugged their stomachs and hung their heads in pails as forty-knot El Norte winds rocked their ridiculously over-crowded boat and tossed it from one gut-twisting wave to the next like a toy most of the way from Mexico. Now, weak-kneed and stinking of vomit and diesel fuel, they were not prepared for the first one of them to die without a fight.

Forty-five minutes had gone by, each minute adding to the dreadful notion that the mission itself, like Roque, was doomed. Then, when they feared they'd have to leave him behind, their commander ordered the boat's searchlight turned on, even though it would give away their position. They heard Roque's voice again, much weaker, filled with fear more than insistence.

"Here."

Mejías, the pilot, spotted him first, and then several others helped to fish Roque out of the water. They pulled him on board, dripping cold water and fear. Once more, it seemed, misfortune had threatened their God-forsaken mission, but they had managed to avoid disaster. They looked to their *jefe* for reassurance. Fidel Castro remained resolute, and they pushed on.

Circling to find Roque had confused the pilot and thrown the boat further off course. By the time the lookouts spotted flashes from the Cabo Cruz lighthouse, the first strands of day had already started to weave through the darkness. A blue mist clung to the surface of the sea as they slid into shallower waters. The dim outline of trees peered out at them through the gray dawn. Silently, the *Granma*'s wooden hull scratched against a sandy bottom and lurched to a halt, unable to go farther or to dislodge itself.

They still were 100 yards or more from the first trees, which they could see in the distance as they peeled off their stinking clothes and put on new olive-drab uniforms with the red-and-black arm insignia of the 26th of July Movement on their shoulders. They pulled on new boots. They pried boxes open and Castro thrust rifles and sidearms still smelling of packing oil into their hands.

Despite the wretchedness of his men, despite the damage already caused by his logistical shortcomings, Castro remained confident. The thought of setting foot on Cuban soil again after nearly eighteen months in exile helped him overlook all that had gone wrong. Such setbacks were insignificant compared to what they were about to accomplish. For the first time in its long, troubled history, Cuba was going to be freed of all colonial chains. It would not have to bear the Spanish colonial yoke that had made Cuba the first of Spain's colonies in the New World, and the last that the decrepit empire surrendered, doing so only after losing the war with the United States in 1898. Nor would Cuba any longer be the corrupt American pseudo-colony that had oozed into existence as the Spanish departed, with Washington propping up one crooked president after another. No, this revolution that they were about to launch would free Cuba once and for all, and though he had not thought out its final outcome, nor realistically assessed how Cuba could be led afterward, or by whom, Castro realized that his revolution would be a battle of ideas, like the one waged by his hero José Martí. He did not need to have an army that was bigger than Batista's to win. For his war he just needed stout hearts and resonant voices to urge them on. He had some sense of what he would do after his victory, and which ideas would triumph, but no definitive plan for how he was going to lead Cuba, or where. That would come later. Now his focus was on fulfilling the vow he had first made in 1955 during a fund-raising trip to New York and then repeated everywhere he went. "We will be free or we will be martyrs by the end of 1956," he had sworn earnestly and repeatedly. It was now just before dawn, December 2, 1956.

The *Granma* was dead in the water. A dingy, piled high with equipment and supplies, was lowered over the side, but it tilted precariously and tipped over, sinking immediately and taking with it many of the supplies the men were counting on for survival. There wasn't time for them to do anything else but jump into the water themselves. Even the lightest of them sank to their hips, and all had to hold their rifles high overhead. The landing had been far off the mark. Instead of unloading at the sandy beach where they expected sympathizers to be waiting with trucks, firearms, and supplies, they were in a mangrove swamp that snared their boots, slashed their arms and hands, and made each step a struggle.

It was morning and they were dangerously exposed. Batista had feared just such an invasion and had put his military on alert. A passing barge had reported that the *Granma* had run aground in an area where no navigator in his right mind would try to land unless his goal was to stay out of sight. With Santiago under his control, the local army commander believed this was the invasion everyone had been waiting for. Army planes found the *Granma* but couldn't pinpoint the invasion forces in the mangrove thicket. They flew low over the area, strafing the treetops indiscriminately. Hidden by the dense forest, Castro's men could practically see into the cockpits as the planes thundered over.

At about 7:00 AM, on the morning of December 2, some three hours after leaving the *Granma,* the first rebels staggered out of the mangroves onto the fine white sand and collapsed. They rested only briefly before the order came to move up the beach and into the thin woods at the edge of the sand. They approached the hut of a local peasant. No one knew whether the man had ever heard of Fidel Castro, and they were relieved when he offered them food and water. They took a moment to scrape the mud from their uniforms. Juan Manuel Márquez, one of Castro's captains, said, "It wasn't a landing, it was a shipwreck," and the others laughed. Just as they were about to taste what the peasant had offered them, they heard explosions. They could not be certain if it was an aerial bombardment or a Coast Guard cutter's long guns, but the explosives came closer, and they had no clue where to go.

Sunday, December 2, 1956
Havana

It was another Sunday in Havana. The old city beat with a genteel laziness that filled the white streets like the echoing clip-clop of a horse-drawn carriage. Sunday had long before been drained of any real ambition in La Capital except for attending mass or visiting family. For those without a strong commitment to either of those powerful poles of Cuban life, Sunday was nothing more than another day, shortened by hours of extra sleep.

Half the day had already slipped by and it was early afternoon by the time R. Hart Phillips showed up at *The New York Times* office on the second floor of the ancient Spanish-style house on Refugio Street, within sight of the Presidential Palace in Old Havana. No American correspondent in Cuba knew more about the country than Phillips, who used her first initial rather than her given name—Ruby—to throw off critics who might not trust a female correspondent at a time when nearly all correspondents were men and women were supposed to stick to writing for the society pages. She had been given a chance to work because a place like Cuba played a distant second fiddle to the greater drama of the Cold War. The focus of the United States was on the Soviet Union, and on containing communism wherever it threatened to pop up. Latin America was largely controlled by right-wing dictators. Interest in the region flared briefly in 1953 when Guatemala's president, Jacobo Arbenz, looked and sounded like a Communist and the CIA engineered a coup to replace him. But Cuba was considered comfortably secure. Batista, a mixed-race former sergeant who was undoubtedly corrupt, governed it with an iron fist. He had first seized power in 1933 and had been in charge on and off ever since.

Though there had been Communists in Batista's early governments, he had chased them out after staging another coup in 1952. Washington tolerated Batista, so long as he cooperated with American needs, and Washington expected a Cuban president to know what those needs were without being told. The United States had been directly involved in controlling Cuba since Theodore Roosevelt's Rough Riders charged San Juan Hill in 1898, but it had resisted the temptation to annex Cuba, as some nascent imperialists had urged. However, Washington found an alternative that was almost as satisfying. The 1903 Platt Amendment to the new Cuban constitution gave Washington the right to intervene in Cuban affairs, making Cuba a virtual puppet of the United States and delaying any significant changes in the nation's social order. American troops landed on Cuban shores several times before the amendment was formally revoked under President Franklin D. Roosevelt in 1934. But even afterward, the American ambassador in Havana remained one of the most important men in Cuba, in some ways more powerful than whoever sat in the Presidential Palace. American officials and journalists saw Cuba the same way that most Americans who traveled there to play and gamble saw it—as a friendly and familiar extension of the United States.

Ruby Phillips had made a comfortable life for herself in Havana. Rough-edged and tough, she was a bundle of nervous energy enveloped by the smoke of cigarettes she was almost never without. She had gotten used to living on little more than milk for weeks at a time because of the ulcers she believed were caused by her work. She knew presidents and generals, and everyone, it seemed, knew Ruby.

That's why she was so furious when, having just arrived at the office that Sunday afternoon, more out of duty than necessity, she took a message from a *Times* editor in New York who wanted to know more about a few paragraphs that had come across the

United Press wire that morning. The report claimed that rebels, led by the mysterious Fidel Castro, had tried to invade the island but were annihilated as they landed. Phillips was used to being tipped off in advance by her network of informants, but this time the network had failed her and she knew nothing about an invasion. She called her contact in Manzanillo, on the southeastern coast of Cuba, and he told her what little he knew—rumors were spreading fast that Castro had arrived in a yacht from Mexico. The army claimed to have killed him and most of the men with him almost immediately.

It took little time for Phillips to confirm that the invasion had taken place. From army headquarters she learned that General Pedro Rodríguez Ávila, the commanding officer of the area, had ordered planes to strafe and bomb the beach and mangrove swamp where the insurgents had come ashore. They claimed to have killed forty of them, including Fidel himself and his younger brother, Raúl.

As she worked the phones, Phillips cursed Castro. For some reason, he always seemed to pick Sundays—the hardest day of the week to get anyone to confirm anything—to launch his revolutions. He had chosen July 26, 1953—a Sunday morning—to attack the Moncada military barracks in Santiago, the second most heavily armed and guarded military installation in Cuba. It was a carnival weekend, and he had hoped to catch the guards sleeping off their previous night's celebration. But the plan quickly fell apart and the soldiers easily routed the invaders. Fidel and Raúl were taken alive, and after a sensational trial, both were sentenced to prison on the Isle of Pines—Raúl for thirteen years, Fidel for fifteen. There they had remained until Batista gave in to pressure from opposition groups to release hundreds of political prisoners, including the Castro brothers. Thinking he had little to fear from the failed revolutionaries who had led so many of their followers to their deaths, Batista signed an amnesty bill. The brothers strode out of prison in May 1955, more fanatically dedicated to revolution than before.

Now, little more than a year and a half after Castro had been freed, Phillips was again chasing his trail. She called the other news service reporter in Havana who worked for Associated Press, but he had nothing more than United Press. Unable to confirm Castro's death, Phillips told her New York editors she had doubts about the story. It frustrated her to know she didn't have much influence in New York, and certainly could not match the authority of someone like Herbert Matthews, who surely would be breathing down her neck once he got news of the invasion. If *he* were to tell the editors not to run the UP report, there'd be no question it would be held; but Ruby didn't have that kind of clout. Hard news was scarce on this December Sunday, and the weekend editors had decided to use the sensational dispatch in part because of the level of detail it contained. The UP correspondent, Francis L. McCarthy, had reported that the army had identified the remains of Fidel and his brother by the documents taken from their bullet-riddled bodies.

Despite her many years in Havana—she'd taken over as correspondent when her husband, James Doyle Phillips, who covered Cuba for the *Times*, was killed in an automobile accident in 1937—Ruby Phillips couldn't convince her editors to hold the story while she checked the facts. It ran in the Monday morning paper on the top of page one. The continuation on the inside pages carried one of the first photographs of Castro to appear in the newspaper. The caption beneath it announced that he was dead.

Few people in Havana knew what had happened on the beach in Oriente, and fewer still were at all shocked by the notion that Castro had led his followers to another defeat. Just like Moncada, they said. And what could he have been thinking? At that moment in late 1956, Cuba seemed an unlikely place for a revolution. Tourism was booming, and Phillips had learned from her interviews with business leaders that economic indicators were about as favorable as they had ever been. Cuba was still paradise, a corrupt paradise perhaps, but life there was good for many Cubans. A revolution in good times—it was puzzling.

Monday, December 3
New York

Herbert Matthews got to his office in Times Square that Monday morning and read the news from Havana with disbelief. He had not seen this coming, not this soon anyway. The tall, thin, slightly stooped member of the newspaper's editorial board did not know Cuba the way Ruby Phillips did, but he usually had a good news-paperman's sense of where the trouble spots were. He had visited the island a few times since Batista's coup in 1952 and had been moderately impressed by the dictator's pragmatic style. Latin America hadn't originally been Matthews's to cover when he became an editorial writer in 1949. But he soon found out that nobody else had any interest in writing about the hemisphere because it played practically no role in the Cold War. Matthews made himself an expert on the region. He took his wife, Nancie, on regular tours of Central and South America, stopping in to see presidents and to take the pulse of capital cities from Montevideo to Mexico City. It was one of the small ways he could compensate for having had to give up the work that had been the consuming passion of his life.

As one of the newspaper's most daring foreign correspondents in the 1930s and 1940s, Matthews had found himself at the center of almost every major conflict in the Western world. He was there during the Italian invasion of Ethiopia and the rise of fascism. He was on the ground during the Spanish Civil War, and later he covered the American invasion of Italy, reported on floundering British rule in India, and kept track of the postwar reconstruction of Europe from London. In 1949, an ailing heart and advancing middle age combined to bring him back to New York.

It was far from a punishment. Matthews was given a spacious office on the tenth floor of the Times Building and was free to travel, to think, and to write. Like the other editorialists, he would not be allowed to sign his name to most of the editorials he wrote. Still, the new position was as close as he would come to the academic world where he always felt he belonged.

But Matthews was a scholar with a deadline, an intellectual with printer's ink on his hands and a soldier's tolerance for danger in his heart. Although he had been with the paper since 1922, and considered New York his home, he felt like a stranger working in the building after so many years outside. For him, the most fundamental rule of journalism was to be out where things were happening. Being forced to report to work in an office every day violated his sense of himself as a pure-blooded correspondent. He was still footloose and ready for adventure when he returned to New York, and he certainly wasn't about to leave reporting for good. Fluent in Spanish and experienced in the affairs of Europe, Matthews wrote both editorials and news articles about Latin America. It was a breach of the newspaper's long-standing policy of separating news from opinions, but it had the blessing of the publisher, Arthur Hays Sulzberger. Years before, Matthews had made a point of becoming friends with Sulzberger and his wife, Iphigene, whom he picked to be godmother to his son, Eric. Matthews's seniority, his extensive experience on the front line, and his imperious bearing meant few dared to stand in his way.

When he read about the bungled invasion in Cuba, Matthews knew virtually nothing of Castro, but he had a strong opinion about Cuba's historic instability. With Monday morning's article about the deadly fiasco still clear in his mind, Matthews wrote an editorial in which he voiced one inescapable conclusion: The Cuban people seemed to have a peculiar nature that invited violence and precluded any chance for sustained stability. In the editorial, which ran in the next day's newspaper, Matthews interpreted the attempted invasion as another psychological symptom of a country too uncertain of its own independence to make a real commitment to democracy. As for Castro, Matthews saw nothing impressive about his harebrained plot, which he called "pathetic." He derided Castro's invasion and the way the rebel leader had announced in advance that he was going to invade Cuba. "Could anything be madder?" he asked.

Matthews had seen more than his share of invasions and insurrections, and he found little to cheer about in this latest incident.

He wasn't convinced that the initial reports of Castro's death could be taken as the truth, especially after Batista's spokesman called the whole invasion another propaganda trick of the Castro brothers. Matthews considered Batista a relatively good president because he had put volatile Cuba back on firm economic footing. But he criticized him for staging the 1952 coup, and later he condemned the dictator's strong-arm tactics toward the opposition. In concluding the editorial, Matthews blithely wrote off Castro's chances of success: "How could a revolution, proclaimed in advance, succeed against a regime like General Batista's, which controls the army and has its loyalty? There was not the slightest hope that a revolt could succeed in the present circumstances."

Tuesday, December 4
Havana

Ruby Phillips took little satisfaction from the latest information coming out of the palace. Batista's spokesman had denied the earlier reports that Castro had been killed in Oriente, proving the editors should have listened to her and not run the unconfirmed wire service article about the invasion on the front page of Monday's paper. Her own doubts had multiplied when she found out that UP's sole source had been an overzealous Cuban pilot impressed with his own heroics. The pilot had even provided the UP correspondent with the location of shallow graves in Punta de Las Coloradas where the corpses of Castro and the other rebels were supposedly buried. All the information turned out to be false, as Phillips had suspected. The body was not Fidel's. But if not, where was he? Had he even been aboard the decrepit yacht? She heard rumors that Castro was still in Mexico.

Phillips did not leave her office in Havana to investigate. She rarely did. After more than three decades in Havana, she believed it was more important to know what was happening than to see it. She got in touch with her sources in Oriente and in the Presidential Palace. They provided her with enough information to file a string of stories over the next few days detailing the army's pursuit of the rebels, as the group, originally believed to have numbered anywhere from 120 to 400, made its way eastward from the coast toward the heart of the Sierra Maestra. Batista was so little concerned about Castro that he did not interrupt his scheduled canasta game. He thought of Castro as a gangster with crazy political ideas. He was convinced Castro was a Communist. That alone, Batista believed, guaranteed that the Americans would back him and not Castro for as long as he wanted to stay in office.

Batista already had at least 600 men in the foothills of the Sierra Maestra, and hundreds of reinforcements were on the way to set up a security perimeter around the forbidding mountains. Army planes were ordered to drop leaflets encouraging the rebels to surrender. Local peasants who encountered groups of rebels in the woods informed military authorities where they could be found. The government even produced one of the captured insurgents, José Díaz, of Pinar del Rio, who said Castro had shot him in the side when he had tried to surrender. By the end of the week, Phillips reported that the surviving rebels, "under relentless attack by Government troops," were on the verge of surrendering.

Friday, December 28
New York

As 1956 came to an end, most Americans thought about Cuba the way Robert Wagner did. The popular mayor of New York City cut short his daily schedule on Friday afternoon, December 28, and ordered his limousine driver to take him and his family to Idlewild Airport to catch a direct flight to Havana. They would arrive in time for dinner and planned to stay in Cuba for a post-Christmas week of fun and relaxation. The death of Fidel, and the elimination of his rebel forces, seemed to make Cuba safe again and took the worry out of going there. Russia and China were dangerous places. So was Eastern Europe, especially Hungary. But not Cuba.

Cuba was still a fantasyland, a foreign paradise about the size of Ohio that could be treated like an American playground blessed with blissful weather and perfect beaches. The big American hotels, and the gambling casinos inside them, attracted even more American vacationers. The lushest gambling palace of all, the Hotel Riviera, built with mob money, was scheduled to open in a few months. American English was graciously tolerated and American dollars gleefully accepted. The money left behind by gamblers and vacationers created a boom for the Cuban government, which took a healthy share of the proceeds for itself.

As temperatures dropped and the excitement of Christmas in New York passed, getting out of the city was on the minds of many residents besides the mayor. Herbert Matthews had accumulated some vacation time, so he and Nancie talked about getting away for a few days in the sunny Caribbean. Though disgusted by Castro's pitiful invasion, Matthews sensed that it was a good time to visit Cuba. He kept track of what was going on by reading the wires and the imperfect reports filed by Ruby Phillips, even though he believed she did not measure up to the standards of the *Times*. He suspected that she had been in Cuba too long, had grown too close to Batista and his circle of thugs to be trusted.

January 1957
Havana

As a fateful new year began, Ruby Phillips published an economic analysis of Cuba. She concluded that Batista was taking care of the country's worst problems by pushing through a huge public works program financed in part by sugar sales, which had been Cuba's economic mainspring for generations. Construction cranes were everywhere, and work proceeded on big public works projects such as a long traffic tunnel beneath Havana harbor to finally link the two sides of the city. It began immediately in front of the Presidential Palace—this way, no one would forget who was responsible for modernizing Cuba. A spike in world demand had forced the price of sugar to surge to its highest level since 1951. The only "discordant note" that Phillips observed was the threat of inflation, and she did not include a single word in the report about civil unrest, though she knew it existed. Batista had lashed out at the resistance movement, ordering a wave of repression that had culminated in what many Cubans called Batista's "Christmas present." A particularly vicious army commander in Oriente, far from Havana's casinos, executed twenty-two men from the urban resistance. To ensure that the government's anti-terrorism message was absolutely clear, the commander ordered the bodies of several youths to be hanged from trees during the Christmas holidays.

Still, Batista seemed to have a solid grip on his nation. Washington was so favorably impressed with the dictator's ability to maintain stability that the U.S. government signed an agreement to guarantee American investments in Cuba. Economic ties between the two countries grew stronger. The *Times* reported that the American and Foreign Power Company planned to start construction on a 10,000-kilowatt nuclear reactor in Cuba, the first atomic plant in Latin America. Cuba's Communications Ministry acted as if there wasn't the slightest threat to the Batista dictatorship. It focused its efforts on banning rock-and-roll dance programs from Cuban television because the shows were "immoral and profane and offensive to public morals and good customs."

Matthews suspected that something else was worrying Batista. It had to be serious enough to explain why he had clamped down on television, radio, and newspapers on January 15, prohibiting them from giving any news of civil unrest for a period of forty-five days. Officially, the reason for the censorship was to prevent rumors from interrupting the sugar harvest. But its real purpose was to keep the rebels—wherever they were and however many had survived the landing—out of sight. The ban raised Matthews's suspicions and made him wonder why there were so many disturbances in a country that seemed to be doing so well. He hadn't been able to trust any news coming from Cuba since censors had taken up posts inside the offices of foreign correspondents in Havana. He wasn't even comfortable with private communications from Ruby Phillips because every letter into and out of Havana was opened, every telephone conversation monitored by the government.

In an editorial published on January 18, Matthews used

Batista's censorship order to drive home the point that there was more going on in Cuba than was apparent from the government's calm reassurances. "Cuba is compounding her undoubted troubles over terrorism by an unjustified censorship of the press and radio. At least one can see nothing in what is known of developments in the island to warrant such a drastic move," he wrote a few days after censorship was imposed. Cuban censors scoured copies of the *Times* and other foreign newspapers for news about the insurgency or student dissidents and the civil resistance in Santiago. Censorship, Matthews argued, conveys a sense of desperation, which seemed unwarranted in Cuba at the time. "General Batista still has the Army behind him," he wrote. "The recent invasion by terrorists has been liquidated. The economic situation is good, with sugar prices very high and the demand strong."

But through his network of sources, Matthews picked up information suggesting that the invaders had not been "liquidated" and that Batista's extreme reaction showed how afraid he was that a loose spark might set off a wildfire. He laid down a challenge for the dictator: "If President Batista has some special, secret information to show that the Cuban situation is graver than it looks," Matthews wrote, "he should come out with it."

A short time after that editorial ran, Matthews received an unexpected call from the *Times*'s foreign editor, Emanuel R. Freedman, who relayed a brief and cryptic message from Ruby Phillips in Havana that set in motion a sequence of events that would sweep all involved into the flow of history.

message from the mountains

"They say you are dead."

—THE PEASANT EUTIMIO GUERRA,
TO FIDEL CASTRO IN EARLY 1957

The ninety miles separating Cuba from the United States never seemed as insignificant as in early 1957. Bulky propeller planes made the trip in no time, and a ferry regularly crossed from Miami to Havana, a kind of postwar riverboat that brought happy-go-lucky gamblers to Cuba's racy shows and raucous casinos. In the boom years of the 1950s many Americans, when they weren't worrying about the bomb, were looking for a good time. And with its new, superluxurious hotels, Havana had begun to resemble New York. Men wore wide lapels and felt fedoras; women wrapped themselves in chinchilla capes at the slightest breeze and giggled like starlets. American cars—Buicks and Chevys and the '58 Pontiacs that everyone on the island coveted—swayed down the wide boulevards and crowded avenues. At night, when the lights from the buildings, tall and small, combined with the rumba rhythm of the Caribbean crashing against the broad seaside boulevard known as the Malecon, Havana became a sensual and sultry seduction—an offertory of glitzy casinos, Cuba Libres, plumed showgirls, and an army of alluring prostitutes eager to show the Americans a good time. Cuba in the 1950s was an easy-to-reach tropical bacchanal, friendly as any American state yet still foreign enough to be exotic.

How could such an Eden be roiled by revolutionary fervor? Matthews was fascinated by the rebels and the character of their leader, about whom he knew almost nothing. Nor did his understanding of Cuba go further than what many others knew at the time: Rarely had that country seen as divisive a figure as Batista, who understood that it was easier to seize power than to give it up. Batista had arrived on the Cuban political scene at the head of a gang of low-ranking officers who in 1933 overthrew the provisional government of Ramón Grau San Martín, who had himself led a revolt that ousted the brutal dictator Gerardo Machado. Though only a sergeant, Batista managed to keep power for himself. He effectively controlled Cuba behind several front men he put into office until he was elected president in his own right in 1940, defeating Grau San Martín. During his tenure, Batista surprised many Cubans by introducing some progressive policies. With an eye on his place in history, he drafted a new constitution with sweeping labor and social security reforms. The document also set term limitations that prohibited him from running for reelection in 1944. Grau San Martín won that year and Batista left office peacefully, traveling with his family to Florida, where he set up residence in Daytona Beach and enjoyed the spoils of his years in office.

But Batista had become addicted to power and could not be away from it for long. While still living in the United States, he entered a race for senator in Cuba, representing the province of Las Villas. He returned in 1948 and founded the Unitary Action Party, which he hoped would be his vehicle for retaking the presidency in four years. But many Cubans were suspicious of him, and when it appeared that he would lose the election, he usurped the process. On March 10, 1952—without firing a shot—he marched into military headquarters, surrounded by officers loyal to him, and reclaimed power, vowing to clear the scoundrels out of the Presidential Palace and restore order to the nation. On that morning, the ousted president, Carlos Prío Socarrás, called Ruby

Phillips and the rest of the foreign press to the palace to defend his government and denounce Batista. A wire service reporter drove by the *Times*'s office on Refugio Street to pick her up, but Phillips kept him waiting while she made herself presentable, telling him she "had no intention of going even to a revolution without lipstick." Batista's daring coup had also scuttled the 1952 congressional elections, including the race in which Fidel Castro, then a young lawyer, was a candidate for the Ortodoxo Party from the poorer districts of the city of Havana.

Few Cubans lamented the ouster of a crooked president, even though most remained wary about Batista's return. A few days after the coup, Batista was asked if trampling the constitution had made him a dictator. His answer was enigmatic. "The people and I are the dictators," he said. He was confident that he had the support of American and Cuban businessmen, and some lingering goodwill left over from his previous term in office. In 1954, Batista won a full term in a phony election in which the only other candidate, old Grau San Martín, withdrew in protest.

Although he spent more time playing cards and throwing parties than governing, Batista ushered in a period of relative prosperity, at least for some in Cuba. Bribes and kickbacks greased the skids for big construction projects, and American mobsters poured money into Havana's casinos. Even the parking meters in Havana blossomed into a lucrative source of graft for Batista and his cronies, and the machines became one more hated symbol of the regime. As Batista grew closer to the Havana Mafia, and his corruption became more overt, what little popular support he had slipped away.

But he had the good political fortune of facing a debilitated opposition. Recent events had undone much of the progress of the 1940s, when Cuba held its first comparatively fair and honest elections. During that time, the Ortodoxos had become a formidable political party with a popular leader, Eduardo Chibás, who used his national radio program on Sunday nights to attack the Prío government and call for honesty and integrity in the palace. Chibás was expected to be a strong candidate in the 1952 presidential elections and would easily have defeated Batista. But out of mounting frustration with the political situation in Cuba, he ended one of his radio programs with a dramatic gesture—shooting himself in the stomach. He died eleven days later. Had he been a poorer shot and survived, it is unlikely Batista would have attempted his coup. But with Chibás out of the picture and no surviving political figure strong enough to replace him, Batista took a huge gamble, and it worked.

This time, however, Batista showed almost none of the political shrewdness that had tempered criticism of his earlier regimes. He and his cronies stole so much that even middle-class Cuban businessmen—accustomed to a certain level of corruption—eventually grew weary of him. Cuba descended into a cycle of violence. As Batista's regime became greedier, resistance intensified. Batista's attempts to stamp out the opposition turned bloodier, inciting yet more violence. Batista believed that his trump card was his relationship with the United States. He said the right things about the evils of communism—as many Latin American dictators had learned to do—and he kept Cuba stable enough for American companies there to proceed with business as usual.

As a lawyer and congressional candidate in the canceled election of 1952, Castro at first tried to challenge Batista's coup in court. That effort predictably failed and he turned to armed violence, which many Cubans believed had been his intention all along. The attack on Moncada barracks had been only the beginning. It provided Castro with a name for his resistance, which became the 26th of July Movement, and catapulted him into the Cuban consciousness, though not necessarily in a positive way. After he was released from prison and sent into exile, he toured the United States to raise money to continue the revolution. Prío Socarrás, the former president, provided the funds to buy the *Granma* in Mexico and prepare it for its historic mission of 1956.

Almost no one in Cuba knew what had actually happened on the beach in Oriente where the *Granma* came ashore. United Press had not backed down from its earlier report that Castro had been killed in the initial fighting. Batista ordered the army to fly reporters over the area, proving that the puny rebellion had been smashed and all was well again in Cuba.

But all was not well. Rumors of Castro's survival persisted. And other groups besides the 26th of July Movement struggled to undermine the regime. In Havana, radical university students nipped continuously at Batista's heels. In politically discontent Santiago, where Cuba's long battle for independence had begun in the nineteenth century, young people and middle-class residents were eager to see the end of Batista once and for all. When his soldiers did not produce Castro's corpse, the government's account of the invasion was undermined. Troops remained on patrol around the Sierra Maestra and people asked who they were looking for if no one had survived.

No one knew for certain whether Castro was dead or alive. His opponents wanted to believe he was dead, while his supporters thought it was strange that nothing had been heard from him, or the troops with him, for weeks.

The truth was that Castro was very much alive in the high peaks of the Sierra, although he had suffered serious losses. Batista's planes had done their job well, scattering the miserable troops, killing some, disorienting others so they became separated from Castro and later were captured. There had been other ambushes, and the survivors had fled into the forest. But Castro eventually reconnected with Raúl and Ernesto Che Guevara, the Argentine doctor he had met while training in Mexico. The rebels had already attacked a remote military outpost and seized a cache of badly needed weapons. As he consolidated his forces and recruited campesinos from the Sierra, Castro was also busy strategizing the battle of ideas. He dispatched Faustino Pérez, a survivor of the *Granma*, to Havana to make contact with the urban faction of the movement. While in Havana, Pérez kept a low profile, knowing he would be arrested and tortured if Batista found out he was there. It was better to keep Batista and the rest of Cuba guessing about Castro until the time was right.

With a government censor in her own office, watching nearly every move she made, Ruby Phillips had to be cautious about the

dispatches she filed in the weeks after the "invasion." She attempted to get around the censors by giving her articles to friends who
were traveling to Miami and asking them to put them in the mail
when they landed.

In early February, she sent a desperate note making clear to her
editors in New York how dangerous the situation in Havana had
become. *"IF ANY OF THIS WERE TO BE PUBLISHED UNDER MY NAME I WOULD
BE DEPORTED IMMEDIATELY,"* she wrote, underlining the words and
typing them in capital letters to further emphasize the point.
"PLEASE BEAR THAT IN MIND." In the memo, she gave an update on
Castro, telling her editors that he had in all probability "escaped
into the hills." Various sources, she said, estimated "that he has
from 500 to 1,000 with him." Although she thought the number
was probably an exaggeration, she believed that if Castro was
alive, he probably had a sizable following. Her observation was
just the first of several miscalculations of Castro's military strength
that she and the *Times* would make.

Phillips was also laying the groundwork for some of the *Times*'s
later descriptions of Castro and his movement, shaping basic
characterizations that would be repeated by Matthews and others.
Castro's insurrection was a "youth rebellion: youth of the island
regard him as a hero similar to the ancient knights," she wrote.
But Havana itself, she determined, was not in a revolutionary
mood. Business was too strong, life too good. From her vantage
point on Refugio Street, steps from the Presidential Palace in Old
Havana, Phillips had little sense of the mounting anger in Oriente
Province, more than 500 miles from the capital and light years
away in revolutionary fervor.

"As I mentioned," she wrote in the secret memo to New York,
"there is no atmosphere for a revolution. However the tension is
growing as the armed forces attempt to suppress the rebellion by
shooting down and hanging both innocent and guilty without
trial."

In a subsequent note to her editors, Phillips devised a code that
she would use to try to sidestep the censors. "If memo arrived
send cable reading PLEASE ADVISE IF TIMES ARRIVING LATE HAVANA."

On February 5, the *Times* office in New York sent a cable saying just that.

Much of Phillips's reporting was passed along to Matthews in New York. He was growing increasingly focused on Cuba. In mid-January, he wrote another editorial condemning Batista's "unjustified censorship of the press and radio" and his continuing attempts to keep the rebel movement out of sight even after it was clear that some of the invaders had survived. Matthews still didn't have much faith in Castro's chances of victory. He believed Batista retained the loyalty of his army, and he suggested that Castro's movement, which he described as a "recent invasion by terrorists," had been "liquidated." He was too far from the action to get a clear sense of what was going on, too removed from the daily turn of events. But then something quite random, involving a journalist from the Dominican Republic and a box of cigars, drew him into the story.

The Dominican reporter was Germán Ornes, a critic of dictator Rafael Leonidas Trujillo, who had U.S. support. Ornes, who lived in exile in the United States, had traveled to Havana to attend the 1956 annual conference of the Inter-American Press Association. When he was ready to return to the United States, the Americans denied him a visa. The three months Ornes spent trying to leave Havana became an international cause championed by Edward "Ted" Scott, a sociable New Zealander who had lived in Havana for many years and wrote a column for the English-language *Havana Post.* Scott also represented NBC in Cuba and shared the office on Refugio Street with Ruby Phillips.

Scott wrote several editorials in the *Post* about the Ornes case and tried to pressure the American government into granting the Dominican a visa. When he realized his efforts were futile, Scott reached out to Matthews, whom he knew only slightly through Ruby Phillips. He brought the details of the Ornes case to Matthews's attention and suggested that an editorial in the *Times* could break the logjam. On January 23, Matthews wrote a strong editorial in which he urged the State Department to grant Ornes the visa he sought, "or say why it refuses to do so."

Ornes subsequently got his visa. Scott thanked Matthews, sending him a box of cigars and offering to host him on his next visit to Havana. Matthews wrote back to Scott to thank him for the cigars and to say that since he had vacation time coming, he and Nancie had been thinking about a midwinter visit to Cuba, although they hadn't yet set a date.

It would be set for them soon enough.

In the Sierra Maestra
January 1957

It was quiet in the clearings where a few peasant huts nestled among the dense backwoods of the Sierra. The *guajiros* who lived there had gone, leaving behind their belongings as though they had been frightened off. As Castro and his men pushed deeper into the Sierra and came upon the settlements, they realized that the paramilitary thugs who worked for the big plantation owners had settled old scores. They had been trying for years to get the squatters off their land; now they were able to force them out by claiming the peasants sympathized with the rebels. Where that ruse had not worked, the paramilitaries warned the squatters that army planes were on their way and they would counterattack the rebels with machine guns and bombs. "Hurry," they told the squatters, "get out before the planes come." The frightened *guajiros* left nearly everything behind and climbed higher into the Sierra.

Castro relied heavily on the peasants who had the courage to stand firm. Most of his supplies, and nearly all his food, had been left behind on the *Granma.* If the rebels were to survive, they needed the local peasants to share what little they had. Castro had been raised on a plantation in Oriente but schooled in Santiago and Havana, so he was at a great disadvantage because he had only the barest knowledge of the wild Sierra. He constantly turned to peasants like Eutimio Guerra for directions and information, trusting them with his life and the survival of his revolution.

Guerra, a middle-aged campesino who always wore a straw hat, lived outside the law. He belonged to a gang of peasants and squatters who stole from the ranchers and had learned how to navigate the steep ravines and overgrown woods to evade the authorities chasing them. Guerra agreed to guide Castro and his men for a while. Then he would run back down the mountain and stay with his family for a day or two before returning to help the rebels again. He kept Castro informed, delivering messages and bringing news of the rest of Cuba. One day Castro asked him if the people in the lowlands were talking about him.

"What do they say about me?" he asked.

"Well, actually, they say you are dead," Guerra responded.

"That I'm dead?"

"That's what they say."

Castro realized it was time to make his presence in the Sierra known. As he headed east, trudging along a ridge parallel to the coast, a peasant guide brought him information about the small military barracks at La Plata, a remote spot deep in the woods. Castro ordered a few of his men to scout the encampment and report on how many men Batista kept there, where they went, and what time they went to sleep. The peasants told him the fifteen soldiers inside were not very disciplined, lazily rousing themselves in late morning and ignoring most military regulations. Early on the morning of January 17, before the dark of night had given way to day, Castro attacked the remote outpost while the soldiers slept. Two were killed, five wounded, and three taken prisoner. He also captured an even more valuable prize—several rifles, ammunition, uniforms, and at least one machine gun.

Castro expected the army to follow him. He zigzagged through the Sierra, setting ambushes and picking off Batista's men. He stopped to regroup and was rejoined by Eutimio Guerra. Guerra had disappeared for a few days following the fighting at La Plata. He told the rebels he had gone to visit his family, but in fact he had been captured by Batista's troops and interrogated. He had lied to the officers, telling them that Castro's army numbered 200 men, divided into two battalions. The soldiers listened to his story

and could have killed him for helping the rebels. But they realized he could be more valuable to them if he rejoined the rebels
and spied on them. They offered him $10,000, along with a posi-
tion in the army that would bring a generous pension. All he had
to do was bring them to Castro so they could capture or kill him.
If that did not work, he was expected to go back into the hills and
put a bullet in Castro's head. Guerra agreed.

At first he guided a squadron of Cuban military fighter planes
over Castro's camp. The planes came in low over the treetops,
strafing the ground with machine guns but not hitting the men,
who hid behind trees and rocks. When he rejoined the rebels the
following day, they did not suspect him. The euphoria of their victory at La Plata had worn off, and now the scraggly troops, low on
food and struggling to believe that their leader knew what he was
doing, were becoming despondent.

Before January ended, Castro made his move. It was time to call
together the varied elements of the insurrection and coordinate
plans to overthrow Batista. He sent René Rodríguez, a veteran of
the *Granma*, to Havana to contact the urban resistance. And he
gave Rodríguez another mission. Castro knew the history of
Cuba's revolutionary struggle and understood how words could
be powerful weapons. General Máximo Gómez, one of Cuba's
heroes, had said, "Without a press we shall get nowhere." History
had shown that small opposition forces could multiply their
strength many times by appealing directly to the people. But no
one in Cuba's long history of revolution had faced a situation as
utterly dire as Castro's at that time. He had fewer than twenty men
with him, a handful of modern arms backed up by antique rifles,
no food and no battle plan except to attack Batista's most remote
military outposts. He desperately needed to let his followers in the
cities know that he had kept his promise to return to Cuba before
the end of 1956 and had survived the dictator's best efforts to liquidate him.

But Batista's censorship remained in place, preventing Cuban
newspapers from publishing information about the rebels.
Besides, Castro did not trust Cuban reporters. Too many had

been co-opted by the government, and he couldn't count on them to publish a truthful account. No, just as the Cuban heroes fighting for independence had gone to an American reporter, Castro realized he needed to see a foreign correspondent, someone who could slide under the censorship and let the world know he was, indeed, alive. The greatest of Cuba's heroes, José Martí, had called in an American journalist a few weeks after landing in Oriente in April 1895. And not far from the foothills of the Sierra Maestra where Castro was now fighting, Martí had been interviewed by that reporter, George E. Bryson of the *New York Herald*. Castro, in another age and another revolution, was prepared to fight a war based mostly on propaganda and images. An interview would be the first volley.

When he reached Havana, Rodríguez contacted Faustino Pérez and relayed Castro's order to bring a correspondent. The time and place of the meeting were not set, nor was there a plan for getting the correspondent into the Sierra. All that would come later. The most important task now was to find an American reporter willing to do what Castro proposed. That responsibility was given to Javier Pazos, a twenty-one-year-old student leader at the University of Havana who had been raised on politics and public policy and was committed to the overthrow of Batista. His father, Felipe Pazos, was a respected economist who had served as president of the National Bank of Cuba before Batista seized power and was now cooperating clandestinely with the rebels. The elder Pazos was part of a formidable group of middle-class Cubans who wanted to see Batista removed. They had no clear idea who would replace him, but that mattered less than seeing the end of Batista's arrogant and corrupt regime.

Javier Pazos soon realized his options for finding a reporter were limited. Only the *Times* had a correspondent living in Cuba. Pazos's father had gotten to know Ruby Phillips during his tenure at the National Bank. The elder Pazos agreed to help and got to work immediately. He called Phillips and arranged to meet her at her Refugio Street office. There he said he was going to share with her the greatest secret of the island, a secret so explosive that if overheard, it could get them imprisoned. But the office, as usual, was swarming with people. Phillips had friends there, along with her maid and manservant, even a delivery boy.

Pazos asked if it would be possible to find someplace more private. Phillips led him to an adjoining room that was open to the hallway. Reluctantly, he whispered his secret.

"You have contact with Fidel Castro?" Phillips blurted out, loud enough for the others to hear. "I can't believe it."

Phillips wanted to know who had come down from the mountains with such news and how Pazos could be certain this person wasn't an impostor. She refused to make any arrangements until she had a chance to meet the messenger.

Two days later, Pazos arranged a meeting at his Havana office between Phillips and Rodríguez, who showed up with two bodyguards. They talked for a long time. Phillips asked for details to verify the story of Castro's survival. Rodríguez described the landing of the *Granma* and the difficulties of the Sierra. The most important issue, of course, was getting a reporter past the army checkpoints and into Castro's mountain camp. Rodríguez was openly concerned that it would be impossible to slip Phillips, a woman, past Batista's soldiers.

He need not have worried. Phillips had already ruled out the idea of going herself. Doing so, she felt, and writing such a provocative story, would have been disastrous for her. Batista would be furious, and in retaliation would have her deported. Cuba was her home. She had raised her daughter there and had built her own house there. Being in one place for so long meant that she had greater access to sources than other correspondents. But to preserve that special access she had surrendered a degree of independence.

Phillips was different in other ways from most correspondents. She took over the Havana bureau following the death of her husband despite having little journalistic experience or training. The *Times* accepted her flawed writing and reporting and allowed her to submit expense vouchers to help pay for the Cuban couple who did double duty as her office assistants and housekeepers. The editors even helped her take an occasional shopping trip to Miami. Simply by being in Havana for so long, Phillips had become the most important foreign journalist in Cuba, and all Cuban presidents from Gerardo Machado through Batista kept their doors open for her. But the trade-off between access and independence had raised questions in New York about her ability to remain objective, and her editors did not trust her to handle the biggest stories. She flew into a rage in 1954 when her editors sent Matthews to cover the Cuban presidential election. "Of course, it is very simple for someone to come into the territory of an established staff correspondent, write a fearless objective story, and return the next day to Times Square," she wrote her editors. "It is I who remain here and am handy [*sic*] target for criticism, justified or otherwise."

Besides her fear of being deported, Phillips had other reasons for refusing to go to the Sierra. She doubted Castro's rebellion could succeed. She knew his history and was well aware of his many failures. She also knew the strength of Batista's army, and the dictator's antipathy toward Castro. Going to interview him when he was likely to fail, as he had in the past, struck her as an unwarranted, even foolhardy risk. She told Castro's men that she would get someone else to do it. But she was reluctant to offer it to a colleague from the *Times*, knowing that there was a good chance Matthews would come, and he had upstaged her once before. Instead, she went to a competing news organization.

Walking back to her office after the meeting with Pazos, she ran into Ted Scott and told him about the secret mission. Phillips offered to let him go in her place. He turned down the chance to go for essentially the same reason that Phillips had said no. He had lived in Cuba long enough to know that violating Batista's censorship would surely get him kicked out of the country. Only someone who could write the piece and leave right away could do it. Scott said he had an idea who that might be.

That same day, Scott had received a thank-you note from

Herbert Matthews for the box of cigars he had sent following the editorial about Germán Ornes. He showed the letter to Phillips and suggested they got in touch with Matthews. That put her into an awkward position. She would look catty and mean-spirited if she turned down Scott's suggestion, even if it galled her to have Matthews there.

Phillips cabled Emanuel Freedman, the foreign editor. She made no specific mention of an interview; the censors would have blocked such a message. She simply made it clear that Matthews should come to Havana. Now. Given all the elaborate arrangements she had made to get her memos to New York, the editors would have understood that the cable calling for Matthews was urgent.

The simple message from Cuba revived some of the passions Matthews had felt when he crossed the battlefields of Africa and Europe as a war correspondent, evoking the smell of airplane fuel and the clatter of the portable typewriter that had made his blood race for so many years. Matthews had turned fifty-seven just a few weeks earlier, on January 10, but he firmly believed that despite his weak heart, he was not too old to go after one more great story. He found the silence and solitude of the editorial board's tenth floor refuge somewhat confining, even suffocating, and believed he deserved another chance in the field. He didn't know exactly what lay in store for him in Cuba, but his newspaperman's sense told him to follow the lead, to take the chance, to go.

It had become all but impossible for him to write sensible editorials about Cuba without seeing for himself what was wrong there. In an editorial that was published just before he left for Havana in early February, Matthews denounced Batista's censorship. He had begun to interpret Batista's extreme reaction as a sign that things must be worse in Cuba than the government was willing to admit. The censorship was hitting home, since it was not limited to Cuban news organizations but had spilled over to the *Times* and other publications. He knew about Phillips's difficulties. Her phones were tapped and her mail was monitored. He knew that censors combed through the early editions of the *Times* that were sent to Cuba and cut out anything they deemed objectionable, including his editorials. Deep inside a cable to the foreign desk that otherwise appeared to be about baseball, Phillips had slipped a message past the censors: "PLEASE ADVISE MR. MATTHEWS TIMES ARRIVED MY OFFICE WITH HOLE IN EDITORIAL PAGE."

In the missing editorial, Matthews seemed to have written off the Castro rebellion, but he raised troubling questions about Cuba's future. "A campaign of terrorism began early in December following an unsuccessful rebellion in Oriente Province, east of Havana," he wrote, referring to the landing of the *Granma* on December 2 and the brief spate of civil unrest that had preceded it. Matthews struggled to explain the continued violence in Cuba. It was 1957, the Cold War was raging, and wherever there was turmoil, Communists were suspected of playing a role. Cuba was no exception, although the evidence of any Communist involvement was sketchy. "One guess being made by friends of the dictatorship is that the Communists have increased their agitation to a dangerous extent," Matthews wrote in the same January 31 editorial. "If so, why does not President Batista say so?" He remained puzzled by how quickly Batista seemed to have lost the support of the Cuban people and by how virulently some Cubans wanted him to go. As recently as a year earlier, Cuba had seemed to be a Caribbean utopia. Now bombs were exploding in Havana and corpses were being found alongside the roads leading from Santiago. "Nothing seems to have happened recently to bring such a development," Matthews wrote. "Prosperity is general and the Government is unchanged."

He dismissed the notion that Castro's inchoate revolution was causing the unrest. And he realized that the only way to understand this turn of events was to go to Cuba and to see it for himself. He finalized arrangements for the trip, taking the unusual step of asking the newspaper to pay for his wife's airfare. It wasn't the first time his editors had received an unorthodox request for funds from Matthews, who always seemed to be living beyond his means. "Please don't consider this as a hold-up, in any sense, as I would understand perfectly if you didn't agree," he wrote to the managing editor, Turner Catledge, just before his departure for Havana. "I cannot leave Nancie alone here for ten days and will take her with me to Cuba and will, of course, pay all her expenses there. Being the top of the season it will cost plenty. Will *The Times* pay her airfare, up and back, or whatever the travel expenses are?" The following day, Manny Freedman wrote to the newsroom accountants: "Herbert Matthews, who is going to Havana on a news assignment tomorrow, has been authorized by Mr. Catledge to list as an office charge round-trip airplane fare New York–Havana for Mrs. Matthews." It would turn out to be fortunate for Matthews that his wife accompanied him on the trip.

They arrived in Havana late Saturday, February 9. The following day, Matthews went to see Ruby Phillips. She explained what was really going on and arranged for him to meet Felipe and Javier Pazos at her office. This time, she had cleared out the hallways so no one was there to overhear them. Matthews asked the elder Pazos if he truly believed that Castro was alive. Pazos admitted that he had never met the rebel leader and that until his son and René Rodríguez had come to find a correspondent willing to go to the Sierra, he too had believed that Castro had been killed in the landing. Matthews asked a few more questions, and then it was Pazos's turn to address a delicate issue.

"Will you send for someone from New York?" he asked Matthews.

"No," Matthews said with such authority that it would have been hard for Pazos to raise further doubts. Matthews's own approach to news, and to life, had long centered on a stoic belief that each man is in charge of his own destiny.

"I'll go myself," he said.

A look of concern came over Pazos, who knew it would be a difficult trip, over rough terrain, into the wildest part of Cuba. Pazos could not conceal his surprise that this balding, rather frail-looking editorial writer dressed in his city suit would even consider undertaking such an arduous journey.

"I'll do it," Matthews responded dryly. He did not intend to allow anyone to stand in the way of this story. He had spent much of his career chasing gunfire. He had the spirit of an adventurer in the grand old sense, even though he always believed that in his chest beat the more sedate heart of a scholar. In a life already filled with so many unexpected twists and turns, here was the door opening on yet another opportunity that no one could have predicted. He leaped at it, as he had already leaped at so many other chances in his long and surprising career.

real soldiers of fortune

He was just a smart, skinny kid from the Upper West Side of Manhattan when he joined the army in 1918 in search of adventure and glory like hundreds of thousands of other young men then marching off to war. Not long after he enlisted, Matthews crossed the stormy Atlantic to Le Havre, on the coast of France, and from there made the quick overland trip to army Tank Corps headquarters at Bourges, midway between Paris and Vichy. It was early November and there he was, eighteen years old and near the center of the action, ready for the kind of drama that had enticed him into giving up a privileged start in the academic world for his turn in the bloody trenches of Europe. If only the war lasted long enough. Books, his beloved books, could wait; he needed to taste for himself the kind of life he had read about as a boy, tales of Vikings and Crusaders, stories so resonant with adventure that they would shape his conception of many things, including heroes, scoundrels, and newspapermen, for the rest of his life. The most important of those books was one Matthews had received as a gift from his mother when he was just nine years old, but which he guarded carefully and kept in his collection until his death.

The book that was so central to the formation of his concepts of life and courage was *Real Soldiers of Fortune,* a popular volume of real-life stories written by Richard Harding Davis, the famous foreign correspondent of the *New York Journal* and later the *New York Herald.* Considered the first modern war correspondent, Harding Davis was also a prolific author of books, both fiction and nonfiction, about some of the larger-than-life people he met on his travels. Matthews's mother had inscribed the book before giving it to him as a birthday present—"To Herbert Matthews. From Mother"—and the dispassionate tone suggests she had no inkling that writing and reporting might become his life's work. But his parents did manage to nurture in him sufficient restlessness and curiosity to last a lifetime, and Harding Davis became one of Matthews's own heroes.

Harding Davis wrote with energetic passion about two basic themes—the transformative power of wars, and the personal heroism of the men who live through them. And he wrote from a heroic tradition as yet untarnished by the horrors of World War I. He switched regularly from fiction to nonfiction, and it was sometimes difficult to know whether he was reporting the truth or just telling tales. *Real Soldiers of Fortune* had been preceded by another popular book on the same theme called *Soldiers of Fortune,* a fictionalized account of a nineteenth-century military hero and diplomat. Harding Davis's writing style in both books was so similar that sections of the nonfiction work could be inserted seamlessly into the novel. Fact and fiction both seemed flexible notions to Harding Davis. His principal goal was writing rousing stories.

Although famous as an author, Davis was also one of the best-known correspondents of the turn of the century, especially after his reporting from Cuba during the Spanish-American War. Teddy Roosevelt had befriended Harding Davis and provided him with extraordinary access throughout the war. Roosevelt was rewarded with stirring, eyewitness accounts of his exploits, including the charge up San Juan Hill, which Harding Davis described as the heroic assault of a fearless leader. Years later, when Roosevelt launched his controversial campaign to win the

Congressional Medal of Honor he thought he had earned in Cuba, he used Harding Davis's war dispatches as proof of his heroism.

Although the vivid accounts produced by Harding Davis had been widely read and generally believed when first published, they were viewed skeptically in later years as conflicting information arose. Harding Davis was attacked for the liberties he had taken with the truth, especially when he wrote about Roosevelt and his exploits in Cuba. He had clearly been seduced by Roosevelt's character and was openly biased toward him and his career, presenting an idealized version on which legends could take root: "Roosevelt, mounted high on horseback, and charging the rifle-pits at a gallop and quite alone, made you feel that you would like to cheer. He wore on his sombrero a blue polka-dot handkerchief . . . which, as he advanced, floated out straight behind his head, like a guidon. Afterward, the men of his regiment who followed this flag adopted a polka-dot handkerchief as the badge of the Rough Riders," he wrote in "The Cuban and Porto [*sic*] Rican Campaigns," his 1898 paean to the war manufactured by William Randolph Hearst to sell newspapers and advance the idea of an American empire. Harding Davis manipulated the accounts to place Roosevelt at the center of the action, and he distorted the historical view of the war by depicting the charge made by Roosevelt as a critical turning point when, in fact, it was not. There were so many exaggerations about San Juan Hill that Harding Davis was called Roosevelt's "personal publicist," a shill who had traded his newspaperman's objectivity for access to the future president and who, in the process, invented the Roosevelt legend.

But Matthews didn't know any of that when he read about the exploits of young Winston Churchill and other heroes in *Real Soldiers of Fortune*. Despite obvious faults, each man portrayed in the book had the courage to leap into history and be part of it, a lesson Matthews was determined to live by his entire life—provided of course that fate cooperated, which it did not in France in 1918.

"I was no hero," Matthews wrote later about his World War I experience with the American Expeditionary Forces, "just a generally homesick boy who reached the Tank Corps center at Bourges, near Langres in Eastern France, just too late to see any action." His unit was never sent into battle, and he spent most of his time on the base there waiting to be shipped back home. It took five months for him to be placed aboard a troop carrier returning to New York. He grew to hate the regimentation of military life, the mindless drills and endless exercises that merely filled the interminable hours of waiting. But other aspects of being a soldier—the handsome uniforms and gleaming medals, along with the genuine camaraderie of men facing common danger—became lifelong loves for a man who considered himself shy and unsociable.

Matthews was surrounded by great events, but he was still young and focused solely on the gauzy romance of the battlefield. He was unimpressed as the victor nations hammered out their flawed and historic peace. He was interested in battlefield strategy and firepower, not diplomacy or historical sweep. He did not even try to read the French newspapers, although he had studied the language while in high school. Peace did not interest him, and he was mightily relieved when his unit was not selected to become part of the occupation force in Koblenz, Germany. Instead, toward the end of April 1919, he was sent home, in time to enroll at Columbia University, not far from his parents' apartment on Riverside Drive in Manhattan, and begin his delayed university training with the class of 1922.

His military experience might have been a disappointment, but it transformed him nonetheless and made him mature beyond his years. He was different from the privileged students at Columbia who had not gone to war. He participated in few activities outside the study hall; his desire for a career as a scholar of Romance languages remained paramount.

College was a serious affair, an introduction to a new life of mature intentions. He worked hard like his father, Samuel, who had carved out a successful life for his family in New York City against considerable odds. Since Matthews's family had come to New York from the disputed European territory claimed by both Russia and Poland in the middle of the nineteenth century, it had assimilated completely, dropping the original family name (lost to history) and all but abandoning its Jewish roots. Samuel Matthews went into the garment industry and did well enough to be able to live on respectable Riverside Drive, take summer vacations in the Catskill Mountains in upstate New York, and fill his apartment with books. Young Herbert and his sister, Rosalie, rode horses in Central Park, and once a horse kicked him, leaving him with a knee injury that never healed completely. As a boy he had contracted childhood tuberculosis that weakened him considerably. After recovering, he set out to build himself up by playing tennis and other sports. He was devastated by the death of his mother, Frances, in the influenza outbreak of 1918. It was a traumatic loss the young soldier-scholar never completely got over. Music had always filled his home and was an important part of his early life. He had learned to play the piano, and he was considered talented enough to have pursued it as a career. But he had linked the music in a powerful emotional way to his mother, and he could not play without thinking of her. His profound grief at her early death prevented him from ever touching a piano again.

Music had gone into hiding, but Matthews found he had an ear for languages and a great thirst for history and classical literature. Columbia's Romance Languages Department wanted him to do his graduate studies there, and his professors tempted him to stay by offering him a teaching position. They nearly succeeded. He was bookish in nature, despite his adventurous spirit, and the academic world enticed him. But he also knew he was essentially a loner and that to be a college professor he would have to open himself up to his students. That was hard for him to imagine, so difficult that he believed he had no choice then but to go in a different direction.

But what? He wasn't prepared for much besides teaching, and his ability to speak and read French, Spanish, and Italian, along with his detailed knowledge of medieval history and literature, did not present obvious professional advantages outside the university. He resorted to scanning the newspaper want ads and in July 1922, he answered one under the heading "publisher," assuming it referred to a New York book publisher. Matthews felt this, at least, was something he could do. There was an opening for a secretary-stenographer, and it was only when he was called in for an interview that he found out that the publisher was not involved in books but rather was *The New York Times* and the job was secretary to the assistant business manager. It paid $25 a week. Matthews had learned to type and along the way had picked up stenography. He got the job.

And he hated it. Although he could handle the responsibilities capably, he had no mind for the business and advertising end of newspapers. He soon switched to working nights, pursuing his graduate studies at Columbia during the day. In 1925, the university offered him a fellowship in Europe, primarily in Italy, where he spent most of his time studying Dante and medieval history.

The *Times* had given Matthews a vague promise of work when the fellowship ended. He had met the then vice president and future publisher, Arthur Hays Sulzberger, before he left. Nine years older than Matthews, Sulzberger wished him luck in Europe and suggested he write to him about a month before returning to see what positions might then be available. Matthews knew he did not want to go back to the business side; it did not suit his temperament. Despite his experience in the army and the time he had spent in Europe both during the war and afterward, he still felt shy and withdrawn, not nearly one of the "real soldiers of fortune" he had read about.

"I do not know what opportunities may be open now," he said in a letter that he sent to the publisher from Paris in 1926. He was a twenty-six-year-old man unsure of his own courage and clearly reluctant to be put back on the front lines. "My whole life has been one long training in literary studies, and if it were possible to get on the book review, I would be very happy at the work, and I believe quite capable. If not, perhaps there may be something in the Sunday Department, or the Editorial, that I could do, or even the News, although I rather doubt my qualifications at general reporting."

The basics of newspaper work did not appeal to Matthews. "Except as a last resort, I would not want to go to straight reporting," he wrote to an editor he had worked for in the publications office. The idea of deadlines, quick interviews, and press conferences was not for someone as withdrawn as he was then. He sought the life of the mind and was intent on making his way by dint of his intelligence and what he perceived of as a budding way with words. And he wanted to keep one foot in the ivory tower. "While I hope to go on working for my PhD at Columbia," he wrote the editor, "it is not my intention to let it interfere in the least with my work."

There was nothing available at the Book Review, or the Sunday department, or any department of the *Times* that interested Matthews. What was available was more secretarial work, this time as a night assistant to the acting managing editor, Frederick T. Birchall. The position put him in the newsroom, or at least in a corner of the news-gathering enterprise, and though it tested his lack of interest in the messy world of global politics, it presented a surer path of promotion, and it paid better than the position he had before. There was also the opportunity, should he want to take it, to write for the newspaper.

Despite his reservations about working in the newsroom, Matthews found, to his surprise, that he could fit in, and as he grew more comfortable there, and more confident, he benefited from the essential dynamic of any newsroom, large or small. Because a newspaper must be created every day, the need for copy and the manpower to edit it into finished form is endless. Newsrooms are in essence like sports teams—on any given day, any member of the newsroom team might end up doing almost any job, no matter how important or routine, depending on what is happening and who else is available. Matthews quickly worked his way through a progression of newsroom positions, taking turns as copyreader, reporter, rewrite man, and eventually, because he had been to Europe twice, as an editor on the cable desk where foreign news was handled.

In the spring of 1929, the publisher, Adolph S. Ochs, who had transformed the *Times* from a failing local paper to a powerful institution, sent Matthews on a five-month junket to the Far East that had been organized by the Carnegie Endowment for International Peace. The government of Japan was trying to smooth relations with an increasingly suspicious and jittery United States. Matthews and eighteen journalists from other American papers were sent on an all-expense-paid excursion through Japan, Korea, Manchuria, and northern China, which then was coming under Japanese economic domination. For Matthews, the trip turned out to be more of an exciting grand tour than a political coming of age, but it did expose him to the twentieth-century geopolitical landscape. And he learned something about himself as he was charmed by the hospitality of the Japanese. He empathized with his hosts; he understood their need to win economic and political domination over neighboring Korea and Manchuria to secure their place in a volatile Orient. He believed that war between Japan and the United States was possible, but he could not connect such thoughts to the Japanese officials he met. At twenty-nine, he was still naive enough to interpret cordiality as a compliment, rather than an effort to persuade. He recognized years later that his warm feelings toward the Japanese had been exactly the sentiment they had intended to create. But he never realized that his sympathies shaped what he saw as the truth and made him vulnerable to being misled.

When his tour of the Orient ended, Matthews returned to the cable desk, filled with firsthand knowledge of the region and a growing recognition that in order to do his job he needed to know as much as possible about the rest of the world. Fond memories of his year in Europe kept him thinking of returning there. There was also the matter of a charming and erudite young Englishwoman named Edith Crosse, who preferred to be called Nancie. They had met on an ocean liner when he returned from abroad in 1926 and were married in New York in 1931. Later that same year, an opportunity arose to go to the *Times*'s Paris bureau to cover business and economic news. It was not the primary position in the bureau, and he did not expect it to bring much glory.

He had not yet developed much interest in politics, and he was all but oblivious to the gathering war clouds in Italy and Germany. But going to Paris would get him out of the New York office and back to Europe, so he accepted the offer.

In November, Matthews and Nancie recreated the ocean crossing he had made with the army in 1918, sailing from New York harbor to France on the German liner *Albert Ballin*. He became number two correspondent in the Paris bureau, a position held a few years earlier by Walter Duranty, the *Times*'s correspondent who had gone on to Moscow, where his coverage of the Soviet Union under Joseph Stalin the year Matthews arrived in France would win a Pulitzer Prize and, eventually, lasting scorn because of its one-sidedness. And like Duranty, who was initially driven to Moscow by the limitations of playing second fiddle in Paris, Matthews was soon looking for an opportunity to put his own stamp on the *Times*'s European coverage.

He arrived in Paris with impeccable timing and a touch of New York class. The son of a tailor, he was a clotheshorse and in 1930s Paris sported tailored suits and fashionable hats. A young John B. Oakes—a member of the Sulzberger family who would go on to become a feisty editor of the editorial page, and Matthews's defender—once recalled seeing him stroll into the Paris office after lunch wearing a gray fedora, beige gloves, and spats to match, jauntily carrying an elegantly glossy malacca walking stick. Matthews wrote energetically about the economic and social difficulties of the Great Depression, hinting occasionally at how the political situation in France and Germany had also been weakened and was paving the way for great conflict.

In October 1935, while Matthews was on the train from Paris to Rome, Benito Mussolini announced that Italy had run out of patience in Africa and was launching a military campaign against Emperor Haile Selassie of Ethiopia. Mussolini wanted to avenge Italian defeats in Africa at the end of the nineteenth century, and he was intent on making the ancient nation a colony of the new

Italy. Regardless of the politics involved, this was the chance Matthews had been hoping for, and he convinced his editors to let him cover the war in Africa. He was determined to make the most of his time there, little realizing that the lopsided conflict in Abyssinia would put him on a path that would last the remainder of his life.

Matthews threw himself into the budding war, traveling to Africa aboard an Italian troop carrier. At last, his Columbia education proved useful. He had studied the Italian language, explored Italian culture, and grown enamored of Italian literature, especially Dante's epic poetry. He had become a close friend and associate of Columbia's greatest Dante scholars and had established a relationship with the Italian poet Benedetto Croce during his fellowship in Italy. He liked Italy and the Italians, and now that Mussolini was steering the country toward a war of questionable moral character condemned by most of the world, Matthews let his feelings toward the Italians show. He felt that as a correspondent, he needed to empathize with the people he was covering, in order to understand their motives and describe their feelings. But empathy spilled over into sympathy. He was not ashamed of his bias toward the Italians. Nor was he concerned that it might undermine his reporting. "If you start from the premise that a lot of rascals are having a fight, it is not unnatural to want to see the victory of the rascal you like," he wrote years later. "And I liked the Italians during that scrimmage more than I did the British or the Abyssinians." He also thought he saw much to admire in fascism. For a time, he believed that the conquering Italians could truly bring civilization and progress to the backward natives of Africa.

If Matthews shipped out to Abyssinia with less than an open mind, he did throw his whole heart and soul into the consuming process of being a war correspondent, quickly establishing a pattern that he would follow for the next four decades. He believed most strongly in the power of eyewitness accounts and insisted on being at the front line with the troops. He vowed to write only what he had seen with his own eyes, and what he knew in his heart to be true. He was skeptical of the correspondents who camped out at the hotels in Addis Ababa, cabling back to their offices detailed accounts of battles they had not seen, filled out with details they harvested from military officials and then rounded out by their fertile imaginations. Matthews was unafraid of the discomforts of traveling with the Italian army through the inhospitable African landscape; rather, he relished the familiar feeling of military camaraderie in a war zone. He often inserted himself and his own exploits into his narratives. His own detailed accounts of the action were some of the longest articles the *Times* has ever published (one that ran for more than 11,000 words cemented his reputation as correspondent), and they were written in the romantic tradition of war as adventure that Harding Davis and John Reed had popularized before the horrors of World War I. Matthews sent this wire dispatch from Asmara, Eritrea, on March 1, 1936.

> The climax to the Italian campaign is believed to have been reached and passed. Other developments, some of which may startle the world, remain to be carried out. Vast distances and rugged territory still lie between the Italian troops and the Ethiopian capital, but it can be said with confidence that for all practical purposes the African conflict has been resolved.
>
> The Italians believe that what lies before them is occupation rather than conquest.

Matthews provided a sympathetic platform for Italian designs on Africa, writing about the military maneuvers in an unquestioning way that later proved embarrassing. But public sentiment in the United States was heavily skewed toward the Abyssinians, and Matthews would learn another important lesson in trying to accurately cover an unpopular cause. So many people disliked Mussolini's bullying and favored the African underdogs that Matthews's accounts of Italian victories were suspect, even when they were accurate. People did not want to read about the Italian army under Marshal Pietro Badoglio, a Fascist hero, handily defeating disorganized and poorly armed Abyssinian troops. Instead, they were willing to believe misleading Abyssinian accounts of Italian defeats and heroic standoffs that never actually took place. "That was my first lesson in the difficulty of convincing people of truths that they do not want to believe," Matthews wrote. It was a lesson that would be repeated less than a year later in Spain.

By the time the Italian conquest of Abyssinia was complete in May 1936, Matthews had spent seven months in Africa, and his first taste of war corresponding had whetted his appetite for more. Despite the ten weeks of utter boredom spent waiting for the Italians to begin their campaign and the merciless assault by flies that tortured him day and night, Matthews felt he had gained valuable experience that the *Times* ought to use in the next war. He also embarked on a separate career writing books based on his reporting. In December 1935, he wrote to his father that a publisher was interested in a book about his experiences in the wilds of Africa. Matthews was hesitant at first. "I don't see that I could do anything but a rehash," he wrote. "I've thought vaguely of a book, since everyone seems to expect me to write one, but since it isn't my line at all I've always dismissed it from my mind." But he hadn't learned thrift or how to handle money responsibly, shortcomings that plagued him his whole life, especially after he and Nancie developed a taste for fine art, the best wine, and luxurious hotels. Since someone was willing to pay him to write a book, he agreed to do it. *Eyewitness to Abyssinia* was the first of a dozen Matthews eventually managed to write. The book reflected his own views on Mussolini and fascism at that time. Years later he repudiated the Fascist regime. "I was slow to see the danger," he admitted, "but not so slow as were some others, and I have fought it as well as the next man."

Matthews had found in Africa the kind of war heroics—the danger and the action—he had hoped to experience in France during World War I. But being a correspondent took a toll. He was separated from his wife and two children for months, a pattern that continued for a decade. He was never able to spend much time with his son, Eric, or his newborn daughter, Priscilla, and the children grew up knowing little about him except for what he wrote and what their mother told them.

Soon after the Spanish Civil War began in July 1936, Matthews begged to be sent to Spain, not because he then believed in the cause that underlay the fighting but rather because he felt that Spain represented the best opportunity for him to further his career. He reminded the paper's managing editor, Edwin L. James, that he spoke Spanish and that he had traveled through Europe. When the *Times*'s regular correspondent in Spain, William P. Carney, got into trouble with censors, James cabled Matthews to say that he had won his argument. Matthews started his new assignment in Valencia in November 1936. Shortly after he arrived, his editors assigned him to cover the Republican, or government, side of the conflict, while another correspondent (eventually it was Carney) reported on the actions of Generalissimo Francisco Franco and his insurgent Nationalist rebels, who opposed the fairly elected, left-leaning government that they feared had become too cozy with the international Communist movement. Franco was intent on restoring Spain's greatness, along with its traditional conservative values. He raised an army in Spanish Morocco, and soon he was backed by Nazi Germany and Fascist Italy, eager to put their new war machines to the test.

The war in Spain was prelude to a much wider and more brutal conflict that was already on its way, but Matthews was not perceptive enough when he arrived to deduce that. What he did understand as he settled in was that this was another conflict that needed to be reported not by rewriting handouts but by slipping off to the front lines, where he could see and smell and hear the brutal choreography of battle, and learn how hard it was to convince readers of a truth they did not want to believe.

But that came later, as did a fundamental transformation of his life and his way of viewing the world. Had he been assigned to cover Franco's troops so soon after documenting Mussolini's triumph in Africa, he might have seen the war differently. In Franco, he would have found the kind of strong military man that had impressed him since boyhood. But his earliest days on the Republican side left a deep impression. "In my first dispatch from Valencia I caught simply some inkling of the heroism and the glory that Spain was to mean," he wrote. The struggle in Spain between democracy and totalitarianism meant less to him than the measures of valor of the men on both sides. Spain was already luring idealists from around the world. They included those armed with no more than pencils and typewriters who would report on the battles in which others died. Matthews's vivid early dispatches were being read by other writers, firing their imaginations.

By the time Ernest Hemingway arrived in Madrid in March 1937, he had read most of Matthews's reporting, and the two immediately struck up what was to become a lifelong friendship. Hemingway quickly became the core of a group of reporters and writers that included Matthews, Martha Gellhorn (who later married Hemingway), Sefton Delmer of the London *Daily Express,* the photographer Robert Capa, and others who saw in the Republican government of Juan Negrín a legitimate and honorable cause. In time though, the war's importance would resonate even more strongly, as the German and Italian support made of the rugged and inspiring Spanish landscape a pitched battle between fundamentally opposed ideologies.

This was also a time of shifting sympathies in the United States, when it was not clear which side represented the gravest danger— Negrín's Republicans (or "Loyalists") and their Communist supporters, or Franco's right-wing Fascists. That put Matthews and the other writers on an ideological as well as a military front that shifted continually. Hemingway's presence on the Loyalist side created a ground swell of sympathy, which was bolstered further by the arrival of the Abraham Lincoln Brigade, made up of idealistic American volunteers, some of them Communists. As passions soared on both sides, Matthews found himself in an escalating battle with his critics and embroiled in an intensifying struggle to report a truth that could be believed.

For all the hardship of living and working in a war zone, Spain also provided intense excitement and white-hot emotions. Matthews lived in the Hotel Florida with Hemingway, Gellhorn, and other writers. Some of them believed that Matthews had fallen in love with Gellhorn. She was infatuated with Hemingway, but she saw a heroic side of Matthews in the intense days of fighting and writing in Madrid. For a time, he took a flat on the edge of the Retiro Park that had a terrace where they would stand and calculate the direction of artillery bombardments. He generally ate well, and there always seemed to be enough good cheap wine available. In the middle of the war, he took time to buy several custom-made suits and a black topcoat with a fine velvet collar from an out-of-work tailor. But when Matthews was at the front, he tended to wear peasant trousers and espadrilles. While in Spain, he also purchased a set of etchings by Goya on Japanese imperial paper for $225, thinking they were worth at least $1,000. "So you see," he wrote his wife in 1938, "although I trust neither we nor our descendants will ever have to sell the set, we have made an investment which makes dabbling in stocks picayune."

In a chummy letter to Nancie that same year, he described some of his efforts to relieve the stress and boredom of the war. "Do write often, dallin, and don't think terrible things that ain't true. The true things are really the nice ones, if you could only believe it," he wrote, though it is unclear whether he was referring to the war or to rumors of his feelings toward Gellhorn. They remained close. At night, when his migraines became especially painful, Gellhorn would come up to his room to massage his neck. Hemingway did not suspect anything. He admired Matthews's perceptiveness and courage, and Gellhorn believed he was the model for Robert Jordan, Hemingway's hero in *For Whom the Bell Tolls*. Hemingway did tell Matthews that with his thinning hair and long nose, he resembled Girolamo Savonarola, the fifteenth-century Italian monk whose zealous denunciation of contemporary vice and frivolity led to the "bonfire of the vanities" and, eventually, his own condemnation and death. Years after the war, Hemingway offered to write an introduction to Matthews's book on the Spanish Civil War and Abyssinia, *Two Wars and More to Come*. Matthews declined the offer, feeling that the book should stand on its own rather than ride on the enormous popularity of Hemingway's name. Hemingway understood, and instead wrote a classic jacket blurb. "Herbert Mathews [*sic*] is the straightest the ablest and the bravest war correspondent writing today stop," Hemingway cabled to Matthews's agents in 1938. "He has seen the truth where it was very dangerous to see and in this book he brings the rarest commodity to you stop In a world where faking now is far more successful than the truth he stands like a gaunt lighthouse of honesty stop And when the fakers are all dead they will read Mathews in the schools to find out what really happened stop I hope his office will keep some uncut copies of his despatches in case he dies."

Hemingway's testimonial was printed as he wrote it, except for the last sentence, which the publisher decided was too indiscreet to use.

Spain also brought Matthews into his first serious conflicts with the editors of *The New York Times* over his reporting. The newsroom struggle, which lasted through the end of the war, sapped his spirit and generated a professional paranoia that would trouble him throughout his career. From then on, he worried that people did not like what he did because they did not like him. As in the Abyssinian conflict, Spain evoked strong passions in readers who based their opinions not on the reports of what was happening on the battlefield but rather on their sympathies and on what they wished were taking place. The brutality of the Republicans, especially toward Catholic priests, who were hunted down and murdered, helped turn public sentiment among Catholics toward Franco, even though his rebel forces also murdered Basque priests suspected of espionage. The decision by the Communist International Committee to support the Loyalists also raised suspicion in the United States.

Matthews initially reported simply what he saw, beginning with conditions in Madrid. Though Franco's troops threatened to take the city, Matthews did not believe the heroic capital would fall to the rebels. Against the wishes of his editors, he insisted on staying there, even as other correspondents fled. Madrid did not fall until the end of the war, but Matthews had already gotten a glimpse of where the sympathies of his editors actually lay. They believed that Franco represented the more powerful of the two sides, and therefore was the more likely to prevail. Matthews perceived a clear bias on their part and was infuriated by way they handled his dispatches when he reported anything that did not coincide with their perceptions or the reports they were receiving from other correspondents.

It was a lesson that was to be repeated over and over through the three years that Matthews spent in Spain. His editors, under intense criticism from Catholics and anti-Communists in the United States, continually questioned Matthews's reporting, often altering his dispatches to soften the tone or shift the inference, usually to Matthews's consternation. He often found himself at odds with Carney, who continued to get his information from Franco's forces. Matthews was challenged by the editors in New York, especially when it came to the role played by Germany and Italy in the war. In March 1937, Franco's forces swooped down toward the Spanish city of Guadalajara, north of Madrid. When the Loyalists managed to stop them before they reached the approaches to the city, Matthews got back into his car and, ignoring the danger, drove to the front, where he got his first eyewitness view of the familiar Italian troops he had followed to Abyssinia.

The battleground was littered with Italian tanks, Italian rifles, and Italian dead. The Loyalists had captured Italian troops and Matthews spoke to the prisoners of war in Italian, confirming their identities and providing proof that despite all pledges of noninterference, Mussolini had done far more than simply lend technical advisers to the rebels as he had claimed. Matthews sent a dispatch to New York emphasizing that the troops and equipment he had seen were "Italian and nothing but Italian." But the editors refused to publish the story as Matthews had sent it. Instead, doubting Matthews's impartiality, editors changed the word "Italian" in his dispatch to "Insurgent." That included Matthews's summing-up phrase, which became "They were Insurgent and nothing but Insurgent."

The tinkering with Matthews's story set off a round of accusations between him and his editors, who implied that he, practically alone among reporters, had accepted Loyalist propaganda as truth. Infuriated, Matthews responded with blistering letters in which he accused the editors of a "deliberate lack of faith" and a refusal to trust that their correspondent saw what he claimed to have seen because they had allowed their own views to color the way the Spanish story was being presented to readers. Matthews felt it was a fundamental issue of journalistic trust, and the conflict with his editors presaged other, more heated battles to come. He was willing to bet his career that he stood on the right side of the issue, challenging the *Times*'s managing editor in one letter to either "trust your correspondent more than you do his competitors or his editors 3,000 miles away, or else you ask for your correspondent's resignation." Although using the word "Insurgent" rather than "Italian" did not make the report incorrect, Matthews's account of Fascist involvement later proved to be accurate, though his editors never acknowledged that, nor did they apologize for making the change in his copy.

It became increasingly clear that simply telling the truth and honestly portraying what he saw were not necessarily enough to convince his readers of truths they preferred not to believe. In order to accurately convey the reality of a complex situation such as a war or a revolution, Matthews believed he had to buttress the raw facts with background and history, to put it all into a context that, presented with passion, represented an emotional recreation of an event, an eyewitness account that came directly from the heart.

It was a view shared by the other writers he knew in Spain, although none of them were newspaper correspondents like him. Rather, like Gellhorn, they wrote for magazines or other publications with ideological bents that were not limited to recounting facts but were expected to wrap events in emotion. Gellhorn disdained the very concept of unemotional coverage and mocked what she called "this objectivity shit." She belittled efforts to pursue what she believed was patently unachievable, even dishonest. Matthews felt his responsibilities as a newspaper correspondent were the same as hers.

For him, Spain had been a great adventure, like World War I, except this time he saw plenty of action. He had begged to take part in the great struggle, and he was intent on seeing it through to victory for his side. Like an enlisted man, he wrote home weekly, telling his wife and his father in New York of his exploits. He lived as though he were part of the Loyalist forces and the International Brigade of volunteers from the United States about whom he was writing. In 1938, as the war was coming to a disappointing end, he saw the International Brigade off. "Good lads," he said in a letter to Nancie, "and may they prosper. Me, I must carry on the war all alone." Matthews remained hopeful that his side would somehow be victorious. In a letter home after the Republican forces were driven out of Spain, Matthews at last threw in the towel and revealed, once and for all, just how much he had invested in a Loyalist victory.

> And so it goes. We got beat proper. I guess at the end I was fighting harder than the soldiers—at least on paper. So long as there was hope I played it up strong, all along. There really were possibilities but they depended on getting material from and through the French and of course they ditched them. Now I got no hope, but maybe they can hang on here for a month or so and in the center another month or so. Then their only hope is a European war in the meanwhile.

The defeat of the Loyalists wounded Matthews, and the scars never completely healed. He went on to write several books about Spain, and about the more horrific conflict it presaged. He was sent to Italy at the start of World War II, and reported halfheart-edly there until Italy declared war on the United States and the Fascists threw him into jail for a few days. He then was transferred to Sienna where, for five months, he was kept in lightly guarded custody, free to stroll and even bicycle around the city. When he was finally released in a prisoner exchange, he became persona non grata in Italy. The paper sent him to cover India for a year. He returned to Italy for the Allied invasion. After the war ended, Matthews was made bureau chief in London, where he and Nancie, along with their two children, lived in the postwar auster-ity for several years. By then, Matthews was well into middle age and uneasy about his future. His relationship with Arthur Hays Sulzberger, who had become publisher in 1935, had continued to deepen. Whenever he needed a special favor, he did not hesitate to take the issue directly to the publisher, as he had done in Spain. In London, the most difficult issue Matthews faced was not con-vincing his editors that his dispatches could be trusted. Rather, he was bedeviled by money problems, brought on by an elaborate lifestyle that could not be sustained on his salary. Sulzberger authorized a $16,000 loan for Matthews to purchase a house in London, over the objections of the paper's accountants, who thought it too risky.

The *Times* extended and refinanced the outstanding house loan several times, but Matthews's constant requests for financial assistance finally strained relations with the New York office. "Granted that he does fine work," the paper's president, Orvil E. Dryfoos, wrote in a memo to the publisher—his father-in-law—in 1959, when Matthews had within a single day gotten approvals from each of them for two separate Latin American trips, "I am always a bit leery about his financial shenanigans."

By 1949, a deeply unhappy Matthews, frustrated by his money problems, facing his son Eric's first year at university, and feeling unappreciated by New York, had succeeded in his sustained nego-tiations with the *Times* for a transfer out of London. He was angling for a seat on the editorial board, where he thought his broad experience would give him standing and authority. But he was not content to simply join the board, nor to give up entirely the footloose ways of a correspondent. Since before the war ended, he and Sulzberger had been discussing a new hybrid kind of position, one in which Matthews would not only write editorials but would continue to travel and to report on the countries and people he would editorialize about. Matthews was headstrong about his views of what a correspondent ought to be and do, and how it differed in substantial ways from routine reporting.

"We are faced with a new situation which calls both for a new type of newspaperman and a different technique of coverage," he wrote in a 1944 memo to Sulzberger. He criticized the newspaper's European coverage and proposed a radical departure. Let the news agencies do spot news, he proposed, and fall back on the old distinction between "reporting" and "corresponding."

"The function of the special correspondent should more and more be to interpret, illuminate, analyze, acquire expert knowledge of his subject and above all to do special articles and stories that the agencies would not go after." Matthews boldly called for raising standards of accuracy, keeping straight news articles shorter, and offering reporters greater training opportunities. And he broached one other subject: "Finally, I think one should add the idea, which I believe was originally yours, of having the important foreign correspondents called in every so often to write editorials for, say three months or so. This will be good for the editorial page and especially good for the correspondent, who can touch home, learn what interests there are among the readers, get in touch with his sources in Washington, etc."

Matthews brought up the dual-appointment idea again in 1948 when the publisher encouraged him to consider a transfer to New York. But he feared that going to the tenth-floor editorial board would be like an old war horse being let out to pasture. He demanded that the new position come not only with reporting opportunities, but with a title: associate editor. Such a move was highly unconventional, and though it might have been salve for Matthews's wounded ego, it would have ignited jealousies throughout the editorial board that the paper's top editors wanted to avoid. Cyrus L. Sulzberger, the newspaper's chief foreign correspondent and the publisher's nephew, was dispatched to London to meet with Matthews and assess the most delicate issues. He quickly sensed Matthews's insecurity, but he advised the publisher against giving him the new title. Cyrus Sulzberger recommended that foreign editor Edwin James point out to Matthews "that this is not a Mexican army filled with official titles and that the important thing is for him to make his arrangement to move next summer and get ready to do a bang up job of writing editorials where he is wanted and needed. A slight job of between the halves coach's talk will help Herb see the thing in its proper light and make up his mind."

Matthews had pretty much decided in early January 1949 to accept a transfer to New York. The decision was cemented in April of that year when Matthews, then forty-nine, suffered a heart attack after a grueling reporting trip to assess the conditions in postwar Germany for a series of special reports. Sulzberger, who had already suffered a heart attack of his own when he was still in his forties, was openly sympathetic. "Awfully sorry about you," he cabled Matthews in his London hospital, "but if 'twas occlusion let me welcome you to my club any event be sure obey doctor cheerio sulzberger."

Matthews spent six weeks in a London hospital, then took another two months at home to convalesce and prepare to move back to New York for the first time since accepting the transfer to Paris in the early 1930s. The world had changed drastically since then, and so had Matthews. The experience of reporting and living through three cataclysmic wars had forced the naive idealist, who had once championed fascism, to evolve into a hardened, though not embittered, realist who lamented the loss of so much energy and opportunity for the world. He still believed passionately in the causes for which the Spanish Civil War stood in his mind: democracy, individual expression, and the flaming desire of people to break free from tyranny. He had lived through the bloodiest years of the twentieth century without injury. He was a celebrated war correspondent who had spent far more time working outside his newspaper's home office than inside it. His injured heart forced him to see working on the editorial board as a kind of semiretirement, but the occlusion he had suffered had not snuffed out the passion he felt for causes, nor his sympathy for the people behind those causes.

Soon after taking his position on the editorial board, Matthews wanted to know who had responsibility for writing about the increasing ferment in Latin America. When he was told that no one in particular was assigned to keep an eye on the area, he took it upon himself to become an expert on the region. He used his relationship with the publisher, and Sulzberger's support of the unorthodox idea of a reporter-editorial writer, to create an influential beat to which he devoted himself for the next fifteen years. He briefly toyed with the idea of becoming a foreign affairs columnist for the *Times* and was in the running to succeed Anne McCormick when she died in 1954. But he lost out to Cyrus Sulzberger, and years later he figured it had been just as well that he had not won the column because he probably would have turned out to be too controversial. Instead, he reported and wrote editorials about the unrest in such places as Argentina, and then sharply criticized the government of Juan Perón in editorials that had a huge impact on the Perón government, which needed to improve its relationship with Washington.

In 1955, Matthews had heard that Perón had ordered 100 or more student dissidents to be held in prison at the Villa de Voto jail and had prohibited the Argentine newspapers from publishing a word about them. Using a false Argentine name and hiding his identity as a newspaperman, Matthews managed to get into the prison to interview some of them. The following day he flew to Chile and wrote a detailed article about the detention of the students. The article, and an accompanying editorial that he had arranged to be written in New York, caused an uproar in Argentina. A few months later, Perón was thrown out of office. An American television series called *The Big Story* dramatized Matthews's adventure and made him, briefly, a hero.

Matthews might have been savoring another appearance on

The Big Story as the turmoil in Cuba started to escalate. He had made his first reporting trip to Cuba after Batista seized power in 1952, and by the time Castro ran the *Granma* aground at the end of 1956, the necessary elements for big trouble were starting to fall into place. But they were subtle signs, not obvious to most Americans. Having witnessed firsthand the handiwork of dictators in Europe and strongmen in South America, Matthews was more finely attuned than most to approaching turmoil. He noted the island's relative prosperity compared to the rest of Latin America, but he was also aware of Cuba's violent history and the deep resentment many Cubans felt toward the United States because of its frequent interventions. He knew it was a situation worth watching.

dawn in the sierra

American tourists vacationing in Havana in February 1957 played on sugar-white sands during the day, then lined up to see the new Elvis Presley film, *Love Me Tender,* in a local movie house at night. Since most of them stayed at the classic hotels in Old Havana or at the flashy new American ones with their huge casinos near the waterfront in El Vedado, they never heard the small bombs that went off after dark almost every night on the outskirts of town or in the poorer neighborhoods, and they were mostly unaware that rebellion was brewing in Cuba. The bombs were usually placed where no tourist or Cuban civilian would be hurt—near a power line, or a telephone exchange—and they were meant not to maim or kill but to interrupt normal operations in the city and to weaken the confidence of local people in the government that was powerless to stop the violence.

The increasing chaos in Cuba was a concern to the U.S. government, but not a big one. Some American travelers had been frightened by the reports, but in the overall scheme of things, Cuba, and indeed all of Latin America, was considered acceptably secure since the CIA had taken care of the nasty problem with

President Arbenz in Guatemala a few years earlier. Nothing that happened in the hemisphere was anywhere near as galling to the Eisenhower administration as having to sit back and watch the Soviet tanks invade Hungary in 1956 without being able to lift a finger to stop them. No crisis in the hemisphere seemed likely to end up like the grisly standoff on the Korean Peninsula where American GIs had to be left behind to keep the Communists in their place. And though there were rumblings every now and then about Communists in Latin America, strongmen like Batista could be relied on to keep them in their place.

When Herbert Matthews arrived in Havana on a flight from New York late Saturday, February 9, he told Cuban immigration officers that he and Nancie were on vacation from a cold and wintry New York. They looked for all the world like a pair of middle-aged tourists, well-to-do snowbirds who could afford to hop on a plane and leave the winter behind. Of course, this was no vacation. There would be a week before he headed to the Sierra, and he worked hard to take the pulse of Cuba during that time, noting every blast, every furtive figure on the street, every noisy convoy of police or soldiers that rattled through the old city in an intimidating show of force. The meeting with Javier and Felipe Pazos had piqued his interest. By Monday morning, they still had not revealed the details of his trip to the Sierra. But while he waited, Matthews was intent on finding out as much as possible about the deteriorating conditions in the country, despite the appearance of calm and the hordes of tourists.

He and Nancie had once again checked into the Sevilla Biltmore Hotel, one of the old capital's most elegant lodging places, and his favorite whenever he came to Havana. It was close to both the Presidential Palace and the *Times*'s office, and the old hotel, with its elegant lobby and luxurious accommodations, had a European air, which made Matthews feel at home. One of the first signs he noticed of the new pall over Cuba came as soon as he looked for a copy of the Sunday edition of *The New York Times*. He knew from past trips that it usually arrived on a plane from Miami more or less on time the same day it was printed. But since

Batista had imposed the censorship measures at the beginning of the year, the paper was often days late and arrived with holes where articles that mentioned civil unrest had been cut out. The February 8 edition of the paper originally carried an article, written in New York, that said the rebels in Oriente numbered 500, and were putting up fierce resistance and killing many of Batista's best troops. The article was never seen by anyone in Cuba but the government censors and Matthews, who had a chance to read it before leaving New York. Although reporter Peter Kihss got the number of rebels wrong, his article undoubtedly influenced Matthews when he tried to independently assess Castro's strength later that week. Even the copies of the newspaper that went to the American embassy were cut up until Ambassador Arthur Gardner formally protested.

Matthews began the week of interviews by stopping at the embassy on Monday morning to talk to Gardner, John Topping, the embassy's chief political officer, and Richard Cushing, the information officer. He did not mention his plans to go to Oriente Province for the interview. Matthews was suspicious of Gardner because the ambassador had become extremely friendly with Batista, which made him very unpopular with the Cuban people. Although it was more a courtesy call than an attempt to gather information, the meeting would eventually prove to be a flash point between the two men. Whereas Gardner said little of importance, Topping provided useful insights. He had his own sources in the Cuban underground and had managed to put together a comprehensive account of Castro's landing in December and Batista's frustrated efforts to pursue the survivors. Although he could not say with certainty whether Castro was still alive, Topping provided some early estimates of rebel strength that Matthews took with him into the mountains. The army had caught up with the rebels at Alegría de Pío and had killed up to thirty of them in a fierce ambush. After that, Topping said, the army tried a different tack. Instead of hacking through the wilderness to pursue the rebels, army commanders offered fair trials to those who surrendered. Another twenty to twenty-five of Castro's followers had been rounded up this way. He said that left a core of no more than thirty men in the hills, with or without Castro. In the following weeks, they were joined by about 100 others, some armed, most of them campesinos willing to provide food, refuge, and information. The embassy estimated that another 400 insurgents and sympathizers were hiding in Oriente, ready to join the movement if the call came. Matthews noted everything. So far he had gotten at least three separate estimations of Castro's strength— from Ruby Phillips's note to New York, Peter Kihss's February 8 article from New York, and now the embassy's account of the landing's aftermath. All three sources concluded that the number of rebels in the mountains was fluid but that there were probably several hundred, with more waiting in the wings.

After leaving the embassy, Matthews saw a number of American businessmen in Havana, including Walter W. Schuyler of the United Fruit Company, who filled him in on some of Castro's early background. Schuyler knew Castro's father, Angel, who had come from Spain to fight in the Spanish-American War and never returned. He went to work for United Fruit as a laborer but later went into business on his own, gradually accumulating contracts and land. He ended up owning a sugar plantation in Oriente, and in his later years also operated a general store. It was in the store that Schuyler said he first met Fidel, who then was no more than a tough farm child raised with chickens and pigs. His father had done well enough to send him to private school, first in Santiago, then in Havana. By the time he enrolled in the University of Havana, he had developed a complex view of the world. Despite all the privileges of his own youth, many made possible by his father's work with United Fruit, Castro developed an anti-imperialist and anti-capitalist streak that intensified as he got older. He embraced violence as a legitimate way of bringing about change. In 1947, while still a student, he took part in a failed attempt by Dominican exiles and Cuban radicals to invade the Dominican Republic and overthrow dictator Rafael Leonidas Trujillo. Most were arrested before they got anywhere near the Dominican coast, but Castro managed to escape by jumping overboard. The following year, he traveled to Colombia to take part in anti-American protests timed to coincide with a meeting of the new Organization of American States. After a protester was killed, rioters rampaged through the streets of Bogotá, the capital, for several days, and the chaos they caused nearly toppled the Colombian government. Castro, then only twenty-two, was at the head of some of those street riots, and the experience was a political awakening for him.

Schuyler told Matthews that the business community feared that an open revolt that brought down Batista would inevitably plunge Cuba into chaos. Castro, the hotheaded gunslinger, wasn't strong enough to take over, the businessmen thought, and if Batista were ousted Cuban history would repeat itself once again. As corrupt as Batista was—and the businessmen in Cuba all agreed that Batista's greed was insatiable—any military junta that took over from him would be even worse. "We all pray every day that nothing happens to Batista," Schuyler told him.

Matthews went to see former president Ramón Grau San Martín. Grau believed that Batista's censorship would end up backfiring on him. By blacking out crucial information about the rebellion, the censors had created a poisoned atmosphere in which rumors festered and even the best-informed Cubans couldn't be sure of what was happening. The government said Castro had been killed in Oriente, but if so, why were thousands of troops still there, and why the censorship?

Matthews tried to make sense of the military situation in Cuba. The army was under a great deal of pressure and was handling it in a chaotic way. The same day that Matthews had been to the U.S. embassy, Ambassador Gardner had handed over to Batista seven American tanks, still painted "U.S. Army," that would obviously be used to put down rebels, since Cuba did not need them for national defense. While Batista spent lavishly on uniforms, housing, and other privileges to keep his army loyal, the troops that were sent into the Sierra grew increasingly frustrated. They had not been trained to fight a guerrilla war, and duty in the Sierra was becoming dangerous. Batista had ordered the army to make examples of all those who were found to be sympathizing with the rebels. Former Ortodoxo Party senator Pelayo Cuervo, who had become a leading voice of opposition to Batista, told Matthews that such moves inflamed Cuban sentiment against the government, especially among the younger generation of Cubans, those who were increasingly siding with the Fidelista insurgents in Oriente and who saw the army as their enemy.

By the end of the week, Matthews had touched base with most of the important political, business, and economic figures in Havana. He did not see anyone from the Batista government because he feared that doing so might raise suspicion about his presence in Cuba. To prepare for his trip to the mountains, he bought special clothing that made him look like a rich American on a fishing expedition. He was also advised that the nights could be uncomfortably cool in the Sierra, so he brought along a heavy coat and hat. Finally, he got word from the rebels in Havana to be ready to go on Friday, February 15. The plan was only generally worked out by then. Matthews would be picked up and driven 500 miles across Cuba to Oriente. Where the interview would take place, and how Matthews was supposed to find Fidel, still hadn't been determined. But Matthews had decided that the best way of getting past the cordon of troops surrounding the Sierra was to bring along Nancie and pretend to be a couple of middle-aged American tourists out with some young Cuban friends.

At 5:30 PM on Friday the 15th, as Matthews was finishing packing his bags, the telephone in their hotel room rang. "You will be picked up in an hour," Fidel's men told him, "be sure you are ready." The interview was set for the following night in the mountains. Castro had agreed to come down from the high peaks to the lower slopes of the Sierra so Matthews would not have to do too much climbing. Even so, there would be some rough going, because that part of the Sierra was wild, without passable roads or horse trails. They would have to move on foot, and be prepared for some hardship. Matthews rushed Nancie to get ready, but she had just mixed an expensive Italian hair coloring and insisted that she couldn't possibly leave in an hour. When Matthews reminded her that they were not going for a drive in the country, she reluctantly poured the mix down the drain and prepared to leave. By 6:30 they were set to go, but there was no sign of the Cubans. They waited one hour, and then another. Finally, Matthews took Nancie to the Floridita restaurant for frozen daiquiris and a platter of moro crab. Matthews confided to her that many young Cubans were risking their lives to smuggle him into the mountains, so it was important to be discreet during the long trip.

The Cubans finally pulled up to the Sevilla Biltmore at around 10:00 PM and loaded Matthews's luggage into the car. Ted Scott, the *Havana Post* columnist who had invited Matthews to Havana, spotted them as they prepared to leave and shouted, *"Buen viaje,"* which startled Matthews because he didn't know that Ruby Phillips had told Scott anything about the plan. They drove through the night along the central highway across the spine of Cuba, stopping frequently for tiny cups of strong, sweet coffee. In the car with the Matthewses were Javier Pazos and a couple who were introduced only as Marta and Luís. Matthews later learned they were Liliam Mesa, a Havana socialite and Castro supporter, and Faustino Pérez, acting chief of Castro's movement in Havana. The anti-Batista forces in the capital were preparing a new offensive, but Pérez's top priority was getting Matthews in to see Fidel.

Crowded into the car, they passed the hours on the rough road singing Cuban songs or talking about the revolutionary movement for which they were risking their lives. Matthews was enthralled by this secret passage through Cuba, but Nancie was cold, tired, and hungry, and not at all thrilled to be still driving by the time the sun came up the next morning. They decided to stop for breakfast, but hardly did so with discretion. Rather, Mesa, who was behind the wheel, got so confused that she stopped three times to ask a policeman for directions to a good hotel where they might eat. But the camouflage worked, and no one suspected their real mission. After *café con leche* and sweet rolls, they were back on the road and nearing the military roadblocks surrounding the Sierra Maestra.

A soldier stepped into the road in front of them. It was the first real test of their plan. He peered inside the car, checking out the young Cubans in the front and the American couple in the back. They all held their breath for a second, their hearts racing. Because she had been unable to do her hair at the hotel, Nancie had grabbed a white "pillbox" hat that resembled a chimney pot, fashionable in 1950s New York, to hide her hair. The hat must have impressed the soldier. He took a quick look around the car and smiled, then waved them through.

They ran into other roadblocks before they reached the rendezvous point outside Manzanillo, a town in Oriente that flanked the Sierra. There, a pair of schoolteachers who fervently supported Castro offered to put up Nancie for the night while Matthews continued on into the hills. Graciously, they asked her if she wanted her dress pressed while she waited for him. Matthews took advantage of the break and rested in the safe house, anxious to get going and well aware of the role that foreign journalists had played in Latin American history. It would be hard not to think of that in Cuba of all places, because it was William Randolph Hearst and correspondents such as Richard Harding Davis who had incited the Spanish-American War by publishing accounts and images that were distorted beyond recognition. It wasn't just Cuba, either.

A few years after the Spanish-American war ended, it was Mexican dictator Porfirio Díaz's interview with an American correspondent, James Creelman, published in *Pearson's Magazine* in 1908, that had set off the spark that led to the Mexican Revolution. Díaz told Creelman that after twenty-seven years in power, it was time for him to retire and open space for someone else to lead Mexico. He welcomed the formation of an opposition party and promised to support a transfer of power. Francisco I. Madero, a wealthy northern landowner, used that statement as a call to form a party and build a base for his own campaign for president in the 1910 election that was to conclude Díaz's long reign. But in the end, Díaz did not keep his word, and instead of retiring, the eighty-year-old war hero and business advocate announced that he would sacrifice himself for the nation once more by running for reelection to an eighth presidential term. No one doubted that the election would be rigged. When Díaz was declared winner, Madero called for the Mexican people to rise up and on November 20, 1910, the first great social revolution of the twentieth century began.

Matthews knew that journalists' interviews rarely had that kind of history-making power. Even so, he was sure that he had one hell of a story on his hands, if he could get into the Sierra to see the mysterious rebel leader. But that seemed less likely as complications arose. Castro had also decided to coordinate his forces more effectively and make clear his plans for a national uprising. He had called together his regional leaders from around the country for a meeting that would start right after he finished the interview with the American journalist. After regrouping at the safe house in Manzanillo, a number of those leaders drove off to rendezvous with Castro, leaving Matthews behind. When the courier who was supposed to drive him into the foothills finally arrived, he took Javier Pazos aside and told him they would have to wait an extra day because by now the area was crawling with Batista's troops. An open Jeep with four soldiers had been stationed in the middle of the main road they would have to use. The driver said that trying to get past the roadblock would be suicidal. But Pazos refused to wait, knowing that Castro would not accept any excuse for his failure to show up with the correspondent. Reluctantly, the driver agreed to find another route.

They left the safe house at about 7:00 PM. As planned, Nancie stayed behind with the rebel supporters. Matthews had changed into darker, heavier clothes and now had a new cover story. If they were stopped, he planned to identify himself as a wealthy American plantation owner who only spoke a few words of Spanish. He intended to say that he was being taken to a village at the foot of the Sierra to look over a farm he was interested in buying. Javier Pazos, who spoke English, was to tell the soldier he was along as a translator.

An afternoon downpour had inundated the rough roads leading to the Sierra, making them all but impassable. The driver,

Felipe Guerra Matos, lived in the area and, like many of the peasants there, knew by heart all the back roads and unmarked trails.
It wouldn't be easy, or fast, but he thought he might be able to get
by Batista's patrols by driving alongside the cane fields and over
the rough roads until they got close enough to the meeting point
for them to walk in. The men knew it would be dangerous, but
they were confident that Matthews's presence would provide safe
cover. Before they left, they gave him a roll of bills—$300 in all—
that they were taking to Castro. If they were searched, it would be
easy to explain that the money belonged to the American planter.
In reality, Castro would use it to pay local peasants for any food or
supplies that the rebels took from them.

Despite their precautions, the group ran into an army patrol
and was stopped. A soldier peered into Guerra's Jeep, asking
them who they were and where they were going. He looked suspi-
ciously at Matthews, and at the others, but finally waved them
through. They drove through the fields of rice and sugar cane,
plowing through the unmarked farm roads and across streams in
the dark. They remained on the lookout for the patrols that
Guerra had seen earlier and managed to avoid them all.

It was midnight before they finally arrived at the spot where
they were supposed to rendezvous with Castro's men. Matthews
and the others started hiking up the lower reaches of the Sierra.
They followed the rough terrain up and down, slipping at times
in the heavy mud, squeezed by foliage so thick and wild it seemed
more like the Amazon jungle than eastern Cuba. They came to a
river, dark and angry that night after the downpour earlier in the
day, and had to wade across, knee-deep in the cold rushing water.
On the opposite side they climbed a steep slope, still dripping wet
and cold, before reaching what they thought was the spot where
they were supposed to meet the mysterious men who would take
them to Fidel.

No one was there.

They did not know if they had gone to the wrong place. Or perhaps they had to push on a bit farther. Maybe Castro's men had
gotten tired of waiting and had decided to push on without them.

The Cubans left Matthews and scouted the area, signaling to each other in the toneless whistle they used, hoping to make contact with the scouting party without attracting the attention of either Batista's soldiers or a rebel patrol that was not expecting them.

The only sounds were the night voices of the forest—the screeches of animals and the heavy drip, drip, drip of raindrops shaken loose from the trees. All hope of meeting Castro that night disappeared, and the men stopped at a muddy knoll to figure out what to do. The bright light of an incandescent moon broke through the underbrush, casting eerie shadows behind the tall trees and spiky bushes. Matthews and two others were made to wait while Guerra and another Cuban continued up the mountainside, hoping to make contact with Castro's men.

For the next two hours, Matthews sat in the mud, waiting and thinking. Though he wanted to note every sound and every motion, sleep laid a trap for him. Despite the cold and the wet ground, he let his head fall to his knees and he dozed briefly, awakened only by swarming mosquitoes.

Finally, out of the darkness, came an unmistakable sound—the two flat notes of the secret code indicating the other men were returning. Both sides whistled across the void until they found each other in the darkness. They had come upon an advance patrol in the woods, and one of the scouts had returned with them to guide everyone to the mountain outpost where they would find Castro.

The scout was a local man to whom the hills were as familiar as his mother's name. Matthews struggled to keep up. Although there were no markings on any trees, no visible sign of a road, or path, or even a trail, the guide moved as though it were broad daylight, paying little attention to the gangly middle-aged American who could barely keep from falling in the mud. But Matthews pressed on, and in time they came to an area of level ground where the scout stopped. He whistled. For a few seconds there was silence. Then, they heard the welcome sound of the return whistle.

They marched farther into the forest, which by now was bathed in bright moonlight. The scout whispered that the camp was nearby. Castro would come shortly after dawn. With a few hours remaining until sunrise, the Cubans offered Matthews a few crackers to eat and spread a heavy blanket out on the damp ground where he could rest. In tones barely above a whisper, they talked of rebels and of revolution.

"I'd rather be fighting here for Fidel, than anywhere in the world now," said one Cuban who had seen Batista's soldiers drag his brother out of his store to be shot. The others talked about the injustice of the regime, and they dreamed openly of a day when a new, fairer government would provide security and justice for all Cubans. A short, wiry black man who wasn't afraid to let Matthews print his name said he was in charge of the group. "I am Juan Almeida," he said, "one of the eighty-two." The others told Matthews their own histories. A few had lived in the United States. One said he had been a minor league baseball player. They said they couldn't find enough to eat in the mountains, where almost nothing edible grows, so they relied on local farmers to bring them supplies, and they always paid for what they took. Another one of the eighty-two came by—a thin-faced, round-shouldered man with longish hair. He said he was Raúl Castro. He struck Matthews as slight and pleasant, a famously flawed misreading of the man's character, but it reflected Matthews's frame of mind at this time. After the long hours in the car from Havana listening to the litany of the 26th of July Movement's idealistic goals, the dangerous journey into the Sierra, the difficult passage to the rendezvous point, the lack of food and sleep, Matthews had lost much of the skepticism he had felt about the rebels when he was in New York. Given his self-confessed passion for underdogs, and for the causes about which he wrote, Matthews was easily won over by those he covered, regardless of their politics. That is why it was possible for him to root for the Fascist Italians in Abyssinia, and a few years later support the leftist Loyalists in Spain.

Here he was now at the beginning of another revolutionary movement, another passionate cause, a civil war in its earliest stages, where words and images were far more important than guns or military strategies. Matthews was just starting to understand the players and the complex dynamics of a Cuba in which the normal conditions that made a Latin country ripe for a social revolution did not exist, but revolution was in the air anyway. He could not know then exactly how the story would turn out, but he was determined to see it through to its end.

impenetrable fastnesses

Castro pushed through the spindly *guaguasí* trees and the heavy underbrush dripping with morning dew to greet the surprised American correspondent he had kept waiting much of the night. It was just after dawn, and Matthews was muddy, hungry, cold, and in need of a shave and a hot shower. But this was why he had come all the way from New York, this was the reason he had decided to forgo a comfortable career in the university, this was the kind of encounter with history that for so long had made him feel most alive. Castro strode into the clearing with the sun just breaking through the clouds and dawn seeping into the day. He wore fresh army fatigues and an olive-gray cap, and he carried a long rifle with a sharpshooter's telescopic lens.

"We can pick them off at a thousand yards with these guns," he boasted to Matthews soon after greeting him, brandishing the rifle as though it were a trophy. The impact of every word could hardly have been more dramatic. It was a classic scene of encounter, the historic meeting of two forces ineluctably drawn together by fate. Matthews already had a substantial amount of information about Castro's life, his movement, and his history, but he needed to find out much more. Castro knew nothing about Matthews except that he was an American and that he wrote for the *Times*. And because Castro had spent several months in New York trying to raise money, he had an idea of the newspaper's standing, and the potential value that an article in the American newspaper, free from Batista's censorship, would have for his faltering movement. Castro controlled the setting, the timing, and to a large extent the content of the interview. Both men were intent on using each other to suit their own needs. Castro saw Matthews as a conduit for his ideas, a public address system with a pen who would relay an important message to the world. Matthews saw in Castro a way to prove that he could still parachute into a physically difficult situation and scoop the competition. Castro meant for Matthews to be impressed, intimidated, and perhaps even frightened by his talk of picking off soldiers. But Matthews was too busy recording what he saw to react with fear.

"Taking him, as one would at first, by physique and personality, this was quite a man—a powerful six-footer, olive-skinned, full-faced, with a straggly beard," Matthews would write in the first of three articles based on the interview. As the day lightened, he quickly reassessed his surroundings at the temporary camp set up for the interview. He realized that no one but Castro was even half his age, and that the rebels who followed him were fired with the white heat of revolutionary youth. "How young!" he jotted down in his notes. Although the fighters he saw were less than twenty-five years old, their firearms were ancient, cast-off American rifles and one machine gun of questionable reliability that the rebels claimed to have taken during a raid on an army base weeks before. Matthews could see now that some of the men wore rough and mismatched uniforms, while others were dressed in tattered civilian clothes. One had on a white shirt that, though filthy, was incongruously bright against the verdant foliage—hazardous attire for a guerrilla.

"I'm first," Matthews noted, clearly savoring the scoop he would bring back as the first reporter—American or Cuban—to visit the rebel camp and return with the remarkable story of Castro's survival. He had not brought a notebook or a typewriter. Instead, he was using eight-and-one-half by eleven lined sheets of writing paper folded in three so they fit in his left hand while he wrote with his right. At six foot one, Matthews was used to towering over the people he interviewed. Now he found himself looking straight into Castro's brown eyes, and he was captivated by how they flashed with intelligence and daring. He noticed his "extraordinary eloquence" and his "overpowering personality." Even the rebel's beard, a wispy, incomplete set of dark whiskers, made an impression on him, though he couldn't know how significant a part of rebel iconography that beard was to become. But by stressing Castro's youth when he wrote about his interview, and mentioning his beard, the long hair of his followers, and their audacious attempt to challenge the existing order, Matthews was identifying essential elements of Fidel's rebel character for Americans who would, soon enough, watch their own youth adopt some of the same features as they marched into the radical and rebellious 1960s.

Matthews was being subjected to Castro's flair for the dramatic. As the interview unfolded, Castro crouched close to him and whispered, warning that columns of Batista's soldiers surrounded the area where they were meeting, a small ridge on the hardscrabble farmstead of a local man named Epifanio Díaz. The area was dense with foliage and a cold mountain stream ran nearby. He knew that the army intended to liquidate the remnants of his rebel forces before the period of censorship was scheduled to end on March 1. He leaned toward Matthews, who wore a dark overcoat and a common cap, and put his lips close to the correspondent's ear. Castro spoke in a hoarse whisper and with an intensity that made everything he said resonate with possibility.

Matthews did not realize it, but he had not ventured far into the Sierra at all. The meeting place was barely twenty-five miles from the city of Manzanillo, hardly the heart of the forest. But the terrain was wild enough to have made it difficult for any army patrol to reach them. The main line of the army's encirclement had been set up about sixteen miles from where they were meeting, but no paved roads and only a few trails rutted with the tracks of ox carts traversed the hilly land in between. This was dangerous territory for the army but a good region for the guerrillas. The heavy forest also provided some camouflage to hide them from low-flying air patrols.

The rebels had laid out a blanket for Castro and Matthews, and offered the American some of the food they were surviving on in the mountains—tomato juice, coffee, crackers, and ham. Castro said the local peasants who provided the food were paid generously for their products and praised vigorously for their support of the revolution. The $300 Matthews had carried in would be used for that purpose, he said, and there was plenty more money where that came from. People all over Cuba supported their efforts to get rid of Batista, Castro bragged—some of them so rich and powerful that it would be a surprise if their names were revealed.

Castro could speak English, but he made it clear that he preferred to conduct the interview in Spanish. Matthews obliged him, although he continued to take most of his notes in English, translating as he went along. As the conversation progressed, Castro interspersed it with talk of his larger goal for a free and independent Cuba, one governed by the rule of law and respect for the rights of all Cubans. Matthews could easily see how Castro's courage and leadership inspired those who followed him, and he listened attentively to Castro's battle plan.

It was to be a classic guerrilla campaign, one in which the deep cover of the Sierra would obstruct and confuse the regular army that was pursuing the rebels. Surprise and stealth were to be their principal tactics—attacking the soldiers when and where they least expected it, then disappearing back into the folds of the Sierra. There the rebels' small numbers became a tactical advantage, every tree and bush a trusted ally.

Castro told Matthews that Batista's soldiers were not prepared for this type of mountain offensive and were fighting badly, but his own men had become well adapted to guerrilla warfare during their extensive training in Mexico. Even with the government's uncontested superiority in the number of troops and the quality of weapons, the soldiers could not do much more than hope to accidentally run into a rebel patrol and capture or kill the men before they fled. When the soldiers retreated to their barracks, he said, they were liable to be attacked while they slept or to be picked off by a long-range rifle shot without even knowing they had been targeted. Batista's men were becoming demoralized, whereas the rebels felt stronger and more confident every day. Castro told Matthews that the army had executed some of his men after capturing them to set an example of what could happen to rebels who challenged the government. But he treated his prisoners humanely and eventually freed them, a gesture intended to win over a broader swath of the Cuban people.

Castro was aware that Batista's censorship had prevented most Cubans from hearing anything truthful about the movement. "You will be the first to tell them," he said. Matthews knew that he had sensational news at hand, a once-in-a-lifetime drama. For a free-press stalwart like him, such a story served many purposes, but his principal goal was to break the silence Batista had imposed. He found the very idea of government censorship abhorrent. An article about Castro on the front page of *The New York Times* would render the censorship meaningless, and figuratively resurrect Fidel from the dead.

As a lawyer and a student of revolution, Castro understood the importance of a sympathetic press. He knew that to win over Matthews, he would have to convince him that the rebels were dominating the Sierra and growing stronger every day. Little about the encounter had been left to chance. Celia Sánchez, who joined Castro in the mountains and would become his closest confidante throughout the revolution, had taken charge of putting the temporary camp in order so that Matthews believed the disheveled troops were an army. They were in sorry shape after two and a half months on the run. Their clothes were shredded, their shoes battered and muddy, some held together by lengths of electric wire. She told them to clean themselves up as best they could. They wiped the mud off their rifles and marched in military formation close enough for Matthews to see them. One wore a shirt that was so tattered it had nothing but threads holding it together in the back, and he marched sideways so Matthews might not notice that he looked more like a vagabond than a soldier. But it is hard to imagine that Matthews did not spot him, and the attempted ruse, immediately.

Contemporary accounts of that day do not mention any attempt by the rebels to actually march in circles around Matthews to fool him into believing their numbers were greater than they actually were. And the topography of the meeting place makes it unlikely that such a scene ever occurred. The clearing where Castro met Matthews was a ridge that jutted out over the small stream that the local campesinos called the Rio Tío Lucas. Because the stream ran around the site on three sides, Batista's soldiers could not sneak up on the rebels without being detected. But the layout also meant there was not enough room for Castro's men to have marched around Matthews without him noticing.

Nonetheless, there was ample stage directing during the encounter. While Castro and Matthews talked, one of the rebels, Luís Crespo, returned to the temporary camp from a scouting expedition and reported to Raúl Castro, who took him aside. Crespo was to become a bit actor in the staged performance that was unfolding. With fresh instructions from Raúl, Crespo rushed over to Castro, who was still deep in conversation with Matthews, and interrupted.

"Mí commandante," he blurted out. "We've succeeded in reaching the second column."

Castro played his part in the revolutionary drama well. "Wait until I'm finished," he shouted at Crespo.

He then turned to Matthews and explained that the men and equipment around them constituted the first-column headquarters unit and that the Sierra was strung with columns of rebel soldiers. The place where they sat was well guarded, he said, and nothing moved without their knowledge. The rebels had sized up their enemy and knew its size, strength, and strategy.

Matthews wrote in his notes that Castro believed Batista had

3,000 men in the field surrounding the rebels, while his men walked in cells of seven to ten, and "a few of 30 or 40." He quoted Castro saying, "I will not tell you how many we have, for obvious reasons. He [Batista] works in columns of 200; we in groups of ten to 40, and we are winning. It is a battle against time and time is on our side."

Matthews had to weigh that information against the independent estimates of rebel strength that he had brought with him into the mountains. During the week he spent interviewing sources in Havana, he had been told that Castro's original group of eighty-two on the *Granma* had been cut down to no more than fifteen, but had subsequently rebuilt itself and attracted enough new recruits to constitute a fighting force of several hundred, with hundreds more Castro sympathizers throughout the Sierra. Matthews had the presence of mind to count each one of the individuals he saw during the interview, although the forested setting was confusing and he focused most of his attention on what Castro was saying. He figured that he saw about twenty-five men and women at the temporary camp. He could add to that number the 26th of July Movement leaders gathered in the safe house in Manzanillo, along with the scouts and guides who had helped him reach Castro's camp. In all, Matthews figured he had seen or heard roughly forty individuals, which seemed to correspond to Castro's description of "groups of ten to 40" and suggested that they were part of a larger force. It was a calculation that squared with what he had been told by several different sources, and he saw nothing to suggest it wasn't accurate. Had he written that Castro was holed up in the mountains with no more than a dozen rebels, his dispatch would have raised eyebrows in New York since it contradicted what had already been reported in the *Times* and what Ruby Phillips had told the editors in her memos. Such a low estimate, though in fact closer to the truth than the hundreds some had assumed were with Castro, would also have been challenged by the American embassy and nearly all the Cubans Matthews had spoken to before heading to the Sierra.

The entire interview lasted about three hours. Matthews asked only a few general questions and Castro put on an impressive display of oratory. Matthews was impressed by the way Castro's "brown eyes flash; his intense face is pushed close to the listener and the whispering voice, as in a stage play, lends a vivid sense of drama." One of Castro's men brought over a box of cigars. Castro took one and offered the box to Matthews, who was also a cigar smoker. Both lit up and as the air filled with the aromatic smoke, they talked of politics and Fidel's cloudy political aims. Matthews asked if what he had heard was true—that Castro was going to use the strength of his forces to declare his own revolutionary government, assuming control of Oriente Province and making Santiago a new capital.

"Not yet," Castro answered, as though he simply needed to determine the right time for doing so. "I will make myself known at the opportune moment. It will have all the more effect for the delay, for now everybody is talking about us. We are sure of ourselves."

As Matthews puffed on his cigar, he tried to assess the man in front of him. Fidel clearly had enormous self-confidence, and his belief in himself, and in his cause, was the fuel that fired the passion of the men around him. But Matthews thought he also detected a few weaknesses. He did not think Castro had a firm grip on complex issues of national economy. Nor did he see evidence that he was a great military leader. Apparently, his was a revolutionary mind, and a political one.

Castro made his political ambitions clear, though he could not describe how he intended to achieve those goals. Nationalism was at the core of his revolution, he said, and that meant he also stood against the forces of colonialism and imperialism that he believed oppressed Cuba. He was angry with the United States for continuing to support Batista and provide him with weapons that were being used against the rebels in the Sierra and against Cubans all over the island. But that did not imply that he was anti-American, he told Matthews. "You can be sure we have no animosity toward the United States and the American people," he said. Matthews did not challenge him, although he had gotten a glimpse of

Castro's ambivalent feelings toward the United States during his interviews in Havana.

Matthews thought he detected strong democratic strains in Castro's revolutionary goals. He embraced liberty, democracy, and social justice, and his overriding goal was to restore the constitution that Batista had violated with his 1952 coup d'état. Holding new elections, said Castro, the former congressional candidate, and giving Cubans back the democratic right to choose their own leaders—that was the principal goal.

Matthews ascribed other goals to the insurgents as well, though he outlined them only in general terms. Repeating observations first made by Ruby Phillips, he classified the movement as principally one of youth, and he tagged Fidel "the flaming symbol of the opposition" to the Batista regime, even though he knew that there were strong leaders in other opposition groups. He described the 26th of July Movement as revolutionary, and he classified it as socialistic and nationalistic, but definitely not communistic. He adhered to a formal definition of Communists that included only those who belonged to the Communist Party and who took orders from the Central Committee, a narrower focus than that taken by many other observers. He knew that Castro intended to force Batista to leave office, but he could only vaguely predict what might happen once power was vacated. "It amounts to a new deal for Cuba," Matthews wrote, describing the rebel's vision for a new Cuba as being "radical, democratic and therefore anti-Communist."

"Above all," Castro told Matthews that morning, "we are fighting for a democratic Cuba and an end to the dictatorship. We are not anti-military; that is why we let the soldier prisoners go. There is no hatred of the Army as such, for we know the men are good and so are many of the officers."

However, he did not hesitate to boast about his prowess in picking off those same soldiers with his telescopic rifle and fifty others like it that he said his men carried. Here Matthews clearly was insufficiently critical. Had he demanded to see the other rifles, Castro would have been caught in an outright lie. At that time there were no others, and even after the rebels procured additional ones, there never would be fifty. Further, Fidel said, when the revolution triumphed, soldiers would be paid $100 a month, substantially more than the $72 a month they received now. He had the money to pay for this and all his other plans; to prove it, he had one of his men bring over to the blanket a package wrapped in a brown cloth. Inside was a large pile of peso bills. Matthews estimated that there must have been about $4,000 in the stack.

By this time, the coolness of the night was a fading memory. It was about 9:00 AM and the Caribbean sun was blazing. Suddenly, a bomber roared overhead and the unfortunate rebel with the white shirt had to be pulled into the bushes to keep from being spotted. The army plane continued on to higher elevations in the Sierra, where it dropped its explosives, far from the rebel camps. "They bomb every day," Castro said, signaling that the interview was over. It was time for Matthews to head back to the city.

"You have taken quite a risk in coming here," Castro said, and for the first time he acknowledged Matthews's own mission. If anything could stand for the moment when a personal relationship developed between the two men, this would be it. Sharing danger, as they had shared food and cigars that morning, brought them together in an unspoken pact. Matthews had already signaled a willingness to believe in Castro. His questions during the interview had been straightforward and even gentle, not intended to cross up Castro or catch him in contradictions. He did not challenge Castro's assertions, not even those that must have seemed most improbable, such as Castro's claim that the ragtag troops had won many battles with Batista's well-equipped regular army. And now, at the end of the interview, Castro was expressing concern for the American's well-being. With great sincerity he assured Matthews that he would be returned without trouble. "We have the whole area covered," he said, "and we will get you out safely."

Before he left, Matthews had one last request, one that again brought the two men together on the same side in a shared goal.

He handed Castro the folded-over sheets of paper on which he had been taking notes and asked him to sign his name to them. There would be doubters, he said, but the signature would authenticate the interview he had conducted with the rebel leader who was believed to be dead. He also asked one of Castro's men to use a small box camera to photograph the two of them together, smoking their cigars and talking about the roots of revolution.

After the interview ended, Javier Pazos led Matthews back down the hill to a farmhouse where they waited for the jeep to take them the rest of the way. Matthews was driven back to the house in Manzanillo where Nancie had spent the night. There he washed and shaved, changing out of the muddy camp clothes, tired but bursting with anticipation. He had something to eat before being driven to Santiago, where he interviewed three professors from the University of Oriente who were followers of the 26th of July Movement. Matthews considered their support a sign of the movement's popularity in middle-class circles.

Later that day, Matthews and Nancie took the afternoon flight to Havana. Although he was pressured to leave right away, and Ruby Phillips encouraged him to get out before anyone discovered what he had done, Matthews insisted on remaining in the city a while longer to interview student leaders, including José Antonio Echeverría, president of the Student University Federation, a potential rival of Castro's who didn't always see eye to eye with him. Matthews was taken to the students' hideout in the El Vedado district of Havana for a secret meeting with Echeverría and other fanatic youths dedicated to Batista's overthrow. "We are accustomed to clandestine struggles," said the twenty-four-year-old architectural student, whose friends called him "El Gordo" (the fat one). "Cuban students are never afraid to die," he boasted. Soon enough, they would have the chance.

As Matthews knew, their interview was only part of Castro's plan for that day. For the first time since Castro had returned to Cuba, he was calling together the national leaders of the 26th of July Movement. He intended to coordinate their efforts and tame competing factions. One group wanted to disperse the fighters on several fronts in the mountains and in the cities. Castro insisted that they concentrate all their weapons and funds on the Sierra. Castro was also worried about opposition groups such as the radical students in Havana that were larger and more powerful than his own and would challenge him for control of the anti-Batista movement. He intended to leave no doubt that only one person could be in charge, and he was that person.

After Matthews left the clearing, Castro had one other important matter to take care of before he could start the meeting with national resistance leaders. He was convinced that the peasant Eutimio Guerra was a traitor, spying for Batista's army. During the previous weeks, Guerra had ingratiated himself into the rebel group, and one night Castro had even shared a blanket with him. Guerra lay on the ground next to Fidel with a .45 pistol in his hand. All he had to do was to pull the trigger. His target was inches away, unguarded and utterly vulnerable. But he couldn't do it.

As Matthews hiked back through the forest, Castro sent several men to find Guerra and bring him to a clearing near the spot where the interview had taken place. When they frisked him, they found a pistol, three hand grenades, and a letter from the local army commander guaranteeing his safe passage through the region. He even wore a brand-new pair of army boots, a reward for the information about the rebels he had provided, and an unmistakable symbol of his betrayal.

Guerra fell to his knees and begged to be shot immediately. But Ciro Frías, one of Castro's men, insisted they wait while he humiliated Guerra, reminding him of how much he had benefited from being with the rebels and how ruthlessly he had betrayed them. Guerra, his head bent, asked only that the revolution take care of his children. The day had turned stormy. As thunder crackled, one of the men shot him through the head.

Three days after Matthews's interview, Castro composed his first public message since the landing in December. He planned for the manifesto to coincide with the publication of Matthews's article. In it, he outlined briefly how, despite rumors spread by Batista, they had not only survived but had regrouped into an effective fighting force that had the army scared. He described the battles they had won. Exaggerating his victories and painting the army in the worst light, at one point he even suggested that the soldiers had run off and left their dead behind to be picked at by vultures.

"Can Batista go on hiding from the country and the whole world what is happening here?" he wrote. "The interview we had in the heart of the Sierra with *The New York Times* correspondent will be published with photographs any minute now."

Batista's censorship kept the manifesto out of the newspapers and off the radio, and few Cubans knew of its existence. But within days they would know much more.

After interviewing Echeverría and the student leaders, Matthews had completed every stop on his list but one. That night, he and Nancie visited Ernest and Mary Hemingway at the Finca Vigía, the couple's estate outside Havana. The Cuban Revolution would keep the two old friends from the Spanish Civil War in touch with each other for a long time. After the visit, Matthews returned to the Sevilla Biltmore and prepared to leave Cuba, anxious to begin work on the articles. He worried about getting his notes and the photographs of the meeting past the customs inspectors at the airport. If the notes were discovered, there could be trouble, especially since they carried Castro's signature.

"They're dangerous," Nancie told her husband. "Let me carry them."

She took the seven pages of folded notes and stuck them inside her girdle, certain that the Cuban inspectors would not dare to look there. They took the earliest flight available, departing Havana for New York on Tuesday morning, February 19, two days after he had left Fidel in the clearing in the Sierra. As the twin-propeller plane cleared the sky over Havana and headed out over the Caribbean toward Key West and southern Florida, Nancie excused herself and went to the plane's lavatory. She came back with the wrinkled notes. Matthews was already writing the story that he believed would breathe fresh air into his career.

In the first few lines of what later became three long articles based on the interviews in Cuba, Matthews laid out his extraordinary story, and put himself smack in the middle of it forever.

Fidel Castro, the rebel leader of Cuba's youth, is alive and fighting hard and successfully in the rugged, almost impenetrable fastnesses of the Sierra Maestra, at the southern tip of the island.

President Fulgencio Batista has the cream of his Army around the area, but the Army men are fighting a thus-far losing battle to destroy the most dangerous enemy General Batista has yet faced in a long and adventurous career as a Cuban leader and dictator.

This is the first sure news that Fidel Castro is still alive and still in Cuba. No one connected with the outside world, let alone with the press, has seen Señor Castro except this writer. No one in Havana, not even at the United States Embassy with all its resources for getting information, will know until this report is published that Fidel Castro is really in the Sierra Maestra.

a chapter in a fantastic novel

Old Havana rested on three principal points of power in 1957: the embassy of the United States, Batista's ornate and heavily guarded Presidential Palace, and a few blocks away, the lovely Art Deco offices of the Bacardí rum company, one of the most powerful and well connected firms on the island. Inside the seven-story tan and pink building, with its three-dimensional brick chevrons and the letter B worked into the wrought-iron grating over the ground-floor windows, Bacardí's president, José "Pepin" Bosch, oversaw a vast enterprise that turned Cuba's main crop, sugar cane, into a high-value export identified around the world with Cuba itself. This, and his family's extraordinary wealth, gave the firm a standing in national affairs equivalent to a government secretariat powerful enough to have on its payroll important national figures like Felipe Pazos, the former head of the National Bank of Cuba, who, like Bosch himself, was being drawn ever more closely into the anti-Batista revolutionary movement.

Men like Pazos and Bosch were old enough then to have lived with Batista most of their adult lives, and they had watched uneasily as he grew ever more arrogant and corrupt. Batista toyed with

Cuba's constitution, running in presidential elections and, when it suited him, bypassing the law and seizing power. His legal term was scheduled to end in 1958, but there had been growing suspicions within Havana's elite that Batista would try to have the constitution amended to allow him to run for reelection in another crooked contest. The moderate political opposition, ever hopeful of a peaceful transition back to constitutional rule, had at first attempted to negotiate with Batista and had had some initial successes. During the 1954 election campaign, they had demanded the release of all political prisoners and an amnesty for all political exiles. In a halfhearted attempt at compromise, Batista had released all the prisoners, including the Castro brothers, and he had allowed Prío Socarrás to return from exile in Miami.

Over time, however, it became clear that Batista was using such actions to delay any real move toward constitutional rule. By early 1957, just a year before the next scheduled elections, it was apparent that Batista's illegal government could only be ended by force. Then, with the dictator finally out of the way, a new regime—moderate, responsive, and more to the liking of men like Bosch and Pazos—could be installed. The disruption, they believed, would be minimal and Cuba could get back to business as usual.

Several groups besides Castro's were causing trouble in Cuba at this time. For the most part they operated independently of each other, with different approaches, competing leaders, and constituencies that did not overlap. Castro's old political party, the Ortodoxos, remained actively opposed to Batista but it restricted itself to political organizing and refrained from violence. In April 1956, about forty army officers who did not support Batista planned an uprising that was to be led by Colonel Ramón Barquín, a well-respected commander. They were betrayed and Batista threw them all in jail. In another attempt to topple the regime, a group of Prío Socarrás's supporters attacked a barracks in Matanzas. But the uprising was quelled, and the former president was taken into custody and once again forced into exile in Miami. The student movement in Havana, led by Antonio Echeverría, regularly planted bombs throughout the city and hoped to ignite chaos that weakened the dictator. The radical nature of the students and their inexperience made it impossible for the middle-class businessmen of Havana and the power brokers like Pazos and Bosch to support them.

For moderates who wanted to see Batista removed, there seemed no alternative but to support Castro's movement, whether or not Castro himself had survived. At the very least, he had fulfilled his vow to return to Cuba by the end of 1956, and his legend was growing, even in the face of his apparent demise. No one had heard from him for months, but in the absence of any solid information, rumors filled the air. And as Batista's reprisals grew more gory, as the bodies of students and dissenters were found on street corners and along the roads leading from Havana and Santiago, as others simply disappeared after attending a meeting or speaking out against the dictator, support for the rebels slowly increased. If they somehow managed to force Batista from power, no one expected them to govern. In a post-Batista world they would have to share power with the other dissident groups, along with their elite backers and the military. It was thought that a moderate, constitutional government could be formed to balance the competing interests. But that would come later. First, Batista had to be removed.

Pazos had initially been brought into the 26th of July Movement by his son, Javier, but by now he had become a solid ally and part of the movement's urban wing, moderate in politics though radical in opposition to Batista. While Matthews was in the Sierra, Pazos asked to see Mario Llerena, a leading intellectual who had returned to Cuba after years of teaching Spanish at Duke University in North Carolina. Llerena now headed the Committee for Cultural Freedom, which opposed Batista's attempts to control the media. Llerena and Castro had met in Mexico during the preparations for the invasion. He had agreed to provide intellectual and planning support. His academic training and moderate politics could help put flesh on the ideological bones of the insurrection, which had until then been vague and unfocused, promising a restoration of the constitution and an end to injustice without offering any details. Llerena had done extensive political writing, and he was no friend of the illegitimate

Batista regime. But neither did he want to see one corrupt government replaced by another, as had happened so often in the past. Like many other moderates, he believed that a rebel movement of youth had the possibility of presenting something new for Cuba, if it was committed to legitimacy and legality.

One day shortly after Matthews interviewed Castro, Llerena walked the three blocks from his office to Pazos's in Old Havana, and their conversation quickly turned to the 26th of July Movement. Pazos said that, in time, the rebels would be able to force out Batista and make room for a new, constitutional government in which the modest reforms begun under Grau and Prío could be resumed. Pazos handed Llerena an analysis of Cuba's economy and a restructuring plan to reduce or eliminate many of the nation's problems. It was the same report that Castro had shown him in Mexico. Pazos had helped put it together.

But Pazos said he hadn't asked Llerena to come to discuss economics.

Llerena, a slight man with a dignified air, was surprised when Pazos told him that he knew, with certainty, that Castro was alive and fighting in the Sierra Maestra, where an American correspondent had gone to interview him.

As a sometime journalist himself, Llerena understood how damaging Batista's censorship had been. The silence was threatening to smother the movement before it could take hold. An article in an important American newspaper beyond the reach of Batista's censors could end the silence and begin the revolution.

But even an American newspaper would be stopped by censors. Pazos said he was looking for someone to fly to New York when the article came out, have it reprinted, and airmail copies to the most important people in Cuba.

Pazos passed Llerena an envelope containing a round-trip ticket to New York, along with extra cash to cover his expenses while in the United States.

Pazos then handed Llerena a telephone directory and the *Havana Social Registry*. "Here," he said, "for names and addresses."

*   *   *

Matthews got to work soon after he landed in New York, drinking in the secret satisfaction of knowing he had the greatest scoop of his life. He realized it had been purely accidental that he had been called in to interview Castro. But that did not take away from the fact that it had required a great deal of planning, and not a little pluck and courage, to get by the sentries without being caught. He had never doubted that the risks were worth taking or that he was again being given the opportunity to leave a mark on history.

It had been almost twenty years since the controversies over his reporting in Spain, and many of the editors that Matthews had sparred with then were no longer around to raise questions about his objectivity. The newspaper was widely suspected of having a liberal bias, though it had stood up to withering accusations during the McCarthy hearings. But the paper could not shake off the reputation of being soft on communism. That charge had also been leveled against Matthews during the Spanish Civil War, though he denied it. He was now a member of the editorial board, which put him in a peculiar position to be writing news articles about a budding revolution that he also analyzed on the editorial page. Still, Matthews had the publisher's blessing for his dual role, and his earlier articles from Argentina had proved that combining commentary and news made him one of the most powerful writers in the region.

If any editors retained reservations about Matthews's objectivity, they did not raise them now. Instead, they seemed willing to do everything they could to give his exclusive story big play. They had Matthews write not one but three separate articles about Cuba, pulling together political and economic analysis with the sensational material from the interview. The first article gave the big news that Castro was alive, and told the story of Matthews's trek into the rebel camp. The second article focused on Batista and the revolutionary mood in Cuba, and the third put the current troubles in historical context, while also looking at other groups that were trying to compete with Castro's for power and popular support. Because they were certain that no other paper had the Castro story, the editors held the series all week so they could start running it on Sunday, when circulation is nearly twice as high as during the week. That left Matthews little more than three days to pull the whole thing together, which would have been impossible for a less well organized writer. While Matthews worked on his pieces, the paper's Promotion Department trumpeted the upcoming series in house ads within the news pages, highlighting the possibility of a revolution in Cuba without giving away Matthews's big news.

In those days, there were no remote newscasts or satellite phones. Simply getting to a troubled place could be news, and "exclusive" could refer to something truly unique and sensational. Here, the paper had a story in which it was certain that its correspondent had gone where no other reporter had been, and returned with a story no one else had—a trophy specimen of a scoop. The newspaper advertisements revealed that Matthews had just returned "from a visit to that seething republic. And he brought back with him a story that's sure to startle the world." Vowing to get around the censorship that Batista imposed, the ad promised that the series would reveal how the Cuban people were feeling about Batista. It went significantly beyond what Matthews would report when it claimed that the articles would explain why Cubans were violently anti-American. And, without mentioning Castro or his movement, it predicted that "the old order is approaching its end."

Matthews had little trouble putting together the articles the way he wanted. There were only a few contentious points in the editing, the most significant being questions about the $300 that Matthews had carried in for the rebels. He originally included that incident in the first article, but it struck Theodore Bernstein, then the night managing editor, as being open to misinterpretation. It would either have to be thoroughly explained that the money belonged to the rebels and that Matthews had agreed to carry it only as a precaution in case their car had been searched or left out all together because readers might interpret it as a sign that Matthews was getting involved in the revolution. In the end, Bernstein asked for it to be cut, and Matthews complied.

News about Communists was everywhere in 1957. Juan Perón was suspected of plotting a return to power in Argentina, where, according to American political analysis, he would install a Communist regime and become the Stalin of Latin America. President Eisenhower marked the fifteenth anniversary of the Voice of America by issuing another warning about the dangers of the "Red peril." Elvis Presley was being drafted into an army that was ready to tangle with Communists anywhere in the world. American newspapers were filled with such articles as the final touches were being put on Matthews's series. The first article ran on Sunday, February 24. The early city edition came off the printing presses on Saturday night, as usual, and had a limited circulation in New York City. It was also trucked to the airport to be flown to distant markets, including Miami and, later, Havana. Matthews's article dominated page one and was accompanied by a striking photograph of Castro standing beneath a jungle canopy, holding the telescopic rifle that he had boasted of to Matthews. The expression on his face in that photograph was benign, even humble, as though Matthews had merely stumbled onto him while wandering along a path in the Sierra. The headline, "Cuban Rebel Is Visited in Hideout," put the emphasis on Matthews, while the subhead, "Castro Is Still Alive and Still Fighting in Mountains," foretold a broader story.

After seeing a copy of the first edition, Matthews complained that the photograph alone was not sufficiently convincing to prove that he had actually seen Fidel. His experience with readers and his own editors who doubted his eyewitness reports from Spain had made him especially sensitive to such things, and he now anticipated a similar reaction. He got his notes from the Sierra and suggested that Castro's signature would reassure readers that the interview had truly taken place. He ripped off the bot-

tom one-third of the last page of his notes and a layout editor past-
ed it onto the front page below Castro's photograph. There, in
the rebel's florid handwriting, were his signature and the silent
testimony of the words "Sierra Maestra, Febrero 17 de 1957."

Photo credit was given to *The New York Times*.

Llerena was already in New York when the article came out. As
soon as he had landed he got in touch with a small group of
Cubans in New York and New Jersey who were willing to help.
Since the first article had indicated that there would be two others, Llerena waited until the series ended before sending anything back to Cuba. The second was published on the front page
on Monday, February 25. The third article ran inside the first section of the newspaper two days later.

Llerena got to work. He clipped the articles and laid them out
on cardboard sheets, which he then brought to an offset printer.
While the printer was running off thousands of copies, Llerena
and his helpers scanned the Havana directory and the *Social
Registry* for names and addresses. In all, they mailed between
3,000 and 4,000 copies of the series to Cuba, certain that each one
would then be read, passed along several times, and talked about
at every office, café, and restaurant in Havana within days. Despite
Batista's censorship, everyone would know that Fidel was alive,
that the movement had survived.

While he was in New York, Llerena went to see Matthews, who
welcomed him enthusiastically. Llerena had no doubt that
Matthews was a friend of the revolution. He later wrote that he
found the writer to be openly sympathetic. Matthews told Llerena
about his own trip to Cuba, and he spoke highly of Castro, with
whom, he said, he was most impressed.

Matthews, thrilled by the effort to skirt the Cuban censors,
offered Llerena advice. Llerena recalled that Matthews suggested
he try to get an appearance on American television, perhaps
adding to the drama by disguising his identity and allowing himself to be called a secret agent of the rebel underground in

Havana. He could present the goals of the revolutionary movement to a curious American public while further exposing the abuses of Batista's regime. Matthews called CBS News in New York, and Llerena was given an appointment there for the following morning.

After Matthews's articles appeared, every major news organization wanted to get in touch with the Cuban rebels. The newsmen at CBS discussed with Llerena the kind of program appearance that Matthews had suggested. The news director expected Matthews to accompany Llerena on the broadcast, but when he called Matthews to ask him to participate, the answer was no. Matthews felt that appearing on camera with Llerena would make it seem that he was part of the revolutionary movement and raise doubts about his editorial positions on Cuba.

Without Matthews, the man who had found Castro, to lend credibility, the news director was uncomfortable about broadcasting an interview with Llerena, and the project was killed. Nonetheless, CBS was keenly interested in the situation in Cuba and wanted to get its own crew in to see Castro. The director invited Llerena to stay for lunch with a few other newsmen, including Robert Taber, a documentary filmmaker who had a particular interest in the Cuban revolution. They asked Llerena to help get Taber in to see Castro, and he agreed to do everything he could to arrange the interview.

Llerena returned to Havana to begin preparations for the television crew's visit. He found that the country he had left only a few days before had been turned upside down during his absence.

Each copy of the Sunday newspaper with the first part of Matthews's series was delivered in Cuba with a section of the front page missing and another hole inside. Under Batista's censorship rules, an individual censor was assigned to every newspaper circulated in Cuba, and the censor responsible for the *Times* had immediately ordered the article, along with Castro's photograph, scissored out of each copy before it was distributed.

But no censorship could completely suppress news as sensational as what was contained in Matthews's articles, especially in a place like Cuba, so close to the United States and so filled with revolutionary tension. Travelers who flew to Havana that Sunday from New York and Miami brought the uncensored newspaper with them, and within hours, the story had spread by word of mouth all over the capital.

In the Presidential Palace, Batista was as confused as he was furious. He had believed his officers when they told him Castro was dead. Then he had trusted them when they said he was still in Mexico. When they reported that the Sierra was encased in a "ring of steel" through which no rebels, or reporters, could pass, he had taken them at their word. He turned to Edmund Chester, a former American newsman who worked as an aide, to help him put togther a response. Chester also believed Castro was dead, and he drafted a statement, in English, that would be released by Cuba's minister of defense, Santiago Verdeja. Chester framed the blistering statement as a response to a cable from the *New York Herald Tribune*, the *Times*'s chief rival, which had pressed the government for an official reaction to the articles.

"Before anything else, let me assure you that the opinion of the Government, and I am sure, of the Cuban public also, is that the interview and the adventures described by Correspondent Matthews can be considered as a chapter in a fantastic novel," Verdeja's statement read. Then he pushed the button he knew would incite the greatest reaction in the United States, by linking Castro with communism: "Mr. Matthews has not interviewed the pro-Communist insurgent, Fidel Castro, and the information came from certain opposition sources."

Like most Latin countries in the 1950s (and the United States as well), Cuba had a Communist Party that was well established, though not very powerful. The Cuban Communists were agitating for Batista's removal, but they were not generally cooperating with Castro's movement, which they considered too violent and unpredictable. "Communism has little to do with the opposition to the regime," Matthews wrote in the second article of his series.

However, Raúl Castro and Che Guevara, who had clear Communist connections, were gaining more influence with the 26th of July Movement. Matthews wrote that Batista still had the upper hand and, if he could stave off his rivals, would finish his term in office, which was scheduled to end in February 1959.

The third article was, in some ways, the most accurate, but it received the least attention. It outlined in detail how the budding insurrection in Cuba was different from others that had come before. For the first time since the establishment of the republic, the old order would be challenged by a new way of thinking. Matthews noted that the confluence of forces—the disillusioned middle-class businessmen, the angry university students, and the hard-core rebels in the Sierra—all wanted to end the revolving door of corrupt strongmen and establish a rule of law. The ongoing struggle, he wrote, "is more than an effort by the outs to get in and enjoy the enormous spoils of office that have been the reward of political victory." He warned that this would not be just another political game of musical chairs. Rather, Castro planned a sweeping social revolution that was likely to be marked by some anti-American sentiments. Cubans had resented the open interference by the United States in Cuban affairs since the end of the Spanish-American War and were especially incensed because Washington continued to sell arms to Batista. Matthews focused more intensively in the final article on Echeverría's radical student movement than on Castro's guerrillas, but since he had not needed heroics to get to Echeverría, the portrait fell flat.

Verdeja, Batista's defense minister, repeated the government's claim of not knowing whether Castro was alive or dead. But even if, by chance, Castro was alive, Verdeja said, he did not command forces that were anywhere near the size or strength reported by Matthews. He rejected Matthews's claim that the Cuban economy was hindered by corruption. In the end, he denied that the interview had ever taken place, going so far as to lay down a challenge to Matthews and the *Times*.

"It is noted that Matthews published a photograph saying that it was of Castro," Verdeja's statement said. "It seems strange that, having had such an interview, Matthews did not have a photograph taken of himself with the pro-Communist insurgent in order to provide proof of what he wrote."

Matthews responded quickly. Along with the photo that had run on the front page, Matthews had brought back several others. They were of poor quality, badly composed, and so out of focus that they were considered to be too amateurish to run. But after Batista's government issued its challenge, the editors went back over the photographs and selected one that left no doubt that Matthews had been with Castro. The photograph showed the two men sitting together in the forest: Castro is lighting a cigar, while Matthews, a cigar in his mouth, is taking notes. Matthews was wearing a heavy black overcoat and a cap. Castro, seated alongside him, wore military fatigues. The print was so blurred that it had to be retouched in the composing room to give some lines more definition. The day after the series was complete, the paper published the text of Verdeja's statement along with the photograph and a response from Matthews. "The story about Fidel Castro surely speaks for itself," he wrote. "It is hard to believe that anyone reading it can have any doubts." He went on to explain that Verdeja had received the early edition of the paper that was flown to Cuba and had not seen Fidel's signature, which was used in later editions.

"The truth will always out," Matthews wrote, "censorship or no censorship."

The pro-government Cuban newspaper *Prensa Libre* continued to doubt Matthews. It criticized the photograph and said it was so indistinct that the person claiming to be Castro could have been a guerrilla from Ireland or Cyprus. And if the interview had truly taken place in Cuba, the newspaper asked, why was Matthews wearing a heavy coat and a hat? Another pro-Batista newspaper, *Ataja*, called Matthews an outright liar.

The anti-Batista newspaper *Revolución* was printed in the garage of a nondescript middle-class house in Havana. Carlos Franqui, editor-in-chief and an active member of the July 26 underground, wrote about Matthews's interview and helped distribute the newspaper clandestinely. Franqui and a friend loaded a car with copies of *Revolución* and had set out to deliver them in the exclusive sections of Havana when they were stopped by a patrol car. They so feared being caught with the papers, Franqui said later, that had they been carrying guns, they would have preferred to shoot their way through rather than submit to a search. But they had no weapons, and when ordered to pull over, they did so, expecting to be arrested.

The police, however, were looking for expired license plates, and while Franqui idled on the side street with the trunkload of incriminating newspapers, the police stopped other cars and pulled them into a line behind him. Franqui took advantage of the distraction. He and his friend unloaded the newspapers into a taxi. Franqui stayed with the car while his friend left with the damning evidence.

The drivers were ordered to a nearby police station, where their vehicles were impounded until they came back with valid license plates. As the long procession stopped at a traffic light, Franqui looked back and saw a copy of *Revolución* on the backseat of his car. The headline: "Fidel in the Sierra." He grabbed the newspaper, walked over to the patrol car, and leaned in to ask the officers if they had his driver's license. While they were distracted he dropped the newspaper, letting it blow away onto the streets of Havana.

Matthews's story in *Revolución* was soon being read all over the capital. The thousands of copies of the articles that Mario Llerena had mailed from New York were being delivered. Everywhere, Cubans talked about the Sierra. They carefully pronounced Fidel's name, as though just saying it made them insurgents. And they all talked of Matthews, the American who had found Fidel and brought his news to the world.

Throughout his long career, Matthews had never experienced anything like the reaction to the Cuban series. He was inundated with congratulatory telegrams and letters, many from expatriate

Cubans. "We bow before you as a reporter for being the first person to tell the world the truth about Cuba," Castro's sisters Lidia and Emma told Matthews in a Western Union telegram from Mexico City. Raúl Chibás, brother of the political martyr and radio host, Eduardo Chibás, had become a Castro sympathizer and sent a box of cigars and a congratulatory note in appreciation for Matthews's "admirable help in favor of Cuban democracy." Richard Cushing, the press attaché at the U.S. embassy in Havana, sent a personal note just as the series ended. "Strictly unofficially, and from a professional point of view, I want to convey my congratulations to you for a piece of journalism reminiscent of the best of a bygone age," Cushing wrote. "Needless to say, your series caused a lot of seething indignation in high quarters" within the embassy. The FBI agent in Havana wrote to Washington asking for information about Matthews and stating that the Cuban government "has initiated an all-out campaign to show that Castro and his group are Communistically inclined, that Matthews, if not a Communist, at least has leftist tendencies, and that all revolutionary activities against the Batista Government . . . are Communist inspired." The U.S. embassy, the agent noted, could not substantiate the Cuban government's claims.

American newspapers picked up the story of Castro's survival. The *Chicago Tribune* ran an abridged version of Matthews's series, spreading it out over five days and reporting that the articles were "becoming a Cuban national issue." John A. Brogan, Jr., of the King Features Syndicate, sent Matthews a note expressing his "heartfelt congratulations on a newspaper job well done. It reminds me," Brogan wrote, "of the good old Hearstian accomplishments."

Matthews's articles, and the sympathetic way he described Castro, made the rebel leader seem like an American hero and put Matthews into the role of mythmaker in a postwar age when Americans were accustomed to larger-than-life figures and hadn't yet become cynical about those they admired. Matthews had not merely reported that Castro had survived the invasion. He had called him "the flaming symbol of the opposition to the regime" and had said that great numbers of Cubans from all walks of life were with him, "heart and soul."

Such soaring rhetoric elicited rhetoric to match. Eight honor students at the University of California at Berkeley wrote to Matthews to tell him that his articles had inspired them to head down to Cuba, where they intended to hire Jeeps, disguise themselves as anthropologists, and climb into the Sierra to help Fidel. Other readers sent glowing letters of praise, and one from Piermont, New York, was spurred to poetry.

> *Your ancestors fought like Castro and like him*
> *In peril of your life, you braved the guns*
> *Of night patrols. In dripping forests dim*
> *With rain, where the icy stream of danger runs*
> *In the veins you found him—and your story*
> *Of his fight adds luster to Old Glory.*

Matthews became a hero in Cuba. "Without a doubt, Mr. Herbert L. Matthews of *The New York Times* has been, in the last few months, the focal point of Cuban citizens," wrote the *Vocero Occidental* of Pinar del Rio, the busy provincial capital city west of Havana. Matthews was described as "a tall man, thin, half bald, a simple dresser, silent as a tomb, precise as a Swiss watch, a perfect Anglo-Saxon, with eyes that are fixed when he speaks and gestures that are always deliberate. He smiles every once in a while. He smokes like a chimney, but he prefers the finest of our cigars." The public adulation left Batista raging against both Castro and the man who had resurrected him from the dead.

The regime refused to accept reality. The day after the photograph of Castro and Matthews appeared, Batista's chief commander in Oriente, General Martín Díaz Tamayo, denied that Matthews had been able to sneak past his troops in the Sierra. He called the interview with Castro "imaginary" because no one could have entered or left the restricted zone in the Sierra without being detected. "In my opinion this gentleman was not even in Cuba," Tamayo said. "Someone furnished the imaginary information and then his imagination did the rest." Tamayo refused to concede that his sentries had failed miserably, and he tried to discredit the newspaper by calling into question the motives of the reporter: "This interview is prefabricated with the purpose of aiding the psychological war which is going on in the country. I do not know where we will go if we listen to rumors of this type."

A week after the series ended, Batista agreed to an interview with Jules Dubois, the Latin American correspondent of the *Chicago Tribune*, who, like Matthews, was becoming increasingly involved in the Cuban story. Dubois was also active in the leadership of the Inter-American Press Association, and he wanted to ask Batista for assurances that he would not try to shut off the flow of news again.

Batista, however, wanted to talk about Castro, and about Herbert Matthews. He tried to insist that Matthews had never been to the Sierra. Dubois, who knew Matthews fairly well, assured him that there was no way such a thing could be faked. Batista hadn't even been convinced by the photo of Matthews together with Castro, although eventually he would be. At this time, though, all he was willing to concede was that Castro, perhaps, had not died in the botched invasion.

Batista believed only what he wished to be true, and he was allowing his emotional response to deepen his troubles. On Sunday, March 10, Batista gave a speech at the army headquarters of Camp Columbia on the outskirts of Havana. He publicly repeated what he had told Dubois during the interview a few days earlier: Castro was a Communist, manipulated by the Kremlin. His nascent insurrection was not a bid for freedom but part of a Communist conspiracy that would bring trouble to Cuba. It was a line of thought that U.S. ambassador Arthur Gardner had accepted and had repeated a few weeks earlier when Matthews had stopped by to see him before heading to Oriente. But neither Matthews nor Dubois believed it. Neither did the State Department at that time.

As proof of Castro's survival mounted, Batista had to grudgingly admit that Castro was still alive and that Matthews had managed to see him. "The interview, in effect, had taken place and its publication gave considerable propaganda and support to the rebel group," Batista wrote years later, when he recognized the importance of that hushed Sunday morning meeting in the mountains. "Castro was to begin to be a legendary personage and would end by being a monster of terror."

A rare combination of factors contributed to the impact of the articles, and the many events they helped set in motion. They did not create Fidel from nothing, but they did change his image from hotheaded loser to noble rogue with broad ideals, a characterization that appealed to a large spectrum of Cubans as well as Americans. He immediately became the leading figure in the opposition, causing jealousy in the other groups and some dissension within the 26th of July Movement between those in the Sierra, who felt all resources should be devoted to the military campaign, and others in the cities, who thought Castro could be most useful as a symbol, sending back messages and money from a safe exile in Mexico or the United States. The impact of Matthews's image of Castro was immediate, and it continued to spread for months and years to come, leaving its mark on two lives, two countries, and history.

the best friend of the cuban people

When Che Guevara first heard a radio report about Matthews's articles, the living breath was being squeezed out of him. Chill nightly rains had brought on his asthma, and he had lost his asthma medicine somewhere in the chaos of the previous ten weeks in the Sierra. When it got so bad that he could barely walk, he decided to hole up in a coffee grove near the thatched-roof hut of a peasant, Emiliano Leyva, who had offered the rebels shelter. It was the end of February, and with the sugar harvest well advanced and the island comparatively quiet, Batista had decided to lift his forty-five-day censorship order a few days early. While Che waited for his asthma to loosen its grip on his scarred lungs, the first uncensored radio broadcasts were put on the air.

Che had not been present during the interview with Matthews. All he knew of it was what Castro had told him—that Matthews seemed to understand what they were trying to do and had not asked any tricky questions intended to trip him up. In answer to one of Matthews's questions, Castro told Che he had described himself as an anti-imperialist who objected in the strongest terms to the United States selling arms to Batista, arms that would, undoubtedly, be used against the rebels. Now, free of the censors' restrictions, the radio reported how the American reporter had made a fool of the army's chief of staff, General Francisco Tabernilla, by skirting his supposedly impenetrable security ring. And it mocked the ineptitude of the government because Batista's minister of defense claimed the whole episode was a fantasy, which it clearly was not.

In months to come, Guevara's appreciation for what the interview had contributed to the rebels' cause would grow substantially. Eventually, he would declare that for the small group, Matthews's brief visit had been worth more than a military victory.

The first few months of 1957 were a critical time for the rebels. The meeting of national leaders and Castro's interview with Matthews marked the movement's first steps out of the mountains and toward its final goal—Havana. But the same months were among the most difficult for the small band. Che considered this time "the most painful days of the war." Militarily, they were weak. Supplies were low. Morale, despite what Castro had told Matthews, was wavering. For every peasant who joined the rebels, another wandered off and quit or, worse still, betrayed the group for a few pesos by telling Batista's officers where they could be found. Che had been separated from the main group time after time, and he continually struggled with his aching lungs. He was so hobbled by asthma that he had arrived six days late for a meeting with Fidel. By the time he got there, Castro was long gone.

While Che waited at the Leyva family farm for reinforcements to come from Santiago, he also heard that a group of radical students lead by José Antonio Echeverría had attacked the Presidential Palace. At this time, Echeverría's followers outnumbered Castro's. Although the two headstrong leaders had agreed in Mexico to cooperate, they had radically different ideas about how to achieve their goal. Echeverría wanted to go after Batista himself, assassinating him and opening the door for someone else who would restore constitutional government. Castro worried that eliminating the leader of the corrupt system didn't necessarily end the system itself. He feared that killing Batista would simply provide an opportunity for another crooked politician to take over without righting any of Cuba's serious political failings.

Echeverría, as leader of the radical opposition at the University of Havana, had the students working out details of their subversive plan when they heard about Matthews's articles. He saw how quickly Castro was becoming a living legend, and he hastened to regain momentum for his own movement. The students had already worked out their strategy—a direct attack on the palace while Batista was inside. A similar attempt the previous year had been scuttled when Batista somehow got word of it in advance. Following Matthews's articles, with all Havana focused on Castro, the plotters realized that they risked losing everything to the 26th of July Movement if they waited any longer.

Just over a week after Matthews's series ended, fifty men huddled together in a Havana apartment, waiting for a telephone call to spring into action. Dozens more kept their rifles, pistols, and machine guns at their sides, prepared to start the revolution.

The palace sits in the center of Old Havana, facing the sea. City streets skirt it on three sides, and the grand entrance is yards behind the remnants of the ancient wall that once surrounded the city. Just after lunch on March 13, the first fifty invaders crashed through the front gates in several cars and a red and black truck with the words "Fast Delivery" in English painted on its side. Echeverría led a raid by a smaller group on the broadcast studio of Radio Reloj, a popular Havana radio station, and took it over. Batista had again been tipped off, but he did not know exactly when the attack would occur. He sat in his office, reading Jim Bishop's book *The Day Lincoln Was Shot.*

With guns blazing, the attackers shot their way into the palace, quickly reaching as far as Batista's second-floor office. But as they burst into the ornate room, their hearts sank as they realized the dictator was not there. He had taken refuge on the third floor, which could only be reached by a special elevator the attackers did not know about. As Echeverría, presuming the attack had succeeded, breathlessly announced the death of the tyrant from the Radio Reloj studio, the invaders fired on the third floor but were turned back by Batista's more powerful defenses. They retreated, and in the ensuing chaos many were killed. Echeverría destroyed the radio station's control panel with an explosive, then ran outside to join his triumphant co-conspirators, where he was shot dead by police. The battle between the students and Batista's presidential guard spilled out into the adjoining streets. The thick exterior walls of Ruby Phillips's office, a block away from the palace, were riddled with bullets.

In all, thirty-five young men, including Echeverría, were killed that day, along with five palace guards. One of Castro's chief competitors had been eliminated. And like Castro, Batista was reported to have been killed, only to return to play a far more important role in Cuban history. The day after the assault, a hale-looking Batista appeared at an award ceremony with Ambassador Gardner, who presented him with a ceremonial golden telephone. To many Cubans, this was a symbol that Batista had not only survived the attack, but retained the U.S. support he relied on to stay in power.

Matthews was quickly developing a strong network of sources in Cuba who told him what was happening and what was yet to come. He had established himself as the primary contact with the rebels and their anti-Batista sympathizers. As Batista's government fumbled its response, looking increasingly inept and powerless, moderate Cubans were encouraged to become involved in efforts to oust him. One of them was the conservative anti-Batista economist Rufo Lopez-Fresquet who, in early April, told Matthews that his series of articles had created an expectation that Castro was planning a spectacular attack that would clear up any doubts about his presence or the strength of his troops. Lopez-Fresquet believed the articles had made Castro a hero, greatly helping him to recruit reinforcements.

At the same time, Matthews was deepening his contacts with the Washington establishment. Because he had uniquely shaped the Cuban story and had created an image of Castro and his young rebels fighting heroically, and successfully, in the mountains, he influenced the way the story played out. And because he also wrote editorials for the *Times*, diplomats and Washington officials sought his opinions. Matthews freely offered his views on the Cuban situation and outlined steps to resolve the crisis. He acted as a kind of special ambassador, hoping to improve relations with Havana. It was not an unfamiliar role for a foreign correspondent in the mid-twentieth century. By involving himself in the diplomatic process, Matthews followed in the footsteps of other correspondents, including Walter Duranty, who helped bring about U.S. recognition of the Soviet Union in the 1930s.

Matthews traveled to Washington in May for talks with Secretary of State John Foster Dulles. The second Eisenhower administration has just begun, and Matthews encouraged Dulles to accept the pro forma resignation of Arthur Gardner as ambassador to Cuba, even though Gardner had gone directly to President Eisenhower to ask to stay on. Matthews believed that Gardner's closeness to Batista, and his sympathy for the dictator, blinded him to the atrocities taking place all over the island. Gardner had become a liability, Matthews insisted, and his continuing as ambassador would stand in the way of improving relations between the countries during the transition that Matthews believed was coming.

Although it is not clear that Matthews's recommendation tipped the scales against him, Gardner was forced to resign. In his place, Eisenhower named another one of his friends. Earl E.T. Smith was a successful businessman and fund-raiser who had never held a diplomatic position and who did not speak Spanish. But Smith had been finance chairman of the Florida Republican Committee during Eisenhower's campaign, and the posting was his reward. On the recommendation of several officials at the State Department, Smith made time during his briefing schedule to travel to New York for an off-the-record lunch with Matthews.

The two met at a midtown Manhattan restaurant for a two-and-a-half hour lunch, during which Matthews freely gave his views on Cuba, Castro, and the inevitable fall of the Batista regime, toward which he now showed obvious disdain. Matthews made it clear to the new ambassador that he felt it would be in the best interest of the United States for the dictator, the latest in a long line of corrupt Cuban rulers, to be replaced—a view he had already expressed in editorials for the *Times*.

Smith felt the strong views Matthews expressed during their New York lunch were similar to those of the nonpolitical career professionals who operated on the fourth floor of the State Department. Smith believed they had been influenced by the Robin Hood image of Castro created by Matthews's articles. Such views clashed with the message he was getting from the White House, which continued to back Batista, as it supported other right-wing, anti-Communist strongmen throughout Latin America, because he represented the lesser of two evils during the Cold War.

Although Matthews had not actually compared Castro to Robin Hood, he had made him seem like an impassioned outlaw dedicated to aiding his suffering people. Smith didn't know what was in store for him in Cuba, but he knew, after the briefing with Matthews and the fourth floor, that the Castro rebellion—in either its attempt to gain power or its violent failure to do so—would be one of his primary responsibilities as ambassador.

He also believed he would eventually be forced to counter Castro's growing legend. The revolution was young, and the rebel army small, with few military victories. Castro's most successful thrust by far had been the coup he scored with the Matthews interview. Following the debacle of the student assault on the palace, Castro came to a greater appreciation of the power of propaganda, and he, along with core leaders of the insurrection, wanted to organize another show of force to which they would invite American newsmen. Rebel leader Armando Hart came to Havana to discuss the idea with Mario Llerena and other leaders of the civic resistance.

Llerena, who had the most experience with journalists, suggested they contact Matthews and invite him to defy Batista's soldiers again by returning to the Sierra. Hart rejected the idea, saying Castro had made it clear that they should find someone else. The

reason, he told Llerena, was that Castro considered Matthews and
the *Times* to be sympathetic and already solidly on the rebels' side.
By showing support so openly, Hart argued, Matthews had diminished his value to the movement. Better, it was decided, to try
someone else now, and turn again to Matthews in the future.

Llerena suggested that an American television crew be brought
in to see Castro. Such a project had already been tried once but
had failed. Robert Taber of CBS had flown to Cuba shortly after
he met Llerena in New York and spent several weeks waiting to
see Castro. He went back empty-handed, but Llerena promised to
call when another opportunity arose. Now Llerena flew to New
York to make arrangements. It didn't take much to convince the
television crew to return to Cuba, and the following day he, Taber,
and a cameraman, Wendell Hoffman, boarded a nonstop
National Airlines flight to Havana, pretending to be missionaries
on a research trip to film Presbyterian schools in Cuba.

Taber and Hoffman easily evaded Batista's security at the airport. They were rushed to the Sierra, where Hart's wife, Haydée
Santamaria, along with Celia Sánchez and other rebels, led them
to Castro. By then, he was camped much higher in the Sierra than
when he had talked to Matthews. Carrying bulky camera and
sound equipment slowed them down, and Hoffman filmed the
arduous climb to Castro's camp near Pico Turquino, the highest
summit in Cuba. Like Matthews, they highlighted the danger of
crossing the army's security line, and they put themselves squarely in the center of the story. It was a theme that was later repeated in many of the succeeding news reports—despite the fact that
the very numbers of reporters making it through Batista's "ring of
steel" showed how ineffective the blockade truly was.

Taber and Hoffman spent several days with Castro. When the
program *Rebels of the Sierra Madre: The Story of Cuba's Jungle Fighters*
was broadcast on a Sunday evening in May, it left no doubt that
Castro was alive and still in the Sierra Maestra. In the half-hour
program, Taber repeated some of the same sympathetic and heroic myths about Castro that Matthews had told. He showed the
rebels paying local campesinos for supplies, and he allowed the

fighters to boast about the deadly accuracy of their telescopic rifles. Taber knew that Matthews had stolen all the glory of finding Castro, so the black-and-white documentary focused in part on a long interview with three young Americans who, after reading Matthews's reports, had left their homes on the American military base at Guantanamo Bay and joined Castro. The Cubans were fighting for freedom, like the heroes of their own American Revolution, they said. Taber would eventually convince Castro to allow the youngest two of them to leave the mountains and return to the city with him. The third, Charles Ryan, who was twenty, stayed behind.

Throughout the program, the rebels were always shown in sympathetic poses, drawing water ingeniously from hanging vines, peering through dense undergrowth with their rifles poking through the foliage, cooking over open fires, even raiding a beehive in a tree stump for its honey. Critical commentary was limited to Taber's concerns about the careless way the men handled their firearms, which resulted in one of them accidentally shooting himself in the hand while Taber was there. Taber ended the program by handing his microphone to Castro and allowing him to speak directly to the American public in halting English. Castro demanded the end of arms shipments to the Cuban government, and he criticized Batista's clumsy efforts to hide the truth of what was happening in the Sierra.

"As Herbert Matthews, the reporter of *The New York Times*, said, the truth will always be known, with or without censorship, because there are always brave reporters, like you two, that will always be risking your lives for seeking things out," Castro told Taber, adding, "When the *tirano* [tyrant] Batista learns that two more Americans have made him a fool, he will become furious." Castro claimed again, as he had in the Matthews interview, that all the people of the Sierra Maestra were with him and that the cream of Batista's army was incapable of containing rebel forces. "We always know where he is," he said, speaking of Batista's army, "but he never knows where we are."

The program was edited by Don Hewitt, who would later go on

to create *60 Minutes* for CBS. It was not shown in Cuba, but parts of the interview and still photographs taken during Taber's journey were made into an article in *Life* magazine, which did get distributed in Cuba. As Batista fumed, the myth of Castro—and the American reporter who invented that myth—grew.

Matthews learned just how much of an impression his interview with Castro had made on ordinary Cubans when he returned to Havana in June. He had come to interview Batista and report on the growing unrest. Crowds of supporters greeted him at the airport, and there were more friendly faces waiting for him outside the Sevilla Biltmore Hotel. To them, Matthews was not just a newspaperman who had taken advantage of a lucky break. He was the bearer of a truth that others had been afraid to tell. He was a sympathetic eye on the rebellion, an active participant who had delivered a devastating blow at the most crucial time. He struggled to explain that this was not so, that he was just a newspaperman doing his job. But neither Castro's supporters nor the officials surrounding Batista believed him. Matthews had to deal with suspicion and adulation at the same time. He expected to raise the government's ire and was prepared to deal with it. But the flood of public admiration made him uncomfortable, as he wrote in a memo to managing editor Turner Catledge on his return.

"I never expected and certainly never wanted to be placed in the position of a public idol like Clark Gable or Frank Sinatra. I have discovered on this trip that there is nothing more embarrassing or more tiring than to be a hero and I find it a very painful as well as naturally gratifying experience." He watched his own words become part of the political discourse in Cuba and the United States, shaping the debate and influencing public opinion. His experiences in Argentina and other Latin countries had already shown Matthews how powerful American newspapers could be in the region. Despite lingering resentment toward the United States, and the grossly uneven balance of power within the hemisphere, Latin American governments were often more con-

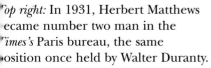

Top right: In 1931, Herbert Matthews became number two man in the *Times's* Paris bureau, the same position once held by Walter Duranty.

Above: Matthews established his reputation as a war correspondent with Mussolini's troops during the Italian invasion of Ethiopia. *Matthews Family Collection*

Right: As a war correspondent in Europe, Matthews rarely got to spent time with his wife Nancie and their children, Eric and Priscilla, except for brief vacations. *Matthews Family Collection*

Above: During the Spanish Civil War, Matthews and Ernest Hemingway were staying in the Hotel Florida in Madrid when it was bombed. Hemingway described Matthews as "brave as a badger." *Matthews Family Collection*

At the outbreak of World Wa II, Mussolini's Fascist government detained Matthews for five months before expelling him. He returned to cover the American invasion of Italy. *Matthews Family Collection*

After Matthews returned to New York in 1949, the *Times* used this photograph in advertisements to trumpet his dual role as editorial writer and roving reporter, calling him "one of the most distinguished journalists of our generation." *Matthews Family Collection*

In 1957 Castro was widely believed to be dead until Matthews made the trek into the Sierra Maestra. At dawn on February 17, 1957, Castro told Matthews he only wanted to restore the Cuban constitution and did not plan to take any power for himself. *Herbert L. Matthews Papers, Rare Book and Manuscript Library, Columbia University*

Left: Matthews's handwritten notes show that he was enormously impressed by Castro during the three hour interview, noticing such details as his "straggling beard" and the way his "eyes flash." *Herbert L. Matthews Papers, Rare Book and Manuscript Library, Columbia University*

Below: Knowing there would be doubters, Matthews asked Castro to sign his notes. Matthews later misplaced the paper and did not see it again until after he retired. *Herbert L. Matthews Papers, Rare Book and Manuscript Library, Columbia University*

Right: The first of three articles Matthews wrote after interviewing Castro in the mountains caused a world wide sensation, and created a dashing image of the bearded rebel leader. Used with permission of *The New York Times.*

Below: Pro-Castro Cubans in New York marched outside the newspaper's Times Square headquarters in 1957 to show support for Matthews and the *Times* for helping the Revolution. *Herbert L. Matthews Papers, Rare Book and Manuscript Library, Columbia University*

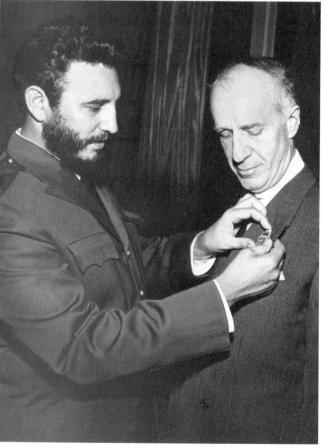

Above: Matthews was celebrating New Year's Eve in Havana when Batista fle in the early hours of Jan. 1 1959. A few days later, Matthews, Nancie, and Rau Chibás, a rebel leader, waited at the airport in Holguin, Cuba, to intervie a victorious Fidel Castro. *Herbert L. Matthews Papers, Rare Book and Manuscript Library, Columbia University*

Left: On his first visit to the United States after his stunning victory, Castro honored Matthews and other reporters for their role in the revolution. The small oval medal says "Sierr Maestra Press Mission: To Our American Friend Herbert Matthews With Gratitude. Fidel Castro." *Herbert L. Matthews Papers, Rare Book and Manuscript Library, Columbia University*

Days after honoring Matthews, Castro publicly embarrassed him at an Overseas Press Club luncheon. Castro claimed he had fooled Matthews into believing he had columns of troops, when he actually had no more than eighteen armed men with him in the Sierra. Matthews stood by his reporting. *Herbert L. Matthews Papers, Rare Book and Manuscript Library, Columbia University*

When Castro returned to New York in 1960, Matthews was often by his side. After complaining about the way he was being treated at the Hotel Shelburne, Castro moved to the Theresa Hotel in Harlem, where Nikita Khrushchev greeted him with a bear hug. *Herbert L. Matthews Papers, Rare Book and Manuscript Library, Columbia University*

Above: After he retired from the *Times* in 1967, Matthews continued to visit Cuba, where he was treated like "a founding father." In 1972 he talked with Juan Almeida, one of the 82 rebels who had sailed with Castro on the Granma in 1956. *Matthews Family Collection*

Left: Matthews understood that his 1972 reporting trip to Cuba would be his last. He continued to try to clear his name and prove that he had been right about Castro and Cuba all along. *Matthews Family Collection*

cerned about American newspapers than local ones because of their influence in Washington, whose support the Latin governments needed to stay in power.

Matthews recognized this, but he had never seen anything like what had happened in Cuba in the four months since his articles were published: "[I]t is really no exaggeration to say that the role we have been playing since February is of far greater importance to Cuba than that of the State Department. The articles on Fidel Castro and the Cuban situation which I did in February have literally altered the course of Cuban history, and the job I have done has also had a sensational impact on Cuban affairs." In public he continued to insist that all he ever did was to allow Castro to be himself, and being so was enough for him to take his place in the history of Latin America. But in these personal memos, it is evident that he was beginning to change his own perception of his role in the Cuban story, from strict impartiality to mounting hostility toward the Batista regime and open sympathy for its opponents. The hubris he had often been accused of came to the surface, and he claimed responsibility for shepherding the revolution for himself and for the *Times:* "I think we can feel proud of the extraordinary power which *The New York Times* possesses in a situation like this, but just because we have that power we also have a responsibility that must be considered at every step."

Ruby Phillips had agreed to arrange for Matthews to interview Batista during his visit, and she accompanied him to the bullet-ridden palace. Batista had stopped giving formal interviews, claiming he was always misquoted. He had insisted that Matthews submit his questions in writing the day before the interview. By the time Matthews arrived, Batista's English-speaking aide Edmund Chester had already written out the answers to his questions. Batista chatted with the reporters informally and off the record. Matthews knew that Batista hated him for what he had written and all the embarrassment he had caused. Nevertheless, he asked Batista tough questions about the growing rebellion. Matthews insisted that Batista would be making a grave mistake to underestimate the strength of the resistance. Batista finally conceded that Matthews was probably right, although he was mistaken about the character of the opposition. "Yes, it is serious," he said, but he insisted that his opponents did not represent a national groundswell against him, that they were mostly criminals, Communists, and paid followers of former president Carlos Prío Socarrás.

Following the meeting, Matthews flew to Santiago to see for himself how much the situation there had deteriorated. He found the usually vibrant city dark and morose. There were bombings almost every night. Rebel sympathizers were being shot, people were disappearing. Although he was under surveillance, he met openly with many representatives of civic and religious groups, all opposed to Batista and his regime, and all willing to risk being seen in order to tell Matthews how bad the situation had become. Over and over they compared what was happening in Cuba to Hungary in 1956, where Soviet troops had crushed the popular rebellion led by Imre Nagy. And they thanked him for bringing three days of peace. While he was in Santiago, they believed, Batista would not dare to attack them.

Matthews described the rebel movement as stronger than ever, with all of Oriente Province in open revolt. Batista, furious, ordered Havana newspapers not to reprint the article. But it was translated into Spanish and distributed by the underground anyway. Shortly afterward, Santiago was again the scene of a revolutionary turning point. Frank País, the urban coordinator of the 26th of July Movement, whose revolutionary mind and logistical skills matched Castro's, was ambushed and killed by the Santiago police. His death eliminated yet another potential rival. And in the continuing struggle between the rebels in the mountains and the opposition movement in the cities—the "Sierra" and the "Llano"—Castro's guerrillas grew significantly stronger because Frank País's impassioned voice had been silenced.

Returning to New York, Matthews again received another outpouring of support. About 400 Castro supporters showed up outside the Times Building on a sunny summer afternoon carrying signs to express their gratitude to the writer who had provided such critical assistance to their country: "Thanks Mr. Matthews for tell [sic] the world the truth about Cuba's democracy." The 26th of July Movement of New York bestowed on Matthews the honorary title of the "Best Friend of the Cuban People."

Matthews kept up his criticism of the regime in both editorials and news articles such as the one he wrote for the *Times*'s Sunday magazine that summer called "The Shadow Falls on Cuba's Batista." Contrary to his prediction a few months earlier that Batista would probably finish out his term in office and leave after the 1958 elections, Matthews now predicted that the end was near and that few Cubans would give Batista any chance of lasting that long. In Cuba, rebel supporters translated the article into Spanish and passed it from hand to hand throughout Havana. René Zayas Bazán, a member of the civic resistance, sent Matthews a photostatic copy of the translated article, along with a congratulatory note: "I must say you have become a sort of legendary hero for the Cubans, for they give you sole credit for having kept Batista from turning the country into another Santo Domingo by publishing Fidel's pictures when you did."

As Matthews became increasingly critical of Batista, his reports contrasted significantly with those filed by Ruby Phillips, who still doubted Castro's popularity outside Oriente Province. Matthews grew suspicious of her, noting her long friendship with Ambassador Gardner and her links to the Batista government. She, on the other hand, resented Matthews and what she perceived to be his overtly sympathetic coverage of the rebels. Also, she was uncomfortable with his dual role as reporter and editorial writer, an arrangement that concerned many people at the *Times*. Phillips's account of the students' assault on the palace was sober and guarded: "Cuba Recovering from Brief Rising." But Matthews's own report on the same incident, written from New York, took a decidedly negative slant: "Cuba Is Still Smoldering Under the Batista Regime." The contradictions in their reporting would confuse readers, draw the scorn of media critics, and intensify the personal animosity between Phillips and Matthews.

The Castro interview had revived Matthews's career and

brought him more notoriety than he'd had since his controversial coverage of the Spanish Civil War. He developed an appetite for more adventures like it, but there was also a darker side to his escapade. He found his strength flagging. Feeling extremely worn, he consulted a doctor. Tests showed that the tuberculosis he had had as a child had come back. He had gone for a checkup in November 1956, before the first Cuba trip, and his X-rays had been clear, leading him to believe that it had been the long night spent in the damp Sierra waiting for Castro that had revived the tuberculosis after so many years. His doctor set him on a course of twenty-seven daily pills to halt the progress of the disease. He had no regrets.

"If the Cuban stories did give me TB," he wrote in a memo, "all I can say is that they were worth it to me and I would do it again."

Tuberculosis would be just one of many medical problems to complicate Matthews's later years. But because it was linked in his mind to the interview in the Sierra, he would never complain about it.

Nor did he let it interfere with his ambition to cover the turmoil in the Dominican Republic as General Rafael Trujillo's brutal regime tottered on the brink of collapse. In summer 1957, he sent a memo to Catledge and Orvil Dryfoos, making a pitch to be sent to Santo Domingo. He argued that if he were allowed to go, his notoriety would precede him and give him and, of course, the *Times* a competitive advantage: "The fact that I was there would be immediately known, not only in the Dominican Republic but all over the hemisphere. I think people would talk to me where they would not talk to anyone else." He tried to make the case that his dual responsibilities for the editorial board and the news desk made him a valuable resource that the *Times* ought to exploit, saying, "When *The Times* has an asset it should use it, even when that asset is abnormal and fits no hitherto accepted category. The rigid concept of a story being 'editorial' simply because it has a lot of necessary personality in it also ought to go down the drain."

The response from the company president and future publisher was the first sign that Matthews's journalistic coup in Cuba could end up bringing infamy as well as fame. Dryfoos was becoming increasingly involved in newsroom affairs, an attempt to combine the business and editorial sides of the paper. "I still feel as I think we all felt yesterday—that Herbert has had enough of this," Dryfoos wrote in a memo to Robert Garst, a night editor in New York. Unlike his father-in-law, Arthur Hays Sulzberger, Dryfoos had no extraordinary allegiance or personal connection to Matthews, and he could look at the unusual arrangement with more objective eyes, realizing how great a breach of policy Matthews's double-dipping in the newsroom and on the editorial board actually was. The outpouring of support by the Cubans who marched in front of the Times Building was seen as evidence that he was already far too close to the story. And there was no appetite for having Matthews intimately involved in any other revolution. "Of course," Dryfoos went on, "if the News Department would want to send Peter Kihss or Milton Bracker [*Times* reporters] to the Dominican Republic that is something else again."

Matthews was disappointed, but he had little time to be discouraged. In October, the Cubans in exile conferred in Miami and signed a unity pact that brought together seven anti-Batista groups, including ex-president Prío Socarrás and his followers. Castro's 26th of July Movement was represented by Felipe Pazos and Mario Llerena, who apparently signed the document on Castro's behalf without first clearing it with him. Word of the pact reached the Sierra when a *Times* reporter in Washington, Edwin L. Dale, managed to break the story. Matthews, on the editorial page, considered the pact a decisive blow against Batista, representing the unification of an opposition movement that had, till then, been deeply divided. But in truth, the pact caused dissension of its own. Castro was furious. He felt betrayed by Pazos and Llerena, and marginalized by the other groups that had signed it without consulting him. His fierce reaction was also a sign of his own ambitions for power, and his reluctance to share it.

Matthews's positions in the articles he wrote under his own byline for the *Times,* and the unsigned editorials that were unmistakably his, had turned relentlessly critical of Batista and rarely anything but supportive of Castro and his rebels. "What we do know today, in spite of the censorship, is that Cuba is undergoing a reign of terror," Matthews wrote in October. "This is a much overworked phrase, but it is a literal truth so far as the regime of General Batista is concerned." Some of the more conservative parts of the resistance in Cuba grew worried as options narrowed and it seemed more likely that Castro, by default, had been anointed Batista's successor.

Mario Lazo, a Cuban lawyer born in the United States and cousin to respected politician Carlos Marquez Sterling, was one of the limited number of Cubans who were suspicious of Matthews. A regular reader of the *Times,* he had been surprised by the emotional tone of Matthews's articles and the overt stance that Matthews had taken in support of Castro. "The most reprehensible act of journalism attributed to a reputable newspaper in my lifetime," was how he later described Matthews's work in Cuba. He believed that Matthews had crossed the line of journalistic objectivity, "in effect, a journalist on a reportorial assignment assumed the posture of an insurrectionist."

As 1957 came to an end, Matthews marked the anniversary of Castro's landing in the *Granma* with a laudatory editorial that further built up the mythology around the fledgling Cuban revolution. "A year ago today one of the strangest and most romantic episodes in Cuba's colorful history began," Matthews wrote. In the editorial, he reprised his own role in the myth, breaking through the wall of Batista's censorship to tell the world that Castro was still alive. Batista's fall was inevitable, Matthews now wrote, and Castro's goal was simply the restoration of Cuba's democracy. He had no doubt that Castro's forces, with the support of Cubans in cities and towns across the island, could overthrow Batista. "Nor is there any question," Matthews wrote with more certainty than was warranted, "of Fidel Castro becoming the next ruler of Cuba." In the end, he bowed to the mixed opinion of Castro in some circles. But he left no doubt about his own feelings: "Whatever one thinks of Fidel Castro, to have survived a whole year with a small force in jungle country against the best efforts of the whole Cuban Army and their modern armament was an extraordinary military feat. As the second year begins there can be no doubt that Fidel Castro has made history."

decisive battles

Another anniversary was coming up, one that in Matthews's mind was every bit as important as the landing of the *Granma*. By February 1958, a full year had passed since his interview with Fidel in the Sierra. He was eager to return to Cuba to report on the progress of the revolution and to assess how much the Castro forces had grown in a year, how much Batista's regime had declined, and what dynamics were likely to shape a post-Batista government. Batista's presidential term was scheduled to expire at the end of the year and an election was supposed to take place sometime before then. Cubans were split about the polling. Some hung on to the notion that only an election could restore Cuba's troubled democracy. But because they had seen many crooked elections before, countless others were skeptical. They simply wanted Batista out. Pressure from Castro was mounting, and there was talk of a nationwide general strike that, if successful, would make Cuba ungovernable. One way or another, peacefully or with violence, the dictator's days seemed to be numbered. It was a great story, and Matthews considered it his.

But the newsroom's editors had a different idea. The early

enthusiasm that the *Times* had shown by advertising Matthews's series had disappeared, and in its place was a growing discomfort with his intense personal role in Cuba. With Sulzberger sick and unable to protect him, Matthews was easy prey for the newsroom editors who had crossed the embarrassing line of Cuban demonstrators expressing their admiration for him. They were uneasy with what they considered to be his uncritical reporting and his clear taking of sides, which he did not deny. It was an old story with Matthews, akin to his experience in Spain, except that he was now both reporter and editorial writer, which made his role in the Cuban story even more suspect. Managing editor Turner Catledge was determined not to let the situation get any messier.

In January, Matthews laid out formal plans to return to Cuba, but Catledge, Dryfoos, and the foreign editor, Manny Freedman, made it clear that they did not want him to go there any more than they had wanted him to travel to the Dominican Republic the previous June. They agreed that someone should take the measure of the insurrection, but it would not be Matthews. Instead they decided to send Homer Bigart, a respected war correspondent who had covered World War II with bravery and common-folk sensibility. But Cuba would be something entirely new for him. He could not string together a simple sentence in Spanish, and he had no background in the web of intrigues common in Latin American affairs.

Matthews was incensed. He fired off a memo to Dryfoos, Freedman, and Theodore Bernstein, by now an assistant managing editor and guardian of the *Times*'s integrity and style. He was a stickler for rules, and for ensuring that they were followed. Bernstein was particularly critical of Matthews's dual role as editorial writer and reporter and saw no reason to depart from the paper's long-standing policy of separating the editorial department from the third-floor newsroom. Matthews believed that his personal involvement in the Cuba story gave him, and the paper, a strong advantage. Bernstein saw his closeness as inappropriate and risky.

Matthews defended his editorials on Cuba and the reporting he had done from there. "I would challenge anyone to analyze the strict, bare, factual elements of the job I did in June and previously in February of last year and show where it was wrong or distorted or not borne out by subsequent events," a cocky Matthews wrote. Once again he felt that his reputation and professionalism were being challenged, just as they had been in Spain. He lashed out at his editors, accusing them of forgetting the paper's promise to provide the most comprehensive reporting possible. He, and only he among American journalists, had been in the Sierra at the beginning, and only he had the kind of access to the rebels that would meet the newspaper's standards. Instead, he was being held back for reasons that escaped him. He felt like a martyr, sacrificed because of his beliefs. "In other words," he wrote, "one gets the news, and deeply and expertly and in a true framework of Cuban history and politics—and this is what should count, not the unavoidable fact that I, as inventor of Fidel Castro, am caught up in the chain of events occurring in Cuba."

The editors thought Matthews was far more than merely "caught up" in Cuban affairs. They were becoming more uncomfortable with the part Matthews had played in inventing the Castro myth. They feared he had crossed the line from reporting on the events taking place in Cuba to participating in them, a charge also made by Batista, who continued to insist that Castro was a Communist and Matthews his stooge. There was no hard proof at this time that the Communists were fomenting trouble in Cuba, but there was little but Matthews's word to say that they weren't. The editors linked Matthews to Castro in their minds and felt it would be better if he were taken off the story. Ted Bernstein cited precedents for removing a reporter because of a personal conflict. The example he used was Clayton Knowles, a Washington reporter who had covered Senator Joseph McCarthy. Knowles had been taken off the security beat because he confessed that he had once belonged to the Communist Party. Bernstein was not accusing Matthews of being a Communist; he was merely making the point that appearances counted. In responding to Matthews's tirade, Bernstein also reiterated his long-standing opposition to having editorial writers work for the news department. "In the present instance," he wrote Matthews, "I see no reason to make any exception to our normal policy." The decision to send Bigart to Cuba stood.

Matthews was not placated, and he sent another scathing memo the following day. "*The Times* is doing itself harm, and will do itself a good deal of harm, if it makes its news policy in accordance with regulations that in theory sound reasonable, instead of adapting its policies to the individuals available and to the type of story that has to be covered." His special access to the rebels was being cavalierly thrown away, his expertise wasted; the paper's overwhelming competitive advantage in covering what was shaping up to be a huge historical event was being tossed aside because of what he saw as a misguided quest for the chimera of totally unbiased reporting, that "objectivity shit" Martha Gellhorn had so disparaged in Spain. To Matthews, who believed that objectivity was unreachable because every reporter naturally took sides, this was the height of self-punishing hubris: "I repeat, I think *The Times* made an undoubted mistake in sending Homer Bigart to Cuba instead of me, and Milton Bracker to the Dominican Republic last year instead of me. But aside from any personal feelings involved, I believe you are fashioning a policy that is harmful to *The New York Times*."

These memos were the opening salvos in a battle within the paper that raged for nearly a decade, and a controversy that was to continue after Matthews retired, right up until his death. The tug-of-war between access that provides insight and closeness that compromises objectivity, is still unresolved.

Bigart traveled to Cuba and, without any of Matthews's heroics, managed to find his way to Castro's headquarters in the Sierra. He spent fifteen days there, and several more in Havana afterward gathering information and trying to understand the Cuban crisis. His series of reports was not nearly as spectacular as Matthews's had been the year before. But they were thorough, and appeared to be neutral in tone, although Bigart brought his personal biases to the story and made spectacular blunders of his own. In the first article, dated February 26, 1958 (exactly one year and two days after Matthews's had appeared), Bigart went out of his way to try to set the record straight, correcting Matthews's pieces without actually saying that he was doing so. The Sierra, he took pains to explain, is not jungle as Matthews had said but "forested peaks," which is a less evocative but a more accurate description of the part of the Sierra where Matthews met Castro. Bigart interviewed Castro outside "a squalid hut deep in the sierra," portraying the rebel leader without any of the swaggering romanticism that Matthews had used, but as simply "resting after a major battle." In a subsequent article, Bigart—who had reported many of the biggest engagements of World War II—analyzed that engagement in more detail, redefining it as a minor skirmish.

Bigart closely studied the rebel encampment and reported only what he had witnessed. "In fifteen days in the sierra this observer saw no evidence of rebel strength sufficient to win a decisive action on the plains," he wrote. But Bigart allowed Castro to boast of his strength and claim he had 1,000 men under arms, though Bigart noted that he could not possibly throw all of them into a single battle—an appraisal that is out of touch with the reality of guerrilla warfare. He pointed out that the rebels did not plan to win only through military action but hoped that with a general strike, they would bring down the regime. He described Castro (inaccurately) as supporting the elections that Batista insisted on holding before the end of the year, which the United States also supported. Bigart never mentioned Matthews's visit to the Sierra a year earlier.

In his next report, also filed from Havana, Bigart tried to apply the military acumen he had gained during World War II to deconstruct a February 16 rebel engagement with Batista's army at what he called Piña del Agua (actually Pino de Agua), concluding that it "will never make an addition to Sir Edward Creasy's 'Fifteen Decisive Battles of the World.'" Bigart seems to have failed to understand the dynamics of guerrilla war, which was not surprising, given his experience with conventional war. Castro did not need to win one of the world's fifteen decisive battles to prevail in the Cuban conflict. Bigart described Castro as being caught in a dilemma, with too few men to defeat Batista's army unless enlisted men decided to defect en masse. Again, he seemed to be looking at the war in Cuba as though it were being fought on the plains of Europe, with large numbers of opposing troops engaged in battle. When Bigart forced Castro to address his doubts about the rebel army's chances of winning, the answer was revealing. "To see our victory," Castro told him, "it is necessary to have faith."

Though he had been sent to Cuba to correct what the editors believed was Matthews's biased reporting, Bigart also apparently took sides, downplaying Castro's chances of winning the war. He paid more attention than Matthews had to the rivalry between the rebels and the urban underground, postulating that the Pino de Agua attack was primarily intended to be an attention-getting ploy to match the stepped-up campaign of sabotage and terror coordinated by the urban resistance. In the third, and concluding, article of Bigart's series, he gave his view of the Cuban crisis. Bigart carefully assessed Castro's strength and Batista's hold on power. Castro's support was coming principally from the middle class and the professionals of Havana who had grown tired of Batista. He pointed out that not everyone considered Castro a hero. There was said to be grumbling about his authoritarian streak, even within the 26th of July Movement. And he wrote that some of the movement's leaders wanted to do something about it before a "cult of personality" arose around him.

Bigart gave a far more critical view of Castro and the rebellion he was leading than Matthews had, but in the end he was wrong about the outcome. Though some of his reports also landed on the front page, they received far less attention than Matthews's had the year before. And Bigart's reporting did not snuff out Matthews's desire to return to Cuba. With stubborn persistence, and a promise to confine his writing to the editorial page, Matthews managed to get himself to Cuba again just weeks after Bigart's articles were published. He and Nancie arrived in Havana on March 14. The Batista government censored three Havana newspapers that tried to note his return to the city. He checked in with his main sources, stopping at the U.S. embassy to talk to Ambassador Smith about the upcoming presidential election, for which he had little optimism. He visited several high-ranking Cubans, including labor leader Eusebio Mujal, who insisted that the Cuban Workers Federation, one of the most powerful labor organizations in Latin America, opposed the idea of a general strike and favored fair elections instead. Mujal's unwillingness to support the strike probably doomed it to failure, but Matthews did not report the labor leader's comments. Instead, he said the strike would cause chaos.

Despite what Ruby Phillips and others told him about Havana's reluctant revolutionary mood, Matthews concluded that the city was ready to explode. Though Havana would never become the tinderbox that Santiago was, even a ripple of revolution in the capital meant that the decisive moment in the struggle for power was imminent. At one point in the copious notes he took during his visit to the city, Matthews acknowledged that he had once again taken sides. "I feel about Cuba somewhat as I did about Spain," he wrote. "One sees the tragedy and wants to share it, to be there, to share, if only as a sympathizer, what the Cubans are suffering." He empathized with the many Cubans he met who were being terrorized by the army or who feared being caught in the battles between the regime and the opposition. Mothers and fathers worried about their sons disappearing, or worse, being discovered some morning lying in a pool of blood on a deserted street corner. Matthews seems to have realized that such intense feelings could end up undercutting his objectivity, but he did not put much stock in objectivity anyway. He admitted, "This is a personal reaction having nothing to do with the professional and more scientific desire to see what was happening. Academically speaking, it is a great story."

No doubt it was a great story, and on March 21, Matthews telephoned the editorial board's receptionist in New York and asked her to pass along a message to the foreign desk. He had a lot of material on Cuba that was theirs for the asking. He didn't say what it was, but he indicated that he did not want to file from Cuba and would prefer to wait until he landed in Jamaica on his trip home. Manny Freedman, the foreign editor, sent a note to Catledge, the managing editor, about Matthews's offer: "My own inclination would be not to take the initiative in this matter. What do you think?" Despite all of his reservations, Catledge knew that Matthews's access to Castro was too good for him to simply reject the material out of hand. He answered warily: "Let's find out what he has." Their response to the story that Matthews sent was predictable. In Matthews's files at the archives of *The New York Times,* there is a March 25 dispatch datelined Pinar del Rio with a note scrawled atop it: "Not used," it says. "Editorialized," meaning that they considered the thrust of the piece to be commentary, and Matthews had to turn it into an editorial if he wanted to see any of his reporting get into print. It was another reminder that Matthews should keep his nose out of the newsroom.

Still, despite repeated objections from his editors, Matthews managed to convince them to publish an article of his datelined Havana (though it appears he was actually in Jamaica by the time he filed it). In the article he laid out a grim assessment of the city's revolutionary fervor. In contrast to Bigart's workaday reporting, Matthews's writing was emotional. His article was laced with drama that recalled his adventure in the Sierra: "The situation today and the situation in February 1957, when this correspondent went to the Sierra Maestra to interview the young rebel leader, Fidel Castro, are startlingly different." He described the general discontent of the previous year but stated that above all there was Fidel, whom he once again described in glowing terms, calling him "the most remarkable and romantic figure to arise in Cuban history since José Martí."

Castro was the symbol of opposition to the regime, and the opposition had become so strong that Matthews felt it was fair to wonder how Batista would manage to survive long enough to plan for elections, which had been postponed from June 1 to November 3. And Washington, Matthews wrote, "is supporting him in this forlorn hope."

Matthews could also be critical of Castro's most misguided actions. When Castro threatened to violently disrupt the rigged elections, an editorial took him to task. "At first Fidel Castro, raising his banner against all this from a dreary hideout in the Sierra Maestra, seemed a sort of Robin Hood. But he appears now to be trying to alienate American sympathy, threatening to shoot any candidates running in the upcoming elections," said an unsigned editorial, probably written by Matthews, as were most of those about Cuba. "We would like to see a democratic government in Cuba and a final end to the suppressions, censorships and outrages of the Batista regime. We know that revolutions, like other sorts of wars, are not Boy Scout exercises. But if he wishes to hold our friendship Fidel Castro must earn it by giving up terrorism, threats and misrepresentations."

Despite his editors' objections, Matthews filed one more story during this visit, declaring that Havana itself was "ripe for rebellion." Castro had declared "total war" against Batista, but his main thrust would not be a military attack. Rather, he told Cubans to prepare for a national strike that would debilitate the regime and force out the dictator. Matthews, writing from Montego Bay in Jamaica, assumed the strike had already begun and needed only a spark to spread widely. That spark, he was certain, would come from Havana, which despite its "calm surface," was roiling with discontent.

Ruby Phillips did not see it that way at all. She had detected little support for the rebels in the prosperous capital. She felt that Castro and his supporters mistakenly believed that their popularity in and around the Sierra was duplicated in Havana. She knew that although men like Felipe Pazos were lending support to the underground, many other business and industry leaders in the city still believed that Batista, bad as he had become, would be better for Cuba than any of the opposition groups, and especially Castro's. And she understood, to a degree that Matthews did not, that organized labor, with its ties to the Communist Party of Cuba, was unlikely to participate in a general strike. "I was so sure that the entire 'total war' in Havana would fail that I told the Castro boys who came to see me that it was premature and stupid," she wrote. "I told them the strike would fail and many of them would get killed."

Many other discrepancies would arise between Matthews and Phillips, and their disparate accounts—biased in their own way on both sides—underscored the difficulty of being objective in the middle of an event as unpredictable and emotional as a revolution. Both were veteran journalists, with long histories in Latin America. Both insisted that they were only reporting what they had seen. They filed contradictory accounts, much to the distress of editors in New York, who did not have complete confidence in either one of them. They preferred Homer Bigart's detached reporting, despite the errors he made. In their eyes, Bigart's inexperience in Latin America had the benefit of insuring that he was a disinterested witness.

The editors were not alone in appreciating Bigart's dispatches from the Sierra. Castro too appears to have welcomed them, as he would all the journalists willing to help the revolution by reporting on it, no matter what they said. Bigart's skepticism did not deter Castro from singing his praises in a handwritten note to Matthews, whom he addressed as "My Dear Friend":

Mi Querido Amigo
We have had the great satisfaction of receiving your friend, Mr. Bipart [*sic*], who made a great effort to get here.

I didn't want him to return home without bringing you a testament of our deep and lasting affection for you.

We have accomplished much since you paid us the unforgettable honor of visiting us.

We hope we will be able to get together so that the Cuban people can pay a great national homage to the brave journalists who, with their generous and noble pens, are helping them recover their liberty.

All of you have done more for the United States than the diplomats and chiefs of military missions.

We are eternally grateful for all that you write about our people in these terrible days of oppression.

I think that we will soon be able to have the privilege of greeting you in our free fatherland.

Fraternally,

Fidel Castro

As Ruby Phillips had predicted, the general strike that Castro called fizzled, collapsing in Havana a few hours after it started. The failure disappointed Castro and revealed his weakness outside the Sierra. The *Times* sent Homer Bigart back to Havana. He filed a critical article, sarcastically recalling the unfounded optimism Castro had expressed during his earlier visit and writing that "evidently, there was more faith than realism" in the way the strike had been planned. The negative tone of the article was subtly underscored by the accompanying photograph, which showed Castro lounging in the sun with an open book on his chest, looking more like a dreamy grad student than a heroic rebel leader. Bigart followed the next day with a spectacularly flawed assessment that began, "The days of Fidel Castro are numbered, according to informed sources." Bigart's "informed sources" were mistaken. Batista apparently believed them, too; Herbert Matthews did not.

Matthews, of course, would prove to be right, but in the days and weeks following the dissolution of the strike, it appeared that Batista might be able to crush the insurrection. Encouraged by the rebels' failure, he sent 10,000 men into the Sierra with orders to liquidate the remaining rebels. It was a much more aggressive effort than any in the year and a half since Castro had shipwrecked the *Granma,* but the rebels were too well entrenched by then for it to be effective. Castro, as overall commander, skirmished with, picked off, and ambushed Batista's demoralized troops. By the time Batista ordered a withdrawal from the Sierra in late July, hundreds of his soldiers had been killed, wounded, or captured.

The failure of the July offensive was a devastating military defeat for Batista, and it brought renewed spirit to Castro's forces after the disappointment of the unsuccessful general strike. But the war that Castro was fighting had, from the start, been primarily a battle of ideas and images, and in that regard, Batista had suffered an even more debilitating setback. In March, Washington had held up the delivery of 1,950 M-1 rifles that Batista had purchased and that were sitting on a dock in New York awaiting shipment to Cuba. Secretary of State Christian Herter sent a telegram to Havana notifying Ambassador Smith that the decision to suspend further arms shipments was made because the Batista government had failed "to create conditions for fair elections," and because of the deteriorating political situation. In reality, Washington was reacting to mounting public pressure to end its overt support of Batista. Matthews's writing, along with constant pressure from Castro's supporters in the United States, had convinced Congress to hold hearings on the Cuban situation, and the State Department expected to have to answer tough questions again if the shipments did not end.

Batista's government objected strongly to the embargo, claiming that the army was being expanded and that worn-out firearms needed to be replaced. Moreover, it was the image of a change in policy that the regime most feared. It would be impossible to keep the decision secret, and once word got out about the embargo, it would be interpreted widely as a show of Washington's support for the rebels. Ambassador Smith agreed with their assessment. "Psychological effect of steps U.S. is taking may bring about overthrow of Batista," he wrote in a telegram to Washington two days after the shipment of rifles was halted.

As Matthews prepared an editorial in support of the suspension, he telephoned the State Department to discuss the embargo and talk more generally about the deteriorating conditions in Cuba. He told C. Allan Stewart, deputy director of the Office of Middle American Affairs, that the rebel movement was better organized than ever before. Reflecting on the recent capture of an illicit shipment of arms in Brownsville, Texas, that was bound for the rebels, Matthews expressed regret that the government could not occasionally turn a blind eye to actions that would bring the whole troubled situation to a quick conclusion. He felt U.S. support for elections under the Batista regime was misguided because the Cuban people would never trust the results.

Although the arms embargo was widely interpreted as a tacit acknowledgment by Washington that Batista's cause was hopeless, the position of the United States was actually more complex. Smith continued to assure the regime that the United States remained supportive. But at the same time, an opposition group that included Raúl Chibás traveled to Washington to discuss the possible makeup of a military-civilian junta that would take over after Batista was forced out. Chibás would later refuse Castro's offer to lead a provisional government, leaving that to a Cuban judge whom Castro favored, Manuel Urrutia.

The split in U.S. attitudes toward the deteriorating situation in Cuba heightened the confusion in Havana, where Smith continued to plead Batista's case. The regime, Smith said in a telegram to the State Department, "has been friendly to and cooperative with US at all times. Whenever US had requested cooperation and assistance in our stand against world Communism GOC [Government of Cuba] has never been found wanting." He again criticized the decision to halt arms shipments and held out hope for a peaceful solution, honest elections, and an alternative future for Cuba that did not include Castro: "So soon after complete failure of highly advertised and long-promised revolution and general strike, it is difficult to believe rebels capable of capturing cities. Past program of rebel unfilled promises is still too vivid in people's minds."

The weapons ban was a debilitating psychological defeat for Batista. As the dictator weakened in the final months of 1958, Castro gained strength. The Communist Party of Cuba finally supported Castro's efforts but did not commit itself to backing him after Batista was overthrown. The presidential election was held in November, but the victory by Andrés Rivero Aguero, Batista's handpicked candidate, only inflamed the Cuban public. In early

December, former ambassador William D. Pawley, President Eisenhower's special envoy, flew to Havana on a secret mission to broker a peaceful transition. Batista rejected the proposal, in part because Washington would not allow him to say the plan had Eisenhower's support. As the morale of the army collapsed and whole battalions refused to fight, the columns led by Che, Raúl Castro, and the other rebel leaders advanced without opposition. The remnants of the revolutionary student movement that had survived the attack on the palace had established their own front in the Escambray Mountains and were on the move. A showdown with Batista was imminent. And once again, with the kind of exquisite timing that newspapermen dream of—aided, perhaps, by a tip from inside the State Department—Matthews decided to welcome in the new year while vacationing in Havana.

The old city was in a somber and cautious mood when Matthews arrived, lacking the gaiety with which Cubans traditionally celebrated the holidays. Even the previous year, which had seen so much bloodshed—the assassination attempt on Batista, followed by the brutal regime's retaliation, an attempted revolt by the Cuban navy at the Cienfuegos Naval Base that Batista had quickly put down, the murder of Frank País, and so much more—the city had celebrated heartily. Christmas trees abounded and the streets had been bright with colored lights. But that was 1957. As 1958 drew to a close, Havana was dark and uneasy. Violence had escalated. The total number of those killed by Batista's goons as they tried to put down the revolt was estimated to be 20,000, though no one knew for sure. Many families feared that celebrating openly would be seen as an indication of prosperity that, indirectly, would suggest cooperation with and support for the regime. The disruptions to business and transportation caused by the opposition bombs had created shortages that meant few families in the capital could celebrate the traditional Noche Buena feast on Christmas Eve. Only a handful of American families put up Christmas trees, and they kept them away from picture windows where they could be seen from the street. Stores in usually busy downtown Havana reported that business was terrible because people were afraid to go out. The dour Yule spirit carried over to New Year's Eve.

Matthews and Nancie checked into the Sevilla Biltmore and planned to spend New Year's Eve with Ruby Phillips and Ted Scott. They had been invited to dinner at the Riviera Hotel with Colonel Charles Barron, one of the owners, and his guests. The hotel's Copa Room was mostly empty as they sat down to eat, the usual crowd reduced to a quarter of its size by a rush of last-minute cancellations. The orchestra played with fervor, despite the circumstances, but the room was heavy with foreboding. Whereas most Cuban families had to forgo a holiday dinner because of the emergency, Matthews and Phillips dined on the Riviera's decadent holiday menu: turtle soup, filet mignon, and Baked Alaska. As midnight approached, Matthews and the others were served champagne and given party hats and noisemakers.

Just before midnight, the son of Jake Arvey, the Chicago politi-cian and Democratic Party boss, offhandedly mentioned to the others at the table that he had seen something odd a few hours before from the window of his house, which overlooked the air-field at Camp Columbia, Batista's army headquarters in Havana. Wasn't it strange, Arvey remarked, that a line of cars happened to be heading toward the airstrip, each one filled with women, chil-dren, and piles of luggage, on New Year's Eve?

Matthews realized immediately what was going on, and he couldn't help feeling a moment of personal satisfaction: Here was what he had confidently predicted from the moment in the Sierra when he had first seen Fidel Castro coming through the dense underbrush in such a dramatic way. Here was what Castro's firm gaze and his impressive character had led him to believe was inevitable. Here was the final result of Batista's greed, and of the American government's misguided support for the dictator. Now, in the earliest hours of 1959, Batista's endgame became apparent. He and his principal supporters were grabbing some of their mil-lions and abandoning Cuba.

As the halfhearted welcome to the new year ended, Matthews and Nancie rushed back to their hotel. Ruby Phillips and Ted Scott returned to their offices and tried unsuccessfully to get information from the palace. There was no answer at Camp Columbia either, nor at any of Havana's newspapers. Local radio stations continued their holiday playlist of festive music.

At around 2:00 AM, Phillips drove to her house in the Havana suburb of Miramar, a few blocks from Camp Columbia. The streets were deserted; even the local policemen who normally stood on duty at the entrance to the traffic tunnel under the Almendares River were missing. It could have been that holiday reveling kept the city's residents inside their houses and apartments. Or, Phillips suspected, something far more momentous had quieted Havana so completely.

No sooner had she entered her home than Phillips heard a big DC-4 straining to lift off the Camp Columbia runway. A second plane followed soon after. Then a third. Phillips's sister, Irma, who lived with her at the time, said she had heard others taking off earlier that night. Then Phillips got a call from Ernestina Otero, a Cuban journalist who reported regularly from Camp Columbia.

"They've gone," she shouted into the telephone, "I'm sure of it."

Phillips got the American embassy to confirm that Batista, his patsy president-elect Rivero Aguero, and other principal figures of the regime had flown off in a squadron of DC-4s. They had headed toward Florida but, in midcourse, veered off to the Dominican Republic, where they landed. With his demoralized army being routed by Castro's rebels throughout half of the country, Batista had desperately attempted to put Carlos M. Piedra y Piedra, the most senior justice of the supreme court, at the head of a provisional government, backed by a few loyal officers who were to form a military junta. Batista felt abandoned by the United States and believed there was nothing left to do but save his own skin.

By the time Matthews and Nancie awoke early the next morning, the streets of Old Havana were mobbed. Cubans, filled with both anger and joy, attacked the parking meters that had become a hated symbol of the dictator's regime. Then they turned to the casinos in the big tourist hotels, including the Sevilla Biltmore. Matthews and Nancie watched as the hotel's gaming tables were ransacked. Gunfire echoed through the streets, and there was general mayhem. It wasn't clear yet who, if anyone, was in charge. Radical students occupied the palace and vowed to defy Castro's troops, who were far from the city. The junta issued orders that were ignored. Nancie Matthews described the scene as "a madhouse."

Ruby Phillips filed the day's principal story, leaving Matthews to check in with his sources and collect impressions for a magazine piece and other articles he planned to write, if allowed. Early that afternoon he ran into Ambassador Smith and other embassy officials coming out of the palace. The two men looked at each other with suspicion, holding as they did very different opinions of the chaos surrounding them. Matthews recalled that Smith gave him "a weak smile and muttered something about 'seeking a solution,'" which he took to mean finding a way to keep Castro from taking Batista's place.

Smith's recollections are different. He said that when they had run into each other on the front steps of the palace, he told Matthews that he and the ambassadors of several other nations had gone to see General Eulogio Cantillo, the military commander of Oriente who had assumed control of the Cuban armed forces when Batista fled, to determine whether the new regime would protect their embassies. Smith felt Matthews did not believe him, and his suspicion seemed to be confirmed when he received a teletype message from the State Department. William A. Wieland, head of the Caribbean desk of the Bureau of Inter-American Affairs, wanted to know whether Smith had gone to the palace to show U.S. support for a military junta that would block Castro's ascension to power. Wieland conceded that he had heard the rumor from Matthews. Smith suspected that Matthews and the career diplomats at the State Department, like Wieland, had developed a close relationship and that both sides wanted to ensure that Washington did nothing "to interfere with his friend,

Fidel Castro, taking over the government of Cuba." Matthews denied that had been his intention.

By this time, a huge gap had developed at State, one that separated the views of Wieland and the other career diplomats from the White House and its political appointees. Allen Dulles, director of the Central Intelligence Agency, believed that Communists had already infiltrated the 26th of July Movement and would play a significant role in a Castro government, a good enough reason for the United States to try to keep Castro from taking over. At a National Security Council meeting a week before Batista fled, the deputy secretary of defense, Donald A. Quarles, declared bluntly that between Castro and Batista, Castro was the greater evil. Vice President Richard Nixon suggested that one way to weaken Castro would be to go after his sympathizers in the United States who broke any law, no matter how minor. But mindful of Matthews and other journalists he considered sympathizers, Nixon cautioned against doing anything that would antagonize the American press.

By then nothing could prevent Castro's victory. His forces swarmed out of the Sierra in the hours after Batista's flight and took control of the city of Santiago. "Now the Revolution begins," Castro thundered, proclaiming Santiago to be Cuba's new capital (he changed his mind a few days later) and calling for a general strike to prevent the military plotters and others from usurping him. He then began his slow, triumphant caravan across the island, traveling in a tank or on the back of an open jeep through frenzied throngs of Cubans who lined up along the 500-mile route to greet the hero of the Sierra. Matthews attempted to fly to Oriente Province to be the first newspaperman to interview Castro but was bitterly disappointed to find that he had been scooped by his competitor Jules Dubois, of the *Chicago Tribune,* who flew to Holguín in a Piper Apache that his editors had chartered in Miami. Dubois asked Castro if Washington's long-standing support for Batista had left the rebels with lingering resentment. At that early moment in the triumph of the revolution, Castro seemed to value tact over the truth.

"If I have had to be very cautious about my statements in the past," Castro said, referring to remarks he had made before about the United States, "from now on I am going to have to be even more careful." In truth, the resentment he felt toward the United States was substantial, and growing.

The rebel army had provided Matthews with a plane, but it developed mechanical problems after he climbed aboard and had to return to Havana. By the time he took off again, he had lost several hours, and he arrived in Holguín after Dubois had already begun his interview. Matthews had not been first this time, but the arranged trip marked the beginning of many favors that Castro would grant. Matthews took comfort in knowing that he was as close to the revolution as any American reporter and knew more about the inner workings of Castro's mind than all but the rebel hierarchy closest to him.

The *Times* reveled in its coverage of Castro's triumph. On January 2, Turner Catledge cabled Ruby Phillips: WARMEST CON-GRATULATIONS ON WONDERFUL JOB STOP KNOW YOU'LL STAY ON TOP OF STORY ALL THE WAY. REGARDS, CATLEDGE.

A few months later, Phillips won a Publisher's Award, a recognition that paid a modest $50. The citation read: "Ruby has given a good account of herself. In the rough, tough job of covering revolution and counter-revolution, ordinarily a man's job in the journalistic world, Ruby has proved to be dependable and tireless." But her editors had made clear their true feelings about her talents a few months earlier when she had asked for an increase in her tiny office budget. In reaching a decision, they had looked critically at her limitations as a correspondent. They had been forced to send in Homer Bigart to ward off Matthews, and they were looking at other correspondents to help cover the action in Cuba. They did not treat her like a regular correspondent. She was heavily censored by Batista, and after so many years in Havana, she was thoroughly entrenched in her ways. "It is true that Ruby is not the best writer in the world," Manny Freedman had written to Turner Catledge, "but it is also true that she is by far the best American correspondent resident in Cuba." When

Castro had landed in Oriente, the wire services had reporters in Havana, but Phillips was the *only* correspondent of a major American newspaper living in Cuba.

Given all the confrontations he had with his editors over Cuba, Matthews didn't expect them to acknowledge the value of his work. Nevertheless, he exulted in Castro's triumph, for it could be said that he had had a hand in it, a remarkable feeling for a journalist used to merely recording events. He was mildly embarrassed when, during the first weeks of the new regime, there was a short-lived attempt to have him named Smith's replacement as U.S. ambassador to Cuba. Jules Dubois publicly endorsed the nomination. Matthews graciously acknowledged the gesture, but conceded that such an appointment would be impossible. He would have been an unacceptable candidate, he said, "considering how involved I had become."

After the frustration of backing the losing side of the Spanish Civil War, and his change of heart with the fading fortunes of fascism, he had finally chosen the winning side in an ideological battle. He was convinced that Castro meant to push Cuba into an entirely new social and economic direction, and he believed that the Cuban Revolution would have a more lasting impact than the one in Mexico or any other since the French Revolution. He had the satisfaction then of knowing that his assessment of Castro's remarkable character had been on target; that despite the odds, the young rebel leader with the fierce eyes and wispy beard had captured the hearts and souls of young people in Cuba, the United States, and around the world. He had more than defended his own role in Castro's rise; he offered no apologies, hid no pride of accomplishment. He had boasted to his editors that the *Times* had done more for Cuba's people than had the United States government and that through him, the newspaper was responsible for helping bring down a murderous regime. He insisted all along that what he had accomplished was the result of fulfilling his journalistic duty, particularly in disrupting Batista's censorship. But Matthews brooked no sentimentality about journalistic objectivity—he had gone after one hell of a story and had quickly decided which side he was going to back. Employing both the news columns and editorial pages of the newspaper, he had become the single most recognizable American voice on Cuba, and he had managed to influence policymakers in Washington.

His sympathetic coverage had helped pressure Washington to suspend the sale of arms to Batista. It had encouraged a number of career diplomats in the State Department to overlook festering concerns about Castro until it was too late to back any alternative. And it had raised Castro, in the eyes of North Americans and Cubans alike, to a position above all his possible rivals and made him a political superstar, the symbol of youthful rebellion and defiance of authority.

It was all an illusion, one that wouldn't last long.

you can fool some of the people

A few days after Castro's remarkable procession into Havana, three of the most powerful newspaper editors in the United States met for lunch and drinks at the fabled "21" restaurant in New York. They had been called together by George M. Healy, Jr., editor of the *New Orleans Times-Picayune* and president of the American Society of Newspaper Editors, for a meeting of the society's program committee. The other members were W. D. Maxwell of the *Chicago Tribune*, Alicia Patterson of *Newsday*, and Turner Catledge of the *Times*. Healy wanted to kick around a few ideas for selecting a speaker for the society's big annual meeting in April. Catledge sent word that he was going to miss the lunch because his gout had flared up, but he invited the others to come to his apartment afterward to continue the discussion.

Healy, Maxwell, and Patterson squirreled themselves away in the restaurant's cozy upstairs dining room. They made themselves comfortable as they drank a few martinis and tossed out names of possible speakers for the upcoming meeting. It was the most important event of the year, and in the past they'd been able to draw presidents and prime ministers. Someone suggested Harold

Macmillan, the Conservative prime minister of Great Britain, who was expected to call an election soon and might find the exposure of a high-profile Washington trip useful. It was an obvious and predictable choice. They went through a few more names, and more sips of their drinks. Then, at almost the same moment, Maxwell and Healy came up with a wild idea: "What about Castro?"

The excitement of Castro's raucous procession into Havana was still fresh in the minds of most Americans who had seen pictures of it. The image of Castro created by Herbert Matthews and copied by CBS and countless other news organizations was widely held—he was the young man of democratic ideals with a beard and a telescopic rifle who had made Batista's army tremble. There was a strong undercurrent of concern about the possibility of Communist influence on Castro's movement, but the conservative figures whom Castro had brought into his original cabinet made the new government seem far less frightening. They were men such as Felipe Pazos, in charge of the central bank, and Rufo Lopez-Fresquet, at the finance ministry, along with the dour presence of Judge Manuel Urrutia, Castro's handpicked president. Taken together they seemed to form a solid team, and not so radical a departure from the Cuban hierarchy that Washington had dealt with in the past. Most newspapers and newsmagazines treated Castro with respect and a certain amount of awe. They forgave the new Cuban leader for his occasional imprudent statement, such as when he declared that if the United States ever tried to intervene in Cuba by sending in the Marines, there would be "20,000 dead gringos" in the streets. Afterward, he admitted that he should have been more discreet.

In Cuba itself, there was a real sense that something new and completely different was forming. The innovative path Castro had undertaken was not only transforming Cuba but was providing the youth of the world with an example of how to bring about change, a shift in perceptions that was just starting to pick up strength in the rock-and-roll days of early 1959. Castro was not yet thirty-three, Che only thirty, and most of the bearded ones—the *barbudos*—who had taken Havana with them were younger than that. It had seemed prophetic when a white dove landed on Castro's shoulder as he addressed the adoring crowds, and he still wore the religious amulet that an old woman had placed around his neck. How bad could he be?

Maxwell, whose paper had published Matthews's 1957 series in its own pages and devoted significant space to Cuba, so liked the idea of inviting Castro to Washington that he immediately called *The Tribune's* Latin American correspondent, Jules Dubois, and told him to start talking to the Cubans in charge of Fidel's schedule. Castro at that time held no public office (he did not become prime minister until February) and was barred by the constitution from becoming president because he was too young. Although he clearly ran Cuba, the editors figured he could be invited as the revolutionary hero he was, without worrying about diplomatic protocol.

Lunch ended, and the party moved to Catledge's apartment on 81st Street in Manhattan. Patterson recused herself because her husband, Harry Guggenheim, the publisher of *Newsday,* had been President Hoover's ambassador to Cuba from 1929 to 1933 and might not approve of the plan. But Maxwell and Healy were taken with the idea. As Catledge poured them drinks, they excitedly let him in on the discussion. No sooner had they settled in for the afternoon than the telephone in Catledge's apartment rang. It was Dubois calling from Cuba. The Cubans, he said, liked the idea. Castro would come to Washington.

Catledge realized that there was dissension inside the *Times* over Matthews's dual role as editorial writer and reporter, and he knew that Theodore Bernstein and others felt his coverage of Cuba had become tainted. The *Times* was already being credited with having helped defeat Batista. Years later, in his memoirs, he would describe Matthews as "a brilliant foreign correspondent, one of the most brilliant in *Times* history." But at this moment he, too, had lost confidence in Matthews's ability to tell the Cuban story straight. Catledge had gone along with efforts to keep Matthews's writing out of the news columns, and he did not think he would have any trouble keeping Matthews away from Castro if he came to Washington for the annual meeting.

But he had no inkling of what bringing Castro to Washington might mean for Matthews, or the paper. Nor could he know that the Cuban story was about to take an unexpected turn that would challenge many existing perceptions about Castro, Cuba, and the United States.

Less than two weeks after Batista went into exile, the *Times* published the first Letter to the Editor protesting Castro's executions of those who had not supported him. "In general, Fidel Castro's victory in Cuba has been hailed as another advance of liberalism and democracy over dictatorship and totalitarianism," the letter writer from New York said. "However, it gives me somehow an uneasy feeling reading in the newspapers that the victorious rebels are placing hundreds of persons—men and women—before firing squads after drumhead trials lasting a few minutes." That same day, Ruby Phillips wrote a page-one story that, for the first time, used the term "blood baths" to describe what was happening in Cuba in the aftermath of the rebel victory. Senator Wayne Morse of Oregon had condemned the summary executions in an angry speech on the floor of the Senate. He called on Castro and the other Cuban leaders to halt the "blood baths."

There were firing squads throughout the island, and the mob chant *"Paredon!"* ("To the wall") echoed grotesquely all over Cuba. Castro argued that he was keeping a personal promise to avenge the thousands who had been tortured and killed during the dictatorship. Quickly meting out justice to a few hundred Batista supporters who had done the regime's dirty work was the best way to avoid an even bloodier demand for revenge. He was so certain he was right that he invited journalists, both local and foreign, into the sports stadium in Havana where the accused were brought to revolutionary justice. He believed the Batistianos were so obviously guilty of the crimes for which they were accused that there was no need to dally long with formal processes, civil judges, or defense lawyers. The accusers—widows, grieving parents, even young children who had stepped in the blood of their slain relatives—came up to the once-powerful police officers and high-ranking army brass who had tried to put down the insurrection, pointed their fingers toward them, and said, "Yes, he's the one." They were then dragged in front of a wall and shot. Castro called it "Operation Truth."

His mastery of propaganda and imagery failed him this time. American reaction to the executions was not at all what he had expected. The initial reports shocked and angered many Americans, and much of the coverage of the Cuban Revolution turned, as though a switch had been pulled, from preening and sympathetic to damning. The honeymoon had lasted only weeks, replaced by a rising tide of condemnation, recrimination, and suspicion that would eventually turn into a flood. The executions were just one turn in the complex story. Because nearly all of his rivals had been either killed or neutralized, Castro had a much easier time than expected of seizing all power without having to share with other opposition groups. The Communist Party, which had been very late to throw its support behind Castro, was seen to be taking a much more active role in the new government, and doubts about Che Guevara and Raúl Castro's Communist links had continued to grow. Despite claiming that he wanted no power for himself, Castro was in absolute control, and he had rejected the idea of holding elections anytime soon.

An angry Castro lashed out at the Americans who criticized the executions, sounding more radical and anti-American than ever before. His public image was changing. In caricatures he was no longer pictured as a messiah. Rather, conservative publications drew him as a barbarian, recklessly leading the corrupt paradise that was Cuba to the edge of an abyss. Matthews was one of the few writers who did not abandon him but tried to put the executions into a revolutionary context. He did not support the killings, but he thought he understood Castro's reasoning for them, and he felt that under the circumstances the executions did prevent further bloodshed, even if they did not meet Western standards of jurisprudence. On one of Matthews's frequent visits to Cuba during 1959, he attempted to cable an editorial to New York explaining, but not justifying, the summary trials. Without a clear sign that the dead were being avenged, he reasoned, mobs would take the law into their own hands, as they had when the Cuban dictator Machado was overthrown in 1933. Within days of his removal from the Presidential Palace, mobs had lynched upwards of a thousand of Machado's supporters and ransacked the homes of hundreds of his henchmen.

Matthews's editorial sounded very much like what Castro himself had said. The publisher rejected it because it seemed to excuse Castro's bloody brand of justice and would make it look as though the *Times* endorsed the killings. Matthews was stunned. It was the first time the publisher had killed an editorial of his; it wouldn't be the last.

Matthews managed to fashion his thoughts on the executions into a news article that was published on January 18, less than two weeks after Castro entered Havana. Matthews tried to analyze the situation from the Cuban point of view, which he would long afterward argue was the perspective missing from most American coverage of the revolution. But many of his critics would see his approach not as empathy, as he had conceived it, but as outright sympathy for Castro and the revolution. After describing Castro as being, in the eyes of most Cubans, "the greatest hero that their history has known," he explained the reasoning behind the executions that were causing such an adverse reaction in America: "[T]he new Provisional Government felt, in the first place, that justice must be done and, in the second place, that, if the authorities did not mete out justice in an orderly way, the people would exercise lynch law and in the process there would be some private vengeance and some innocent victims." The Cuban people were 100 percent behind Castro in this, he said, and condemning their leader meant condemning the people themselves.

That same day, an unsigned editorial appeared in the paper. It was not written by Matthews, though it did mention him by name: "We welcomed the success of the movement led by the devoted Fidel Castro, which Herbert L. Matthews of this newspaper described nearly two years ago as standing for 'a new deal for

Cuba, radical, democratic and therefore anti-Communist.'" The editorial was careful to attribute the conclusion about Castro's apparent distance from the Communists to Matthews, and not to the paper itself. The editorial directly criticized Senator Morse for going too far in using the term "blood baths" and calling for sanctions against Cuba, and it urged Castro to temper his more extreme views: "What we would like to appeal to is the Cuban patriotism of Dr. Castro and his followers. We would appeal to them not to let butchers and torturers go free, but to try them soberly and according to civil procedures."

But Matthews's true feelings about the early days of Castro's revolution were more sympathetic than either the editorial about the executions or his article makes them seem. In notes for a talk he gave at about this time, in which he was careful to point out that he was speaking for himself, not the *Times*, he called Cuba "the happiest country in the world," a nation reborn, with a government of honest, mostly conservative men, "not a government of wild, bloodthirsty rebels." The notes continued:

> In my day the sympathies of the American newspapermen—
> I'm not talking of putting any bias into their coverage—the
> sympathies would have been with a man like Fidel Castro and
> a people like the Cubans who, whatever is said in this coun-
> try today, have performed a great, a noble, a heroic feat.
> They deserve a better fate.

The notes make clear that for Matthews, Cuba was Spain all over again, a heroic struggle of freedom versus fascism. The Spanish Civil War and Cuba's revolution were both passionate efforts of oppressed people willing to die to defend their liberty. The big difference was that, this time, he had picked the winning side. He had not changed much since the 1930s, when he sympathized with the Loyalists and felt that he was objectively reporting what was taking place in battle after battle without letting bias creep into his writing. But Matthews always had a blind spot, never seeing how taking sides could slant his reporting, especially after he started writing editorials and was obliged to do just that—take sides. However, editorial writers were supposed to reflect the paper's views, not their own, as Matthews was reminded when the publisher rejected his editorial on the firing squads.

Headstrong and sure of himself, Matthews openly criticized other journalists for getting the Cuban story wrong, while insisting that he had got it almost 100-percent right from the very start. He ended up isolating himself from most of his colleagues by repeatedly declaring the American press's handling of the Cuban Revolution was "the worst example of American journalism" he had seen in his long career. And he believed that this failure had caused a colossal misunderstanding between the United States and Cuba that poisoned the relationship between the two countries. Castro responded to each mention of a bloodbath in the American press with mounting vitriol, which triggered another round of criticism in the newspapers. Matthews saw a dangerous pattern: "A vicious circle of recrimination and counter recrimination—and soon, of deed and answering deed—had been set in motion, never to cease."

Much had changed in the time between the boozy lunch at "21" and the day Castro and his entourage touched down in Washington's National Airport, where officials were braced for a visit they had not arranged and did not want. The State Department had been quick to recognize the new provisional government, formally acting to do so before Castro had even reached Havana on January 8. But then the executions began, and the State Department started to squirm. Castro was proving to be unpredictable, and they wanted more time to see what he had in mind. The last thing they needed was for the program committee of the American Society of Newspaper Editors to invite him to come to the United States when the situation was still so volatile. The invitation was premature and would force State into a corner, hoping to neither snub him nor offer too many concessions that would later prove embarrassing. Figuring out what to do with the bearded rebel leader would have been tough enough without the editors' ill-timed invitation. But this revolution had been fought in the newspapers from the beginning, and that was not going to change.

The State Department clearly did not want to treat Castro's trip as an official visit. Had it gone through diplomatic channels, there would have been a chance to smooth out the rough edges and put a real agenda into place before anyone arrived. There would also have been more time to gauge the makeup of the new government, and to negotiate objectives and demands behind the scenes rather than having to conduct all business on the fly while the Cubans were in town, or, worse, to have it all laid out in the newspapers. But it was simply too early, the visit too hastily arranged, and altogether the wrong way to begin a relationship with a new government, especially one that came to power at the end of a gun. Nonetheless, Christian A. Herter, the acting secretary of state whom President Eisenhower would soon name as replacement for the seriously ill John Foster Dulles, greeted Castro on his arrival in Washington in April and hosted him at a luncheon. President Eisenhower was wary of Castro and opposed his visit. He couldn't understand why Castro had accepted an invitation from the newspaper editors without even sending a telegram to inform the State Department.

At a National Security Council meeting in March, the president had suggested that State simply refuse to issue Castro a visa. Surely the executions and his anti-American remarks were reason enough to be kept out of the country. Herter convinced Eisenhower that such overt hostility would cause more problems than it solved. Eisenhower gave up the idea and was prepared to meet with Castro if necessary, though he found the prospect disagreeable. No meeting ever took place, however, because by the time Castro arrived in Washington surrounded by his odd team of conservative economists and wild-eyed bodyguards, the president was off golfing in Augusta, Georgia.

In place of Eisenhower, Vice President Richard M. Nixon was supposed to see Castro informally during a weekend visit to the vice president's house. At the last minute, plans changed and

Nixon sat with him for over two hours in the vice president's Senate office. One of Castro's group called the meeting "an out-and-out disaster." Nixon's impressions of Castro were mixed, but despite his reservations he saw in the young rebel leader some of the same aspects of character that Matthews had so often outlined in his articles.

"The one fact that we can be sure of is that he has those indefinable qualities which make him a leader of men," Nixon wrote in a draft summary of their meeting. Nixon's assessment of Castro's communism also coincided, in large part, with Matthews's view: "He is either incredibly naive about Communism or under Communist discipline—my guess is the former, and as I have already implied his ideas as to how to run a government or an economy are less developed than those of almost any world figure I have met in fifty countries." And, in the end, Nixon came to a conclusion that could have been taken from one of Matthews's editorials on Cuban-U.S. relations in 1959. "But because he has the power to lead to which I have referred, we have no choice but at least to try to orient him in the right direction."

During their meeting, Nixon showed Castro secret files indicating that a number of men with Communist ties were believed to be in the Cuban administration, and he expressed concern over the summary executions. As time went on, Nixon's opinion of Castro would turn more negative, and he later suggested to the president that a plan be developed to forcefully overthrow Castro. The groundwork done by the Eisenhower administration became the foundation of the Bay of Pigs invasion two years later.

From practically the moment Castro arrived in Washington, he was interrogated about the presence of suspected Communists in his government. He always denied any connection with them. "I have said very clearly that we are not Communists," he declared before 1,500 people at the newspaper editors' annual meeting. Special precautions had been taken at the Statler-Hilton Hotel where the meeting was held. Anti-Communist groups that did not trust Castro, along with Batista supporters who hated him, had made death threats against him and blanketed the city with pamphlets attacking him. Just before Castro sat down to eat, a waiter changed the dishes in front of him and brought new butter, rolls, and water. His main course had to be cooked separately. Security remained tight throughout the meeting, with policemen stationed around the room. Castro had also brought his own protection, and bearded bodyguards kept watch over him. They even tore apart a microphone in the hotel's ballroom where he was to speak, to make sure no explosives were hidden inside.

After his address, Castro agreed to take a few questions. He was polite, funny, and straightforward, especially when he answered in stilted English. Although he had brought along his top economic advisers, he said, he had not come to Washington to ask for money, nor had Cuba formally requested any economic assistance from the Soviet Union or any other country. Yes, he said in response to another question, he had definitely received everything he had hoped for in Washington. Rufo Lopez-Fresquet, the new finance minister, was even more reassuring in his statements about the visit and the revolution that was taking place in Cuba. He explained that the proposed agricultural reforms would target only land that was not being efficiently used. He denied rumors that the new government was going to confiscate private property, and he said no decisions had yet been made about how to handle the sizable lands owned by Americans.

To the annoyance of the State Department, Castro had expanded his itinerary in the United States substantially beyond addressing the newspaper editors' group. After five days in Washington, Castro boarded a train and headed north, stopping at Princeton, New Jersey, before continuing on into New York City, where he was greeted by the largest and most boisterous crowds of the trip. About 2,000 people, many of them waving Cuban flags, were lined up outside Pennsylvania Station when the train arrived at 11:00 AM. The executions had not bothered them, and they still considered Castro a hero. The New York police had trouble keeping order. Castro drew large crowds everywhere he went in New York, including at Columbia University, where he addressed students and supporters who saw him as the young man who had defeated the dictator, overlooking or making excuses for his other, less enlightened actions.

Matthews had helped arrange a visit to the *Times,* and although the Cubans had not informed the State Department of the details of his visit until he arrived, the Cuban ambassador, Raúl Roa, had told Matthews that Castro had personally asked to see the newspaper's offices so he could thank the *Times* for its role in the revolution. Arthur Hayes Sulzberger had agreed to welcome him, and he made preparations for a sober visit. Castro was scheduled to arrive at 5:30 PM, the publisher notified everyone in a memo, and "Coffee and cigars will be served but *no* drinks!" as though he was concerned that tipsy Cubans might knock over a trophy case. The meeting went off smoothly. Castro thanked Sulzberger and several editors profusely, and praised Matthews. "Without your help," Castro said, nodding toward Matthews, "and without the help of *The New York Times,* the revolution in Cuba would never have been."

No matter how squeamish the publisher and editors might have felt hearing Fidel praise Matthews, it would be nothing compared to their discomfort after Castro addressed the Overseas Press Club, an event that Matthews also helped arrange. The luncheon was held at the Sheraton-Astor House Hotel in New York, and the atmosphere was anything but confrontational. The menu included "Consommé 26 July" and traditional Cuban *arroz con pollo.* It was during this meeting that Castro, for the first time, exposed yet another unpleasant part of his complex character by his willingness to turn on those he considered friends. With the media hierarchy present, and among them no doubt several of Matthews's most vocal detractors, Castro said he was going to let everyone in on a little secret. Matthews recalled watching Castro speak "with a slightly malicious gleam in his eyes," as he tried to make a fool of the man to whom only days before, at the Cuban embassy in Washington, he had awarded a special medal inscribed "Sierra Maestra Press Mission: To Our American Friend Herbert Matthews With Gratitude. Fidel Castro."

Instead of the "columns of 40" that Matthews, in his original article, had reported to be under his command, Castro told the New York press that he had actually had no more than eighteen armed men with him in the Sierra at the time. He said he had given orders for the men to march by repeatedly to fool Matthews into believing the rebel army was much larger. "You can fool some of the people . . . ," Castro said, attempting to repeat Lincoln's famous saying but tripping over the words. After mangling several more attempts, he simply said, "Well, you know what I mean."

Although Castro's account that day was revisionist history, a legend was born, a damning one that haunted Matthews for the rest of his life, and which continues long after his death. It fit snugly into Castro's predilection for shaping myth to suit his own purposes. In later years, Castro's government would downplay, obfuscate, or completely hide the competing efforts of the students and other resisters in the urban underground who had fought against Batista in order to build up the legend of the Sierra fighters. On this evening in New York, Castro was inventing another part of the legend. And Matthews had to sit there as his colleagues chuckled, reveling in his discomfort.

Matthews later acknowledged that his calculation of Castro's forces had been in error, but he never admitted that he had been so naive as to fall for the trick that Castro had described. And there is reason to believe that Castro had revised history to embellish his own myth. By making a fool of one of America's most important journalists, Castro showed that he was capable of making a fool of the United States. But the encounter in the Sierra did not happen the way Castro had described. Matthews had received credible information that Castro led more than one column. It was the information from those sources, and not any ruse by Castro, that led to the exaggerated figure. None of the contemporary accounts of those who were present describe the rebels repeatedly marching around him. Matthews's error was in not reporting that the troop strength figures were from independent sources but could not be confirmed by what he saw, which is what Homer Bigart did after his visit in 1958.

* * *

Matthews acted as Castro's guide and handler during the New York visit, seeing him three times during the week. The entire U.S. trip was an eventful one, but also quite perplexing. Castro had been greeted enthusiastically everywhere but in the White House. His stay was covered with the same excitement as the Beatles' first visit to New York a few years later. His movements were reported in the newspapers and broadcast on television. He was interviewed by Edward R. Murrow while still in his pajamas. His handlers thought he would look too bellicose if he wore his military uniform for the program, but on such short notice, they couldn't find a suit and shirt that fit him. He was interviewed for *The Ed Sullivan Show.* On *Meet the Press,* he was asked pointed questions about his brother's ties to the Communist party and about attempts by the Communists to infiltrate his new government. Castro looked right into the camera and said, in a stumbling and sometimes fractured English, that there were no Communists in his government. "I have read some list that I don't doubt they are saying [that there are Communists in the Cuban government]. If it continues—discovering such Communists in our government— Adam and Eve are going to be Communists too . . . ."

Despite the drumbeat of accusations, Castro himself seemed undecided about communism, and about the United States, at least publicly. No one, not Matthews, despite his access to Castro, nor members of his own cabinet like Pazos and Lopez-Fresquet, knew exactly what was going through Castro's mind. Documents from the Soviet archives raise the possibility that while Castro was in the United States declaring that he was not a Communist, his brother Raúl called him to say that the Soviets had responded to his request for assistance and had agreed to send Spanish-speaking military trainers to Cuba. It represented the earliest signal that the Soviet leaders understood the strategic opportunity that Cuba represented for them in the Western Hemisphere.

Just before he left New York, Castro had one more indirect contact with Matthews. Two of the Cuban women who had accompanied him during the visit called on Matthews and his wife at their Upper East Side apartment. On the surface it appeared to be a social call, but the women let Matthews know how concerned Castro was about the incessant talk of communism. The question of Communist influence would be taken care of once and for all as soon as Castro returned to Havana, the women said. In a memo to the publisher, Matthews relayed Castro's message:

> Fidel says he realizes he must get rid of the undesirables who have forced their way into minor positions. He intends to clear the Reds out of the army. He feels very strongly the importance of good relations with the United States. His feeling about the trip, and that applies also to his entourage, was very favorable. They all feel good about it. He wanted my opinion on his trip also and I said that I thought it was most successful.

He also reminded the publisher just how involved the newspaper was in the Cuban situation.

> In conclusion, I would like to emphasize what you all must have noticed, which is Fidel's youth and all that that means. He really wants advice and guidance and constructive criticism from sources he knows to be friendly, such as The New York Times. As I said before, I think we are in a position to perform an important service for the United States as well as for Cuba by maintaining our attitude of understanding and sympathy with criticism of what we consider bad and praise for what we consider good.

For Castro, the two-week whirlwind tour that was choreographed by an American public relations firm and included stops in Canada and South America, was a propaganda bonanza. He charmed his way through a good deal of the hemisphere and was an especially big hit with the young, who admired his rebelliousness. Arthur M. Schlesinger, Jr., the historian, captured the kind of counterculture magic of his appearance before a stadium full of students at Harvard. "They saw in him, I think, the hipster who in the era of the Organization Man had joyfully defied the system, summoned a dozen friends and overturned a government of wicked old men," Schlesinger wrote. It was the same theme of youthful rebellion that Matthews had described in his first article on Castro in 1957.

But Castro's rock star popularity distressed Philip Bonsal, who became U.S. ambassador less than a week after the United States recognized the new Cuban regime. He lamented the missed opportunity that the trip represented and blamed the failure in part on the editors who met at "21." He felt they had made a grievous mistake in extending Castro an invitation at that moment. A formal visit some time later, after the new Cuban government had had time to grow into its role, could have been better planned, and a visit by Eisenhower to Cuba would not have been out of the question. There could have been a chance to reestablish the historic ties between the two nations and begin a new chapter in their intimate histories. "But the time for such visits was still distant when the editors, so far as I know without consulting any responsible American official, issued their invitation," Bonsal wrote. That missed opportunity haunted him and others in Washington for a long time.

The confusion over Castro and his ambitions was matched by the contradictory interpretations of his revolution that were being reported in *The New York Times*. When Ruby Phillips and Herbert Matthews both filed reports on the same incident, they often reached totally different conclusions. They seemed to have taken different sides in the revolutionary fight, which led to a growing animosity between them. And that enmity eventually spilled out onto the pages of the newspaper.

A clash had been building for some time, despite the similarities of their backgrounds. Matthews and Phillips were about the same age, but they saw the world through different lenses. Matthews was urbane, worldly, and bookish; he carried himself with the air of a university dean or a pinstriped State Department diplomat. He smoked a pipe, quoted Dante, and counted as friends Ernest Hemingway and the Italian philosopher Benedetto Croce. He was a facile writer, author of several books, and a diligent reporter, willing to go anywhere for a story. Since returning from service in World War I and graduating from Columbia University in 1922, he had had only one employer—and had worked his way up at the *Times* from stenographer to distinguished correspondent and editorial writer.

Phillips, too, had worked for only the *Times* in her long career as a journalist. But her exclusive connection to the paper had come about essentially because of a series of happenstances, including the death of her husband. Ruby Phillips was a raw-boned country girl, originally from Oklahoma. Like Matthews, she was as old as the century, born in 1900, and her spirit was as untamed as the frontier where she grew up. Her father, John Hart, was a cattle merchant, the latest wandering soul in a family of pioneers that settled in Tennessee in the footsteps of Daniel Boone. She had her own horse from the time she was four, and she helped her father buy and sell horses and cattle before she was a teenager. She went to school in half a dozen places in Oklahoma, Texas, and New Mexico before enrolling at the University of Las Vegas in New Mexico. She thought she wanted to become a teacher but never finished her courses. Instead, she enrolled at a business school in Dallas, where she learned basic secretarial skills. She bounced from job to job, working for a lumber company, a wholesale grocer, and an automobile company before deciding she needed to get away from the Southwest. She headed for Cuba, where she took a job at Westinghouse Electric.

In Havana, she met and later married another expatriate American, James Doyle Phillips, and helped him establish a small shop offering stenography, mimeographing, and other business services. When University of Havana students ratcheted up their resistance to President Machado in 1931, James Phillips began contributing news items to the *Times,* and he was later taken on as a resident correspondent. Ruby represented the Times World Wide Photographic service and worked closely with her husband, learning the basics of journalism.

When James Phillips was killed in a stateside automobile accident in 1937, the *Times* felt obliged to let Ruby replace him, though the editors were concerned about the level of her journalistic abilities. Within a few months New York came to realize her limitations. "She has not sent much lately, but that is good judgment because there has not been much news of N.Y. interest," an editor surmised in a note to Edwin James, then managing editor. "On what she has sent her work and judgment have been good. Of course, we cannot know, as you remarked, how well she will do until the situation comes to a head again. Whether we care to have her then writing for the occasion is, of course, another question."

Phillips was in the unusual position of being a woman at a time when virtually the entire corps of foreign correspondents at the *Times* and other newspapers was composed of men. Her byline, "R. Hart Phillips," so masked her true identity that as late as 1990, a book analyzing the *Times*'s coverage of foreign policy still referred to Phillips as "he." The combination of taking over for her late husband and working in a part of the world that was only of sporadic interest to most Americans meant Phillips did not command much respect in New York. While she thought of herself as a correspondent, the editors saw her principally as a contract stringer who could call in tips and write routine stories but who would need reinforcing if the story ever got big again.

To her credit, Phillips did not shy away from the challenge of covering Cuba, and slowly, as she gained experience, and as the Cuban story heated up, she won the right to file big stories on her own. She covered Batista's 1952 coup and Castro's foolhardy attack on the Moncada barracks the following year. But when Batista held elections in 1954, the editors sent Matthews to cover them. Phillips felt violated.

Although she had willingly passed up the opportunity to interview Castro in 1957 and called in Matthews on her own, she was not entirely happy with the way he depicted Cuba. Her objections centered on Matthews's portrayal of Cuba's economy, which she felt she knew far better than its politics. She complained to the foreign editor again, this time claiming that Matthews had not adequately presented Cuba's current prosperity: "I shall be glad to write an economic article at any time you want me to do so.

However, it is bound to show that Cuba is prosperous and that things are going well."

In public though, Phillips held her tongue, and if she ever mentioned Matthews, it was only in positive terms, as she lauded his courage and bravery in crossing Batista's lines to get the Castro interview. Matthews also generally kept up appearances. "Incidentally, we should be very pleased and satisfied to have such a correspondent as Ruby Phillips in Havana," he wrote in a memo to the publisher after his triumphant return trip to Cuba in June 1957. There was no hint of animosity as he sang her praises. "She is completely honest, extremely well informed and is so diplomatic that she manages to keep on terms with both the government and the opposition. She is also courageous in a situation that I can assure you requires courage."

Yet he had misgivings about Phillips's talents and her own sympathies, feeling she had been far too close to Batista to honestly represent Castro and the revolution. Just after Castro's visit to the United States, Matthews wrote to the publisher and the paper's top editors that Phillips was unable to cover the Cuban story: "I think it is again obvious how much influence for good *The New York Times* can be. I also think it is obvious that we must have someone go to Cuba at intervals to do a coverage in depth of the situation. Ruby Phillips is unable to do this."

That summer, after Castro signed the agricultural reform laws that raised huge concerns among Americans about the direction Cuba was heading, Matthews again returned to the island, arriving in time to attend a Fourth of July celebration at the residence of Ambassador Bonsal. In letters home to Nancie, who was ill and unable to accompany him, he began the carping almost immediately.

Dear Nancie:
   Starting this already, my first morning, as I am waiting for Ruby to get to the office and there seems so much to say. I haven't seen or heard from Ruby yet! She is a strange creature.

He noted that he was writing the letter well before 10:30 on a Saturday morning and that Phillips had not interrupted her normal schedule because he was in town. Phillips knew that part of his mission was securing a sit-down interview with Castro, something she'd been unable to arrange on her own. Getting it now, she understood, would mean playing second fiddle to Matthews, both during the interview and in writing it up afterward, and she dreaded that prospect. They saw the revolution differently, and that had become so clear by now that other news outlets felt free to comment on it.

In the 1950s, media criticism was limited, but Henry Luce's *Time* magazine was changing that. The *Times*, and especially Herbert Matthews, became an early and easy target. The magazine had become rabidly anti-Castro, and it jumped on the spat between Matthews and Phillips with obvious glee. At the end of May, Phillips had written that the Cuban Communists were working in close cooperation with Castro's 26th of July Movement and were gaining so much power and influence that many Cubans were growing concerned that Castro would be unable to keep them in check.

But at the end of his July visit, Matthews published a front-page article that came to quite a different conclusion. "This is not a Communist revolution in any sense of the word and there are no Communists in positions of control," Matthews wrote. And to back up his conclusions, he added: "This is the overwhelming consensus among Cubans in the best positions to know."

Two weeks later, in a letter to Ambassador Bonsal, Matthews defended his statement that the revolution was not Communist. "I did not in the article deny that there were Communists in secondary positions and an indeterminate element of fellow-traveling, but so far as just about all the leading figures in Cuba are concerned, I feel sure that none of them is Communist and virtually all of them are intellectually and emotionally anti-Communist and when the time comes that we will see ample proof of this," he wrote. Matthews believed that the incessant accusations about Communists were making it virtually impossible for Castro to "take an openly anti-Communist line." He cited support from various sides, including columns by Walter Lippmann, who told Matthews in a letter: "You are playing a gallant and convincing role and we are in your debt."

But criticism far outweighed praise for Matthews's reporting. *Time* referred to him as a "champion of causes," who had found lots to like in various disreputable regimes in the past, including Mussolini's Fascists and what the magazine termed "the Communist-backed Loyalists forces" in Spain. "In clearly choosing sides in Cuba's conflict, Herb Matthews, 59, was following a well-established pattern in his long, award-studded career," *Time* said.

The pressure was getting to Phillips. She developed a bleeding ulcer and was living on milk, crackers, and cigarettes. The Cuban story had taken control of her life, dominating nearly every moment of her days, including her time off. When the Cubans confiscated an American marble quarry on the Isle of Pines, she inherited a parrot that the American owner had left behind. She called the parrot Mickey and kept him in her office, where he would bite pencils and chair rungs, and listen for hours to Castro speaking on television whenever Phillips and her staff had to stay up monitoring the speeches. Sometimes, when she arrived at the office at 11:00 AM the morning after one of the marathon addresses, Mickey was still sleeping in his cage.

It was after one of those speeches that Phillips and Matthews, joined by Tad Szulc, a *Times* reporter who had just come from the Dominican Republic, were finally granted an interview with Castro. They met at 3:00 AM in the lobby of the Havana Hilton, where Castro then had his headquarters. Castro was hungry, so they went to the hotel's coffee shop, where he ordered a large steak and a pile of fried potatoes. He insisted it be an informal, off-the-record chat, and he did most of the talking. He also asked a few questions, directed at no one in particular. One was, "Why don't the Americans like me?"

Phillips was the one to answer. "Why should they like you?" she asked. "You have attacked the United States every time you have spoken since you came to Havana."

Castro hadn't met Phillips before, but he knew her well enough by reputation and had once sent a runner from the Sierra Maestra to Havana in 1958 with a mountain orchid for her. He smiled at her for standing up to him like that. He was used to dealing with headstrong women like Celia Sánchez and Haydée Santamaria. He said he would do something about correcting those impressions in his next televised speech. Later he asked another question of the table, and Phillips again leaped in with an answer.

"Why are the Americans so afraid of communism in Cuba?" she remembered Castro asking.

"If you would take this island and drag it out into the middle of the Atlantic Ocean, no one would bother whether you were a Communist or not," Phillips said, "but you are ninety miles from the U.S., and that's too close."

Castro laughed, then turned to an aide. "So, we are too close."

After Matthews so defiantly declared that the revolution was not Communist in any way, it was *Newsweek*'s turn to point out the inconsistencies between the two *Times* correspondents. "What Fidel Is—Pick an Expert," was the headline. The magazine had asked Matthews about the differing views and quoted him as saying: "You pay your money and you take your choice." Phillips responded: "I'm sending what happens. He's giving the opinions, really." It was just a hint of what was going on between them. "When we were going to see Fidel, you characterized my questions as 'hostile,'" Phillips wrote in a letter to Matthews. "You, of course, have much more experience and authority than I have. I do not believe, however, that an impartial judge would hold that to inquire from Fidel as to where he hopes to secure all of the millions and millions of dollars he is promising to spend on this and that, or the other questions I noted down, were hostile." Obviously wounded by his criticism, she pointed out again to Matthews, as she had explained to *Newsweek*, that he was writing the editorials while she was only reporting the news, "which is not based on your or my opinion but upon what God has permitted to happen to humanity, including the Cuban department of humanity. At no time have I ever questioned your views, as expressed in editorials in *The New York Times*. That is your affair. If other people, like *Time* magazine and *Newsweek*, find that there is a lack of harmony in the news stories emanating from me, and the conclusions and opinions presented in the editorials by you, that is their affair."

Matthews took his complaints about Phillips directly to the publisher. "Through her emotional and technical insufficiencies," he wrote in a memo, "Ruby Phillips has been most incapable of sending a clear and detached and understanding picture of the Cuban Revolution."

The editors believed that Phillips was too anti-Castro, but they thought that Matthews leaned too far to the left. They attempted to mediate by bringing in Homer Bigart or Tad Szulc, but with Castro's suspected Communist leanings more discussed with each passing week, it had become vitally important to have someone whose assessment of the Communist threat would not be questioned. They also wanted an experienced correspondent in Cuba who would live there day-to-day and not just parachute in for big stories. For this job, they picked a young reporter who did not know Spanish, or much about Cuba, but who would know a Communist if he saw one: Max Frankel, the *Times* correspondent just then returning from Moscow.

Communism was the most critical issue of the day, dividing the West along ideological lines and turning the United States inside out. Frankel, then just thirty, knew he was being thrust into an unwinnable position as referee between Matthews and Phillips. He felt he was "being clumsily inserted between feuding writers, both old enough to be my parents and vastly more experienced in the subject." He was given six weeks of Spanish training in New York and a month for political briefings to prepare him for his new post, an assignment he did not look forward to. He was still in New York in September 1960 when Castro showed up to attend a gathering of world leaders at the United Nations. Castro had already made a scene at the Hotel Shelburne, complaining about the accommodations and announcing that he was checking out because the manager had accused the Cubans of plucking chickens and cooking them in their rooms. The dispute actually centered on bills the Cubans had not paid. Castro moved his entourage to the Theresa Hotel on 125th Street in Harlem, where Matthews arranged for Frankel to meet him at the hotel's coffee shop, begging the young reporter to keep an open mind about Castro even though Nikita Khrushchev, also in New York for the United Nations conference, had been photographed giving Castro a bear hug outside the hotel. To Castro's enemies, the photo was taken as proof that he was, at heart and by design, as Red as a Communist could get.

For Frankel, it was a noteworthy introduction. He asked Castro one simple question, then had to sit through an hour-long answer. He glimpsed the inscrutable character of the rebel leader, and of the Cuban government he led. Even his rudimentary Spanish was enough to pick up Castro's inference that Frankel would be sympathetic to the revolution, just as Matthews had always been. Any friend of Matthews, Castro enthused, would also be his friend. There was much for him to tell the American people about Cuba and the revolution.

Frankel arrived in Cuba in early November 1960, with a packet of introductory letters from Matthews. He dutifully delivered them to government officials, including Carlos Rafael Rodríguez, the minister of propaganda and education, and head of Cuba's Communists. Matthews's letters helped get Frankel a late-night interview with Rodríguez, who assumed that he, like Matthews, could be considered friendly to the revolution. The conversation with Rodríguez gave Frankel enough information to write a clear-eyed account of what was transpiring in Cuba. Frankel had lived up to his reputation in the newsroom; within three weeks of arriving in Havana, he had concluded that Castro was a Communist, "not so much by conviction as by conversion and convenience," a power-hungry Latin who understood mob psychology and who benefited from the good fortune of being blessed "with a foolish enemy" in the United States.

In an interview almost forty years later, Frankel did not blame Matthews for having been mistaken about Castro's true motives. "By the time I reached Havana he was well on his way to becoming a 'Marxist-Leninist' and initiating Cuba in the Soviet bloc," he said of Castro. The influence that Che and Raúl had on Castro's thinking could no longer be denied. Castro's tilt to the left had become incontestable, at least to most journalists except Matthews. After Frankel's article was published on November 26, Rodríguez denounced him. Frankel's visa application was denied, and he returned to New York, his duty done.

Frankel went on to become a White House correspondent who traveled to China with Nixon, editor of the editorial page (well after Matthews had retired), and eventually executive editor of the *Times*. He saw Matthews in a critical light, an aging writer "sustained by his mountain adventure and new notoriety," who persisted too long "in his hero worship and apologias for the Castro government." Matthews, Frankel said, was "a romantic who transmuted his understandable opposition to U.S. colonialism in Latin America into excessive faith in Latin radicals. He finally, and belatedly wrote some editorials that you'll find acknowledged Castro's pro-Communist evolution, but tended still to blame the U.S. for losing him." He thought Matthews belonged to a group of newspapermen who are not content to simply explain the world but long to change it. "He was one of those journalists who yearn to give history a hand by directing society toward the good and the beautiful," he said.

Matthews's enthusiasm for Castro's revolution appeared more incongruous as the realities of Castro's vision became more terrifying to Americans. Matthews found himself being criticized by the public, by Washington, and by his own paper. Even though he occasionally scolded Castro in his editorials, he never wavered in his judgment that what Castro was doing was for the good of Cuba. Increasingly, he was becoming a lone voice of support for Castro. He criticized other reporters for their faulty coverage, and he blamed officials in Washington for pushing Castro into a corner where he had no choice but to turn to the Soviet Union for help. There was widespread confusion over Castro's true motives, but that did not deter Matthews, who was secure in his belief that he truly understood what was happening in Cuba.

all out of step but one

Despite the passage of time and events which have transpired
with respect to Cuba, it appears Matthews [blanked-out por-
tion] and has not dampened his enthusiasm with regard to
Castro's communist Cuba.

—TOP SECRET FBI FILE, FROM 1962,
WITH WORDS BLANKED OUT "IN THE INTEREST OF
NATIONAL DEFENSE OR FOREIGN POLICY."

As pressure mounted on him for sticking to his positions on
Castro's communism and Cuba's dark new character, Matthews
grew increasingly isolated. "For a very long time through 1959
and 1960, I felt like Horatio at the bridge," he wrote. His assessment of the revolution as a work in progress, moving inexorably
forward but without a refined master plan and taking no orders
from Moscow, put him out of step with other journalists, including his own editors. "No one else seemed to be able or willing to
present the Cuban side of the story except those who went so far
and so unreservedly and unrealistically to the Fidelista side that
their testimony lost value," he wrote. He was being attacked in
Time and ridiculed in *Newsweek*, and he was making enemies in all
quarters as he continued to defend Castro and deny that either
he or his revolution had clandestine ties to any international
Communist conspiracy to establish a beachhead off the shores of
the United States.

But he was doing more than being careful not to rush to judgment. Matthews was bending over backward to excuse Castro,

ignoring signs that he was in charge of a government that was infiltrated by and cozying up to the Soviets, sometimes in very public ways. Batista had broken diplomatic relations with the Soviet Union after his coup in 1952, but just over a year after taking over, Castro had welcomed Anastas Mikoyan, vice premier of the Soviet Union, to Havana to open a Soviet trade fair and to lay the groundwork for a long-term relationship between the two countries. As the Soviet-Cuban alliance took root, the revolution looked ever more socialistic. On August 6, 1960, the first official act of Cuba's new revolutionary government, Resolution No. 1, had been to nationalize the telephone system without compensating International Telephone and Telegraph, the American company that owned it. Raúl Castro and Che Guevara were becoming increasingly belligerent toward the United States, and the moderates whom Castro had included in his first cabinet were being forced out and replaced with men who more comfortably embraced communism. Antagonism across the Straits of Florida was escalating, and resentment over Castro's renegade regime grew exponentially.

But still Matthews continued to insist that Castro was not a member of the Communist Party and was not taking orders from Moscow. It was difficult to imagine Castro taking orders from anyone, he argued, or for the spirited Cuban people to follow a collective discipline. Naturally then, Matthews's writing was most infuriating to those who were least willing to tolerate even a hint of communism. He became a person of interest to the senators who had devoted their careers to purging the United States of every whisper and shred of Communist sympathy. And he came under the suspicious eyes of J. Edgar Hoover and the FBI. Only a few days after Matthews's articles from the Sierra were published in 1957, Hoover had scrawled a short note to one of his aides, asking, "What do we know of Hans Kohn and also of Herbert Matthews?" Kohn was a well-known historian at City College in New York who regarded nationalism as a threat and dismissed communism in the United States as being "without any importance in numbers and influence." Hoover's interest had been piqued by an agency source who wrote to complain about Kohn and about an article by Matthews, though not one that had anything to do with Cuba. The offending article involved the disappearance of a Columbia University professor named Jesús de Galindez, a severe critic of the Trujillo dictatorship in the Dominican Republic. Hoover's response to that complaint launched what would become a decades-long investigation into Matthews's life and work, a detailed record of his trips to Cuba, and evidence that his phone calls were tapped and his New York apartment kept under FBI surveillance for years until he retired.

At the outset, however, the FBI did not seem all that concerned about Matthews. The FBI agent stationed in the Havana embassy who brought Matthews's 1957 series to Hoover's attention seemed to provide more support for Matthews than suspicion about him: "Available information in this office as well as that available to other interested Embassy agencies, fails to substantiate claim," made repeatedly by Batista's government, that Castro and his movement were "Communistically inclined." The agent could also not find any evidence to support Batista's charge that Matthews "if not a Communist, at least has leftist tendencies."

It would be one of the last times the FBI gave Matthews the benefit of the doubt.

After public opinion in the United States began to turn away from Castro, the bureau significantly increased its monitoring of Matthews. And just as Matthews had gone from hero to goat in the public eye, so too did perceptions of him change at the FBI. In March 1959, a source told the bureau that it was well known in newspaper circles "that Matthews and *The New York Times* had made Castro a hero and if anyone were to destroy Castro it would have to be Matthews and *The Times*," but Matthews had shown nothing but support.

It was the article in which Matthews declared that "this is not a Communist revolution in any sense of the word" that most incensed the FBI director and others in Washington. Vice President Nixon called Hoover early on the morning the article appeared. Nixon, mindful of his meeting with Castro a few months earlier, asked Hoover whether the bureau agreed with Matthews's conclusion. He wanted to know what information was available to show that Cuba was not turning Communist. He also asked Hoover if there was any background on Matthews himself. Hoover said he would check. He sent Nixon a response by courier the next day.

> Dear Dick:
>
> In line with our conversation of yesterday morning, and in accordance with your request, I am enclosing a memorandum analyzing the article which appeared in *The New York Times* of July 16, 1959, relating to the Castro regime as well as a memorandum summarizing pertinent data in our files regarding Herbert L. Matthews, the *Times* correspondent in Havana.
>
> As clearly indicated in the attached analysis, the conclusions of Matthews are in sharp disagreement with information developed by the FBI during the course of our various investigations concerning Cuban activities in the United States, including interviews with numerous sources who have first-hand information regarding conditions in Cuba. Matthews' claims are at variance with the findings of the United States Intelligence Boards, concurred in by the Department of State, the [blanked-out portion] and the intelligence branches of the armed forces, [blanked-out portion].

The analysis went on for several pages, picking apart each of Matthews's contentions about the Castro regime. At one point it even focused attention on the contradictory articles published by Matthews and Ruby Phillips.

Hoover quickly formed his own opinion of Matthews, and it was not a favorable one. In a memo to his top aides in October 1959, Hoover called Matthews's conclusion that there were no Communists in the Castro government "an absolute lie," one that clearly "shows the general line of thinking of Matthews." He dredged up Matthews's reporting from Spain and, disregarding the earlier comments in Matthews's file, concluded that "one can't get much closer to communism without becoming one." Although Hoover wasn't ready to accuse Matthews of being a Communist, he clearly didn't trust a newspaperman he considered to be hopelessly liberal. "[S]ometimes I think I would rather deal with an out-and-out communist than a fellow like this with all his double talk," Hoover wrote in the memo. Such people, he felt, can be dangerous because they "claim they are not a communist and you can't prove it and in their writings they can plant more sinister ideas and I would put Matthews in that category."

Hoover based his conclusions solely on the bureau's interpretation of Matthews's writings and the sympathy he had shown toward left-leaning causes like Loyalist Spain and Castro's Cuba. Though Hoover clearly wanted to brand Matthews a Communist, he could not, not even in confidential memos to the vice president and others with whom he collaborated. The bureau never found evidence to support such a charge. Matthews was not known to have ever belonged to a political party. Nor had he ever taken part in any activity that could be fairly interpreted as political. His own sentiments were clear: He supported liberal causes and despised totalitarianism, despite his brief flirtation with fascism in the 1930s.

When Matthews started writing about Cuba in the mid-1950s, he had supported Batista. But once he saw the regime's true nature, he denounced its censorship and the state terrorism it aimed at the rebels. He understood that Castro dreamed of building a new Cuba that finally, half a century after the war with Spain, would enjoy its first true taste of independence. The creeping influence of the Cuban Communist Party, and the efforts of Raúl and Che to align with the Communists, did not appear to Matthews to be intrinsic aspects of Castro's revolutionary plans. He held stubbornly to his narrow definition of a Communist as someone taking orders from the Soviet Union. Matthews's greatest misstep was in believing too much in Castro's heroism, seeing in him only a man of strong will and stout heart who shaped the destiny of his nation—those qualities that would have made him one of Harding

Davis's "real soldiers of fortune." He was insufficiently critical of Castro's ruthlessness and blind to the flaws in his character.

Hoover did not trust Castro or Matthews. The FBI concluded that "in view of the subject's long history as Castro apologist, it is believed he should be included in Section A of the Reserve Index," the notorious national ranking of Americans whose loyalty the bureau questioned. These writers, actors, politicians, and others were considered just slightly less dangerous than those on another list called the Security Index, who were supposed to be rounded up and detained in the event of a national emergency. The Bureau's primary consideration in deciding where to put Matthews's name was whether, in the event of a war between the United States and Cuba (backed by the Soviet Union), he would side with the Cubans. The FBI concluded that he would not. Nonetheless, his overt sympathies for the Cuban Revolution continued to make him suspect. Matthews's Reserve Index card is a stark reflection of Cold War paranoia: Race—W. Sex—Male. Date of birth—1/10/00. Place of birth—New York City, New York, native born. In the most critical section, the one where the Cold War could become encapsulated in a single stroke of a pen, the box next to "Communist" was unchecked, as was the box next to "Socialist Workers Party." Rather, it was the space on the next line, alongside the label "Miscellaneous (*specify*)," that described Matthews's act of sedition. It had been filled in with the phrase "Pro-Cuban." That was the reality around which Herbert Matthews's life now revolved.

Matthews was far from the only American whom Castro had twisted into knots. The State Department and White House were rank with confusion about Cuba at this time. Caught flat-footed by the swift changes taking place on the island, with few real Latin American experts on hand to put them into perspective, Washington was frustrated in its efforts to understand what was going on and, more important, to predict what Castro would do next. A June 1960 situation report by the CIA and the intelligence organizations of State, along with the military, and concurred in by the United States Intelligence Board and every other intelligence-gathering agency except the FBI, concluded that although the Castro regime looked increasingly Communist, "We are unable to answer the simplified question 'Is Castro himself a Communist?'"

Even members of Castro's inner circle worried about the direction the revolution was taking. Major José Luis Díaz Lanz, head of the Cuban air force, had flown to Miami in a Cuban fighter within six months of the triumph of the revolution to denounce Castro. Díaz Lanz became a source of information for the FBI, and he eventually testified before a Senate committee. A few weeks after Díaz Lanz defected, Cuba's president, Manuel Urrutia, had his own crisis of conscience. Urrutia went on Cuban television to express his concerns about the growing influence of Communists in Castro's new government. Castro was infuriated, and he retaliated by staging one of the most astounding shows of his powers of deception. He reacted to Urrutia's criticism by saying he would not continue to work in a conflicted government. Castro then announced his own resignation as prime minister, only to later stage a mass gathering in Havana where the throng "demanded" that he renounce his resignation. Urrutia, who had no taste for politics, nor any willingness to butt heads with Castro, finally realized that Castro had never intended to share power with him or anyone else. Urrutia resigned and took refuge in an embassy in Havana before fleeing Cuba. Castro made Osvaldo Dorticós, the minister of revolutionary laws, the new president, expecting him to be more obedient than Urrutia.

In the following months, Castro ratcheted up his rhetorical attacks on the United States, especially after Major Díaz Lanz flew a B-25 bomber over Havana and dropped leaflets calling Castro a Communist. When several explosions damaged buildings in Havana and caused casualties, Castro claimed that Díaz Lanz had bombed the city, though there was strong evidence that anti-aircraft fire from a Cuban frigate had caused the damage. It mattered little to Castro, who only seemed intent on whipping up anti-American sentiments. On March 4, 1960, a French freighter, *La Coubre,* carrying Belgian rifles and other munitions that Castro had purchased, exploded in Havana harbor. Castro claimed it was U.S. sabotage, vowing to fight any invasion to the last man.

Matthews was visiting Cuba regularly, spending so much time in Havana that during one stay in early 1960, Raúl Roa, the Cuban foreign secretary, relayed a personal message from Castro: "Tell Matthews that if he wants to become a Cuban citizen I will make a special decree myself." The Cuban hierarchy remained coy about communism, even after Mikoyan's visit to open the Soviet trade fair. The Cubans continued to tell Matthews that the Communists had little power or influence in the government. They did not even control the trade unions. Matthews had easy access to the top figures in the revolution during this trip. Besides Roa, he met with President Dorticós, Finance Minister Rufo Lopez-Fresquet, and Armando Hart, then minister of education. He spent more than an hour with Che Guevara, who told him that what the Cubans really wanted was "independence from the United States, in every sense—economic and political." And this, Guevara said, "is what you really fear."

Matthews countered that what the United States really feared was a "drift toward communism, which in time would lead to a military alliance, a Red base, or something approaching this, perhaps a Communist government in Cuba."

"How is it you do not fear Yugoslavia, and in fact, help her?" Guevara responded. "Yet she is a Communist country."

"Yugoslavia is far away and Cuba is very near," Matthews said. "And we helped Yugoslavia because she is against Russia."

Guevara took the bait. "In other words, you look upon Cuba as a pawn in the military game between Russia and the United States. And we do not want to be that."

During one trip to Cuba in this confusing period, Matthews had lunch with Castro at the Zaragozana restaurant in Havana and asked a provocative question. He wanted to know if Castro's growing antagonism toward the United States was simply a way of making the Cuban people forget unfulfilled promises of the revolution. Castro assured Matthews it was no act. He was simply reacting to attacks by the United States. "I am afraid of what can happen next," Castro told him. "There always seems to be something."

A year later something did happen, and Matthews was not caught by surprise. He had filed a confidential memo to the publisher outlining what he had learned from Cuban exiles in the United States about the preparations for a U.S.-backed invasion. It was then something of an open secret. Since January, several publications, including the *Times*, had published reports about the presence in Guatemala of training camps and large numbers of Cuban exiles. A counterrevolutionary strike had been rumored since Castro's agricultural reform started to look like Soviet-style collectivization. John F. Kennedy had defeated Richard M. Nixon in the 1960 presidential election and had inherited the Eisenhower administration's antagonism toward Castro, along with an ill-defined plan to get rid of him by using a core group of Cuban exiles backed by U.S. firepower. They were to land on the coast, establish a secure beachhead, and incite the Cuban population to rise up against Castro. The most important element of the plan—concerning the extent of direct American military involvement—was still undecided. The exiles had told Matthews that a ten-man council would be ready to take over once Castro was overthrown. José Miró Cardona, who had resigned as prime minister, would be provisional president. Some of Cuba's richest and most powerful men, among them Bacardi's Pepin Bosch, would take other positions in the first post-Castro government.

"I pass this information along because I believe this intervention by the CIA in the Cuban Revolution is bound to come out with a great explosion one of these days and perhaps result in great harm," he wrote in a memo to the publisher. "Those of us who follow the situation closely believe that the CIA is handling this unintelligently and is relying upon men who will be entirely unacceptable to Cuba, whatever happens after the Castro revolution. I think it is also necessary from the news point of view that we all keep up with this development as well as we can so that when it breaks out, we will not be caught by surprise."

The *Times* had received information about the invasion plans from other sources, and by the time the attack was launched in April, at the Bay of Pigs, the paper had already published an article laying out some of what it had learned. But the paper had clearly been influenced by Matthews's controversial coverage of Cuba. The publisher and editors hesitated to print all they knew about preparations for the invasion. Their caution was rooted in concerns for national security and in the stinging criticism the paper had already received for helping Castro come to power. Publishing too many details about the attack could be interpreted as an attempt by the paper to tip off the Cubans. Orvil Dryfoos, who was about to take over as publisher from the ailing Arthur Hays Sulzberger, forwarded Matthews's notes to James "Scotty" Reston, the influential national affairs columnist who then was the *Times's* Washington editor. Dryfoos asked Reston to show the memo to President Kennedy's new secretary of state, Dean Rusk, and ask for comment. "I do not think that we should have this type of information which affects the standing of our government and not give them an opportunity to do something about it," Dryfoos wrote. "Please let me know the outcome."

Matthews had already clashed with Reston several times over Cuba. They had substantial differences over their interpretations of the way developments were unfolding there and had exchanged politely heated correspondence over the possibility of American intervention. Early in 1960, Reston wrote a column in which he foresaw a Communist Cuba aligned with the Soviet Union. He speculated that this turn of events would demand a military response by the United States, something akin to what had been tried successfully in Guatemala in 1953. Matthews felt Reston had not thought through the consequences of supporting such an action. "You should know that this would not be another Guatemala but another Korea," he wrote in a letter to Reston. Knowing far better than Reston the long history of American intervention in Cuba, Matthews believed that landing the Marines would only be the start of a prolonged, and very costly, occupation against which resistance would arise in the Sierra Maestra and other mountainous areas of Cuba. "The guerrilla fighting would go on as long as a single American soldier remained in Cuba," he wrote.

Matthews ignored the obvious signs in disagreeing with Reston's premonition that the Soviets would attempt to use Cuba as a base in the Western Hemisphere. "Personally," Matthews wrote, "I feel quite certain that Cuba under its present leaders will neither go Communist nor come under Communist control or even great influence." As he ended his attempt to persuade Reston, Matthews begged understanding and restated the credentials that made it possible for him to preach to the powerful columnist: "I am sure you will understand my reasons for writing as this is a situation I have studied as deeply as anyone in the United States."

In response, Reston conceded that Matthews probably knew more than he did about Cuba but that didn't mean he got the picture straight. The highly publicized visit of Soviet vice premier Mikoyan; the closer commercial, industrial, and military ties between the Soviet Union and Cuba that followed Mikoyan's visit; and the increasingly belligerent anti-American rhetoric coming from Castro had Reston worried. "You may be right that there is only a remote possibility of this Soviet-Cuban flirtation developing into a mutual security arrangement," Reston wrote from Washington. "I hope so. But I assure you there are many well-informed people here who do nevertheless regard the possibility as less remote than you and who feel that, in this moment when we are out of touch with Castro, it may be useful to make quite clear that this government will not tolerate such a development."

Working out of Miami, Tad Szulc had gathered plenty of information about the pre-invasion plans. Early in April 1961, he was able to file a story that identified the CIA as sponsor of the mission and said it would be launched April 18. The managing editor, Turner Catledge, planned to run it as the lead story on the front page, prominently placed above the fold where it would get the most attention. But first he ran it by Dryfoos, who would not formally take over as publisher until the end of April. In one of his first important judgment calls, Dryfoos felt the article gave away too much and ordered changes. In his memoirs, Reston recalled the tensions of the moment:

"*The Times* was already being tagged as pro-Castro because of sympathetic reporting on his Revolution by correspondent Herbert Matthews. Catledge reasoned that if *The Times* was now seen as tipping off Fidel about the exile force, the paper would be excoriated for helping the dictator stay in power." Years later when he wrote his own memoirs, Catledge stated that he believed Reston had "allowed his news judgment to be influenced by his patriotism." Max Frankel would later write that he understood the pressures the editors were under, but he disagreed with their decision. "Reston was surely right to believe that the paper would have been blamed for yet again saving Castro but not by fair-minded observers." While there was finger-pointing in all directions, the one element that everyone agreed on was that Matthews's coverage had compromised the newspaper's abilities to report on Cuba. Providing Castro with the details of an impending invasion would play right into the hands of the paper's critics.

Pressure to tone down the article also came directly from the Kennedy Administration, which made the request to Reston in Washington. Reston alerted Dryfoos, and eventually agreed with him that protecting national security was the most important consideration. Dryfoos had Szulc's article moved to a less prominent place on the front page and he removed the suggestion that an invasion was "imminent."

By then, Castro did not need a newspaper article to warn him that an attack was coming. Tensions between Cuba and the United States had been rising steadily. Cuba's first attempt at agricultural reform in May 1959 initially appeared to be revolutionary compensation for underprivileged peasants, but when large American landholdings were seized without sufficient compensation, it was the first clear signal of the new regime's true aims. President Eisenhower responded with a partial economic embargo a few months later. The Soviets agreed to buy more Cuban exports and sent crude oil in return, but American companies in Cuba refused to refine it. In July, Eisenhower canceled the quota that specified the U.S. commitment to imports of Cuban sugar, and Castro nationalized all American properties. The United States broke diplomatic relations with Cuba at the beginning of 1961, and a few months after the Kennedy administration took office, the new president was prepared to put into action the invasion plan he had inherited. All the while, Cuba had been cozying up to the Soviet Union, which was sending planes, arms, and civil engineers to industrialize the island. Anti-Castro exiles in the United States were itching for a fight to remove Castro, believing that he had betrayed the revolution by embracing communism.

On April 15 (three days before Szulc's original estimated date), the invasion began with two B-26 bombers piloted by CIA-trained Cuban exiles attacking airfields around Havana. The planes had been painted to look like those in Cuba's tiny air force, a clumsy deception that was intended to lead Cubans to believe that the pilots had defected and were leading an uprising. The planes destroyed most, though not all, of Cuba's air force, and killed seven people in Havana. Presiding over ceremonies for the victims at the Colón cemetery the next day, Castro likened the attack to Pearl Harbor and vowed that loyal Cubans would "defend with these rifles this socialist revolution." It was the first time he had publicly declared that his revolution was socialist.

At about 4:30 AM the following day, Ruby Phillips was asleep when she received a call from the foreign desk in New York telling her the invasion was on. She realized that it was long past all deadlines and the paper had already gone to press. Certain the attack would fail, and realizing she would not be able to write anything until the next day's newspaper, she went back to sleep. Ships that had been boarded in Nicaragua landed at a desolate, swampy area of beach about 100 miles southeast of Havana known as the Bay of Pigs. But in giving the final go-ahead, President Kennedy held back a second round of air attacks, fearing the poorly disguised planes would confirm America's role in the attack. He also refused to order U.S. forces to back up the invaders after they were pinned down in the swamp, sealing the invasion's fate. Castro himself led a column of tanks and soldiers from Havana to repel the exile troops, who were routed or captured easily.

Ruby Phillips and the other American correspondents in Havana were prohibited from filing articles during and immediately after the invasion. Her two Cuban assistants were arrested, her office ransacked, her files and personal belongings confiscated and never returned. She fled on May 19 with only the clothes she was wearing and one suitcase, the sad end of more than thirty years in Cuba. As soon as she arrived in Miami, she wrote a dispatch that poignantly summed up what had happened to the island that had been her home for so long: "Fidel Castro's Cuba is a beautiful tropical island filled with fear and hate."

The end result of the foiled attack: 156 Cuban soldiers killed, 107 invaders dead and 1,189 captured. The Kennedy administration suffered an international embarrassment. The combination of poor planning, a crucial underestimation of Castro's forces, and indecision by the new Kennedy administration had turned the operation into a fiasco, what Theodore Draper called "the perfect failure." The botched effort handed Castro a huge military and propaganda victory that underscored U.S. frustration and helped define the standoff between the two nations. President Kennedy widened the Eisenhower administration's economic sanctions and cut off trade between the United States and Cuba, establishing what would become one of the longest, and most bitter, economic embargoes in history.

Kennedy also pulled the press into the debacle, claiming that articles published before the invasion had contributed to this miserable example of American foreign policy. He lashed out at the press for its "premature reporting" and said the failure of the attack underscored the need for an official secrets act. Kennedy expressed extreme frustration with the *Times* for the way it had handled the story. But following a meeting with editors at the White House to discuss his charges of irresponsible reporting, the president pulled Turner Catledge aside and told him a different story. "Maybe if you had printed more about the operation," Kennedy whispered, half in jest, "you would have saved us from a colossal mistake."

Matthews was called to the White House in July for a talk with President Kennedy. They met in the Oval Office, Kennedy sitting in his famous rocking chair, Matthews on the sofa. During the forty-minute discussion, they went over the president's recent trip to Mexico, and more generally talked about the economic problems facing much of Latin America. It was recorded in the president's appointment book as an off-the-record discussion, and there is no official transcript of what was said. But Matthews, as usual, wrote out several pages of notes afterward that he kept in his records.

At one point in the meeting, he recalled, Kennedy switched gears.

"What do you think of the Cuban situation?" the president asked.

Knowing what the president was after, Matthews said that Castro had come to power without any clearly defined political ideology. He was not a Communist then, Matthews assured Kennedy, but he was determined to bring Cuba a radical revolution. Castro intended to "break the domination of the United States," and that made conflict inevitable.

Kennedy responded that it all seemed like "a Greek tragedy," filled with betrayal and violence.

Matthews said that once the break came with the United States, Cuba was so weakened economically that Fidel had little choice but to turn to the Soviet bloc for assistance. Matthews believed that Washington had mishandled the Cuban situation almost from the start and had boxed Castro into a corner. This was a controversial position because it blamed Washington for creating the conflict and seemed to absolve Castro, a point that Kennedy quickly recognized.

"You don't believe that Fidel, Raúl, Che are Communists?" the president asked.

"No," Matthews said, "not in the sense of belonging to the party and being under party discipline. They were never under any discipline, and the Cuban people are completely incapable ever of achieving the discipline that a Communist regime demands."

They then talked briefly about the failed Bay of Pigs invasion, and Kennedy said he hoped that Castro would release the exile Cuban fighters he had captured. (He did, after the United States paid a ransom of $53 million in food and medicines.)

"Don't forget," Matthews said, "Castro is pure Spanish and very vengeful."

"He ought to be grateful to us," the president said. "He gave us a kick in the ass and it made him stronger than ever." Kennedy acknowledged that he had made some bad policy decisions about Cuba and had not been sufficiently careful about controlling his anti-Communist policy. However, he revealed that the invasion had taught him an important lesson. "If it wasn't for that," he said, "we might be in Laos now—or perhaps unleashing Chiang," referring to Chiang Kai-shek, leader of the anti-Mao counterrevolutionaries in Taiwan who continually threatened to reinvade mainland China.

As Matthews's reputation steadily declined in the United States, his notoriety in Cuba grew. *Revolución* published an homage to Matthews, calling him a great North American. "Heroic was his climb of the mountains of Oriente, where he risked danger of ambush by Batista's troops, in order to proclaim to the world in truthful testimony and with his accurate camera that the hero from the *Granma* had not died," read the article. "What a splendid Cuban Herbert Matthews would make, so upright and so just! So levelheaded and so sincere!"

But Cuban exiles in Miami had targeted Matthews as their enemy, and the first rumors about him began to circulate, quickly making their way to the files of the FBI. Not long after the Bay of Pigs, the FBI's Miami office interviewed informants about a rumor that Matthews had gone to see Batista after he returned from the Sierra in 1957. At the meeting, Matthews was said to have tried to extort anywhere from $300,000 to $500,000 from Batista in exchange for writing articles favorable to the regime. When Batista supposedly rejected the demand because the price was too high, Matthews stormed off to write his articles praising Castro and denouncing Batista.

The stories were based on hearsay and vengeful speculation, but the bureau assigned agents across the United States to interview former Batista officials about them. No one questioned the logic of the rumor or asked why Batista, who had raked in millions of dollars from the casinos and the parking meters in Havana, would have balked at paying such a comparatively paltry sum to save his regime.

Rather, the rumor was treated as though it were fact. Shortly after the Bay of Pigs, Hoover informed Attorney General Robert Kennedy of Matthews's supposed attempt at extortion. He sent Kennedy a memo indicating that Batista himself had confirmed that someone approached him with an offer to publish favorable articles in the *Times* through Matthews in exchange for a substantial payment. The bureau pursued the investigation even after receiving information from sources within Batista's office clearly indicating that Matthews had never made any demands. One of those accounts apparently came from Edmund Chester, the American journalist who was Batista's public relations adviser. Chester told the FBI that Matthews was a "very strong advocate" of Castro and would never have criticized him for any amount of money.

Hoover himself seems to have had no trouble believing the allegations against Matthews. In May 1961, he sent a long memo to the Office of Security in the State Department repeating the charges he had presented to the attorney general. This time he also included a version of the incident provided by a former Batista official who claimed to have been outside the dictator's office while Matthews was inside. After two hours, the official said,

Matthews rushed out of the office in a huff, and Batista came out fuming, calling Matthews a "blackmailer and gangster."

The bureau's attacks on Matthews escalated. In 1961, Matthews published *The Cuban Story*, in which he recounted his initial encounter with Castro in the Sierra and tried to put into context the other events and misunderstandings that had shaded American perceptions of the revolution. The book would turn out to be one of his most popular, though it was attacked by his critics, who saw it as an apologia for Matthews's mistakes. The FBI assigned an agent to "review" it, and the reviewer concluded that "[d]espite the passage of time and events which have transpired in Cuba, Matthews continues to be an apologist for Castro. He is like a recruit in the awkward squad of the Army who believes that everyone is out of step but himself."

The CIA was also keeping tabs on Matthews, intercepting some of his phone calls to Cuba and receiving information about his plans from several sources, including the *Times*'s own Mexico City office, where Robert Benjamin, a temporary correspondent who had served in Army Intelligence, routinely passed along information to the agency. The CIA considered Matthews "a bit naive" concerning Cuba and the real goals of the Castro revolution. Matthews "appears not to have seen too well the problems facing Fidel," and even as evidence that Castro had misled him about his true aims mounted, Matthews was "not yet ready to admit the failure of the revolution."

For Matthews, it was just the beginning of the dark days that would come to hang over his career, and his life.

dark days

Matthews had grown so accustomed to taking an afternoon siesta during the years he lived in Europe that he had trouble breaking the habit when he returned to New York to join the editorial board in 1949. After an ample lunch at a respectable restaurant, he would come back to the solitude of his office and struggle to keep sleep at bay. But as he became more entangled in the Cuban story, such leisure became elusive, and by the end of 1961 it was unlikely he had many opportunities for an afternoon snooze, especially not after Castro broadcast a fiery five-hour speech that began late on the evening of December 1, a Friday. Before it ended in the early hours of Saturday morning, Castro had made Matthews's life hell.

It was one of Castro's typical rambling speeches. It lasted five hours and was marked by so many linguistic feints and rhetorical thrusts that it was especially difficult to follow. A former Cuban journalist who had gone into exile in Miami monitored a radio broadcast of the speech for United Press International. By 2:00 AM Saturday morning, he had sent the first account of the speech's principal points, in Spanish, to the agency's New York newsroom.

An editor then had to translate it into English before putting it out on the domestic wire. The story was finally sent out at 8:00 AM on a quiet Saturday morning, but there was nothing tranquil about its contents: "Cuban Premier Fidel Castro said today he really has been a dedicated Communist since his college days but he concealed his views so it would be easier to seize power." Then, after indicating that Castro said he had kept friendly relations with the United States briefly after the triumph of the revolution because he needed time to consolidate power, the dispatch openly confirmed what many Americans had long suspected, quoting Castro as saying, "I am a Marxist-Leninist and I shall be to the last days of my life." Castro had already declared that the revolution was socialistic in nature, but now, according to the UPI report, he was going far beyond that, vowing allegiance to Marxist principles and tracing his Communist beliefs back to his youth. Such admissions directly contradicted Matthews's strongly held opinion that neither Castro, nor his revolution, had been Communist at the start. Throughout the day, the story underwent numerous revisions that changed the emphasis on certain facts but preserved the central notion that Castro had deliberately concealed his true identity until now.

But Matthews believed that UPI had misunderstood what Castro said. "The speech was a concoction, a composition, a political construction, engineered to fit the particular moment and Fidel's aims," Matthews later wrote. "It was what he wanted everyone to believe."

By this time, though, most Americans accepted Castro's confession as true, and they blamed Matthews again for having misled them. He came under renewed attack, and the criticism this time was brutal. Matthews considered the first few days after Castro's speech "the worst period" of his career. His detractors delighted in pointing out once again how Matthews had allowed himself to be tricked by Castro. Even his friends assumed the UPI report was accurate and that he had been wrong. Matthews worried that what was left of his treasured reputation was being torn to shreds.

Besides Nancie, one of the only people he could trust was his older brother, John, with whom he carried on a decades-long exchange of well-crafted, typewritten weekly letters. Writing to John during these distressing times, Matthews revealed the insecurity he normally kept tightly under wraps. "As you can suppose, that phoney U.P.I. story gave me an awful time last week," Matthews wrote John on December 11. "Before I could check it out I almost felt suicidal even though neither I nor Nancie could believe it. It will still never be lived down because the U.P.I. is naturally not going to admit an error that really cannot be proved against them, and once such stories get around nothing can ever kill them, not even a correction or a retraction." Matthews had also noted that the UPI editor who was making decisions about what to publish was none other than Francis L. McCarthy, the same man who had reported Castro's death in 1956. McCarthy was by this time the agency's editor for Latin America.

Matthews knew the criticism was leaving marks on him and on the *Times*. "People who haven't read my book or only know that I said 'Castro is not a Communist, period' without knowing that I always added I meant not a member of the Communist party taking orders from Moscow (which is still true) would have had a wonderful time anyway attacking me and *The Times*," he told John. And by the time he had turned sixty-two a few weeks later, Matthews came to realize that Castro was not going to let him have a peaceful old age. "It is a pretty tough business, bad for *The Times* and therefore bad for me. A sort of mob psychology has been aroused, and mobs are always vicious."

Some of the sharpest criticism of Matthews came from other journalists. Long before Castro's speech, Matthews had accepted an invitation to give a presentation at the Overseas Press Club in New York about his recently published book, *The Cuban Story*. In it, Matthews made clear that neither Castro nor those close to him were Communists when they came to power. His talk had been scheduled for December 4, two days after Castro's public confession, and Matthews was prepared for the worst. He got just what he expected from his colleagues. "The session was intended to be a crucifixion," he later commented, "always a great pleasure for the mob, and there was an overflow attendance."

In the speech, Matthews made his first concrete objections to the UPI report. Only hours before he was to speak, he got hold of a printed transcript of Castro's speech that had been released by the U.S. State Department. After reading it, he concluded that far from admitting that he had always been a Communist, Castro was in fact apologizing, expressing regret for not having appreciated all the intricacies of Marxist-Leninist thinking in his student days and for taking so long to recognize the values of Marxism. By now, in late 1961, there was no doubt that Castro had embraced international communism. But the critical issue was whether Castro had deliberately concealed his intentions in order to trick Matthews, the 26 of July Movement, his Cuban supporters, and the government and people of the United States. The transcript showed that Castro had said that he had been a "political illiterate" until he graduated from high school. Although he read Marx and was influenced by him, he was not a Marxist-Leninist by the time he left the University of Havana, "not by a long shot," he said. Later in the speech, Castro said he had not yet been a "full-fledged revolutionary" even when he led the attack on the Moncada barracks in 1953, nor when he seized power in January 1959. "No," he said in the official transcript, "I could call myself almost a full-fledged revolutionary."

Many other aspects of the speech were unclear, perhaps deliberately obfuscated by Castro as he laid out some of the difficulties he had with Cuba's traditional Communist Party, as well as what he and they had in common, leading up to his current embrace of communism. Apart from Castro's tortured oratory, there were also questions about the way the news agency had handled the story. The initial dispatch in Spanish from Miami did not make the same sweeping statements as the one that ran on the domestic wire in English. Rather, it began: "Fidel Castro today confessed to being a fervent and absolute believer in Marxism and revealed that the roots of his political creed go back many years to his days as a university student," which is actually closer to the State Department's transcript than to the version of the story that UPI later distributed.

Matthews was not alone in challenging the UPI report. The

respected historian Theodore Draper rejected the agency's interpretation of the speech, as did the *Columbia Journalism Review* and
the *Hispanic American Report,* which was published at Stanford
University by Matthews's friend Ronald Hilton. They all saw the
speech as another bit of rhetorical trickery by Castro. Even so,
Matthews had to bear some of the burden for the colossal misunderstanding.

"Ever since Herbert Matthews went to the Sierra Maestra in
February, 1957, Castro has been toying with sympathetic intellectuals and journalists," Draper wrote. He criticized Matthews's
original reporting on Castro, along with his subsequent uncritical
dispatches about the revolution, and swept everything into the
same category as all of the mistaken perceptions about Cuba that
existed at the time. "The first and most famous of the 'eyewitness'
reports from Cuba set a pattern to this day," he wrote, referring to
Matthews's articles. "It cannot have been merely a succession of
individual aberrations, because too many have been implicated. It
has been more like a mass immersion in romantic 'muck' as
George Orwell called it almost two decades ago."

But "aberrations" have a way of becoming fixed and of taking
the place of the truth. Despite the attempts by Matthews, Draper,
and the others to correct the record, it was the initial incorrect
interpretation of the speech that stuck with most people and
served to further inflame American sentiment against Castro. For
decades to come, Castro would continue to explain his political
evolution, never giving the same story twice and deliberately confounding those who tried to pigeonhole him and his political
ideas. During a discussion with students in Chile in 1971, he
admitted that while he was at the university he developed certain
ideas about society and justice, and his rebelliousness took root.
He adopted what he called a utopian vision of society, which he
later realized might have made him a utopian communist. But, as
he told the Chilean students, he "still hadn't been fortunate
enough to meet a Communist or read a Communist document."
He did not begin to see the light until he came across a copy of
The Communist Manifesto. He read its radical ideas about society
and class, and the notions "hit me like a clap of thunder and I was

won over to those ideas. However, that didn't mean I was anywhere near being a communist!" he told the students. He said he
developed a revolutionary consciousness long before he adopted
a Communist ideology.

Wherever Matthews went and whenever he spoke, he had to
address what Castro had said in that December speech. Whenever
he lectured on Cuba or spoke at a conference on Latin America,
he would be asked how he could ever have said that Castro had
not been a Communist in 1959 when Castro himself had confessed that he had always been a Marxist-Leninist.

As the number of such confrontations mounted steadily, the
bitterness of the protesters increased. The word "betrayal" was
heard more frequently, and it generally expressed the feelings of
many Cubans as well as Americans who watched as Castro was
transformed from hero to villain before their eyes. Most often,
there were suspicions that it all had been deliberate, that a cadre
of Communist sympathizers—including Matthews himself—had
helped Castro dupe everyone into thinking he was a hero. It was
a dangerous game during these Cold War days of spies and suspicions. Castro's number one cheerleader, of course, was believed
to be Matthews. No longer were his readers writing songs and
poems to honor him. The message now was hateful, and readers
did not hesitate to let him know how they felt:

Dear Mr. Matthews,
    Had I done my country that incalculable injury you have I
think I would cut my throat.
    Raymond S. Richmond, San Francisco

Why don't you move to Cuba if you like communist Castro
and his revolution so much? I want you to know that we all
free Cubans, who are suffering so much, hate you from the
bottom of our hearts for all your stupid, communist articles
in favor of the monster. Some time, perhaps very soon, you
will get what you deserve.
                    Marta Hernandez [no address given]

And a Cuban exile group in Venezuela sent a note along with a U.S. penny that was labeled "our contribution for the 'Send Herbert Matthews to his Communist Cuba Paradise Fund.' We are sure that thousands will join us to pay for his one-way ticket so that he can be reunited with his true comrade, Fidel Castro."

Other hate mail arrived at the *Times* simply addressed: "Comrade Matthews."

The newsweekly magazines continued to taunt Matthews. "The longest skirmish of the Cuban revolution has been the one between veteran New York Times editorialist and correspondent Herbert L. Matthews and a great segment of the U.S. press," *Newsweek* said in a press criticism published in October 1961, under the headline, "Only Man in Step?" The article explained, "Bombarded by critics for being too sweet for too long on Fidel Castro, Matthews has announced sourly that the American press has fumbled the whole story." The same month, *Time* took another swipe at Matthews: "In *The Cuban Story* Herbert Matthews wrote, 'Let us note in passing that already in 1948, at the age of 21, Fidel Castro was anti-Yankee and agitating against Yankee Imperialism.' But in his 1957 article, he let Castro say without rebuttal, 'We have no animosity toward the United States and the American people.'"

But Matthews took the most vicious lashing from conservative commentator William F. Buckley, Jr., who believed Matthews was a Communist sympathizer, "the leader of pro-Castro opinion in the United States," whose legacy had been to create a menace that threatened the very security of the United States because he "did more than any other single man to bring Fidel Castro to power." In an article he published in *American Legion* magazine, Buckley accused Matthews of a long list of indiscretions, from fawning over Castro's oversized personality to urging Washington in 1958 to settle the differences between Castro and Batista. But his most savage attack was against Matthews's "ferocious partisanship," a trait Buckley thought the newspaperman had first revealed in covering fascist Italy, and later repeated in Loyalist Spain and Castro's Cuba. "To put it mildly, Matthews was overwhelmed," Buckley wrote. "Castro, he told the world in a series of three articles that made journalistic and indeed international history, is a big brave, strong, rebellious, dedicated, tough idealist."

The consequences of Matthews's bewitching, Buckley argued, were disastrous. "It is bad enough that Herbert Matthews was hypnotized by Fidel Castro, but it was a calamity that Matthews succeeded in hypnotizing so many other people, in crucial positions of power, on the subject of Castro." The headline of Buckley's article became a taunt that followed Matthews to his grave: "'I Got My Job Through *The New York Times*': How one man's opinion, disseminated through an influential newspaper, helped put Castro in power." Buckley had picked up the phrase from an advertising campaign that the *Times* was then using to build up circulation through its Help Wanted section, in which job seekers happily reported, "I got my job through *The New York Times*." Buckley used it to mock the paper, and its correspondent.

While Matthews was under such intense attack at home, he found refuge in Cuba. There he was treated with respect, and for a while that respect seemed to grow exponentially as the criticism he received in the United States mounted. Matthews welcomed the Cubans' reaction. It bolstered his ego to know that at least in Cuba he was honored for his work. "Yes, indeed, this is still my city," he wrote Nancie from Havana. He had become an easily recognizable figure, and Cubans embraced him warmly. The Sevilla Biltmore Hotel boasted in newspaper advertisements that Matthews had stayed there before his famous interview. When he called for room service, a hotel employee said cheerfully: "Good morning, Mr. Matthews, welcome to Havana." He told colleagues in New York that the Cubans sometimes treated him as though he were a founding father of the Cuban Revolution, the one American journalist who, from the beginning, had been willing to tell the truth about what was going on there.

Matthews could count on only a few loyal supporters in these difficult times. Among them were Ernest and Mary Hemingway, who divided their time between their farm in Ketchum, Idaho, and the Finca Vigia in Havana. They watched with enduring fascination as the revolution developed, and relied on Matthews to explain what was happening. Hemingway was battling his own demons, which would eventually lead to his suicide, but he answered Matthews's frequent letters and gave moral encouragement to his old friend. "I am getting into a hassle on this Cuban business," Matthews wrote to Hemingway as the controversy over Cuba raged. He was determined to defend himself, he said in the letter, and restore his name: "I have spent nearly 40 years building up a reputation for professional probity and I am not going to allow anyone to besmirch my reputation at this late date." Hemingway trashed Matthews's critics and stoked his friend's ego. In a September 1960 letter, the novelist related how he had been asked to write a piece on Cuba for the *Saturday Review* but had to turn it down because he was too busy: "I cabled back that I was working and could not do so and considered you the only person absolutely qualified to write the piece. It was a shame that we were not at the Finca to see you and I hope we will be able to talk before too late this fall."

In one self-deprecating letter to Hemingway, Matthews conceded that he felt he was fighting a losing battle. "The worse the situation gets with Cuba, the more I am attacked and the Publisher and others on *The Times* are getting a lot of criticism for having a communist like myself on the staff." Matthews forwarded a copy of *The Cuban Story* to Ketchum two months after the book was published. Mary Hemingway wrote back, calling the book "wonderful and courageous" but saying it was very likely to be either ignored or attacked: "I am afraid that perhaps, in spite of this great effort of yours, you are a voice crying in the wilderness."

In a world gripped by the madness of the Cold War, nothing was innocent and nothing was inviolable. Even Matthews's steadfast admirers in Cuba were willing to use him. Che Guevara considered him a pliable American journalist who could be relied on to present the regime in a positive light. But as Matthews became more discredited in the United States, his usefulness to the regime diminished, and even Castro began to distance himself, although he never completely turned his back on the correspondent who had been so helpful. Still, there was a point when he declared: "I am sick and tired of that old man who thinks he is my father [referring to Matthews]. He is always giving me advice." Castro had deliberately embarrassed Matthews during the 1959 visit to New York, and when Matthews flew to Havana to see him, Castro would sometimes make him wait for days. Embarrassing those who had helped him proved to be only one of the wrinkles in Castro's character.

Despite the indignity of being forced to cool his heels, Matthews always got in to see Castro, and he retained his special access to the Cuban hierarchy through the remainder of his working life. No other American journalist spent so much time with Castro. Government officials always took his calls, and his sources in Havana remained solid. There was no questioning Matthews's privileged position in Cuba and the prominent role he played in the psyche of the Cuban Revolution. But there were continuing doubts in the United States about his sympathies, and those doubts were constantly trumped up by critics who questioned his loyalties. He was quickly becoming that most pitiable kind of journalist—the one muzzled by his own publication.

On January 30, 1962, Orvil E. Dryfoos, the new publisher of the *Times*, sent a succinct and brutally honest memo to Matthews's boss on the editorial board, John B. Oakes. It was a few weeks after Castro's Marxist-Leninist speech and the beginning of what would be a decisive year in the rapidly deteriorating relationship between the United States and Cuba.

> John:
>   I trust that Herbert Matthews will remain:
>   1) out of the news
>   2) and not write for the news department
>   O.E.D.

The mounting controversy over Matthews's biases was becoming intolerable and his support inside the newspaper was crumbling. No longer able to turn to his old friend Arthur Hays

Sulzberger for help, and under a constant barrage of criticism from outside the building, Matthews found it increasingly difficult to pursue the Cuba story and ever more frustrating to be left out of it. Though forbidden to publish news articles about Cuba in the *Times*, Matthews continued to write unsigned editorials. Some were critical of Castro but always in a way that revealed Matthews's desire to see the revolution succeed. For someone like him, who wanted to believe in Castro, it was difficult to watch the endless blunders taking place in both Cuba and the United States.

But Matthews was too headstrong to accept the publisher's limitations on his writing without a fight. For as long as he had worked for the *Times*, he had pampered his ego and supplemented his income by contributing to magazines and other publications. And as he developed his expertise on Cuba, academic publications sought his views. When he returned from a trip to Cuba in 1960, he brought back pages of notes that he believed were important insights into Castro's revolution. But when the *Times* refused to publish them he turned to Professor Ronald Hilton at Stanford, a noted Latin Americanist who had met Matthews in 1954 when both attended the bicentennial celebrations of Columbia University. In 1959, Hilton invited Matthews to be one of the principal speakers at a Stanford conference on Latin America, and later Hilton asked him to become a member of the international advisory board of the *Hispanic American Report*.

Matthews published the rejected article in the *Report*. He stressed the benchmark quality of the revolution, rejecting any notion that it had come about as an "accident of history." He repeated once again his harsh criticism of the press and of Washington's woeful Latin American diplomatic corps. He blamed them all for fostering the prevailing sense of betrayal that Americans felt toward Cuba, while rejecting any blame for himself. "The initial friendliness and admiration for Fidel Castro in this country was based on the naive belief that all he was going to do was to drive away the dictator, General Fulgencio Batista, clean out the Augean stable of corruption, hold new elections, leave the economic structure intact with its dependence on the United States, and carry on as before," he wrote. Matthews described the revolution as evolving haphazardly toward a centralized totalitarian structure, with Castro at its core. He blamed the American press for initiating a self-fulfilling prophecy about Castro being a Communist. "The American press, radio and television, Congress and many American diplomats and businessmen, conceded victory to the Communists long before they had won it," he wrote.

But in the article Matthews had still been unwilling to concede Castro's Communist credentials. Instead, he constructed an almost incomprehensible definition that could have done nothing to call off his critics: "If a label must be given," Matthews wrote of Castro, "he is a pre-scientific, Utopian socialist, not a Marxist socialist." But he proved to be quite prophetic in assessing the most fundamental aspect of Castro's nature and the impact that such a personality was likely to have on hemispheric relations. The Castro revolution was first and foremost a "revolt of youth," Matthews declared, and being so, it was both impulsive and likely to be around for a long time. Castro himself he characterized as "a most formidable young man. He will not back down or surrender easily, and Americans would be prudent to face the fact that a long and hard struggle is ahead if, as seems obvious, the United States is determined to overthrow the Castro regime." The *Hispanic American Report* took Matthews under its protective wing and tried to defend him against critics who claimed he'd helped bring Castro to power. "This is as absurd," the magazine said, "as blaming a meteorologist for a thunderstorm."

It wasn't only Stanford that offered Matthews a safe haven. He found receptive ears on many American campuses, where the Cuban Revolution was judged by more liberal standards. Professors and students who opposed American war efforts in Vietnam supported the socialist revolution in Cuba. Matthews accepted an invitation to speak at the University of Michigan in May 1961, and he told the audience that "once Fidel Castro's regime was labeled Communistic, for the most part it became almost impossible for the American journalists and editors to go against the overwhelming public opinion, although it was the press that created the hostile opinion—like Frankenstein's monster."

That same year, he accepted a $500 honorarium from Hans Kohn, the liberal historian at City College of New York who was an influential scholar of nationalism, to participate in that year's distinguished lecture series. In the first of the three addresses, Matthews used one of his more intriguing descriptions of Castro, one intended to defend both the rebel leader and himself. Castro, he said, "is not certifiably insane; he is not a Fascist and it is most unlikely that he was, or is today, a communist. He is himself, and he fits no category although one can get some vague help from the knowledge that he is a Galician Spaniard by blood, a Cuban by birth and upbringing, and a creature—a very wild creature—of our times." Staking his claim to the title of the North American who knew Castro best, Matthews shared with the sympathetic New York audience his own regrets at the turns taken by Cuba and the United States: "One cannot avoid a sense of profound disappointment that it has had to work out this way, that the Cold War has been brought into the hemisphere, that Fidel Castro has become the most dangerous enemy of the United States ever to rise in Latin America." He tried to distance himself from the Cuban Revolution "in its present form," and yet he urged the audience to look at it as he did and try to understand from the point of view of both history, and the Cuban people, what was evolving: "If you understand, you will condemn and you will condone. You will accuse and you will sympathize. You will see that there is much that is evil and much that is good."

Matthews felt comfortable on university campuses and never stopped wondering what his life would have been like had he chosen to become a professor rather than a correspondent. But Cuban exiles and Cuban-American students opposed to Castro had started to hound him. Several times, he was unable to complete his speeches, and once, at the University of New Mexico in Albuquerque, Matthews was handed a note in the middle of his address that warned him: "You must finish your talk now." The police had been told that someone planned to set off a bomb. One thousand people in the Student Union Building had to be evacuated.

Just a little over two years after he took over as publisher, and following the strain of managing the paper through a disruptive strike, Orvil Dryfoos collapsed and died. He had tried to keep the seriousness of his heart condition hidden from others at the paper, including the man who would replace him—his brother-in-law, Arthur Ochs Sulzberger, who was called "Punch" since childhood, a nickname commemorating a wordplay on his sister Judith's name. Many doubted that the new publisher, only thirty-six, was ready to take over the responsibilities of running the paper, but Sulzberger would prove them wrong. For Matthews, he would come to represent yet another corner where he had lost support, for although the new publisher carried his father's first name, he did not share Arthur Hays Sulzberger's fondness for Herbert Matthews. Matthews was much older than the new publisher, and much more experienced. He sometimes felt the publisher did not grasp the complexities of either Cuba or journalism. The two men would clash often.

Matthews had become one of the most well known American reporters, and one of the least popular men in journalism. He was being attacked regularly at meetings of the American Society of Newspaper Editors, and of the Inter-American Press Association, where he was a director. At one session, several Cuban exiles prodded the association into taking a vote of censure against him because he had written in an editorial that the association had become politicized over the Cuban issue. "It is not true, as has been implied, and even said here, that we have been justifying Fidel Castro or what he does," Matthews said in his own defense. "We are not supporting him. We are opposing him. This does not mean that we have to agree with everything that the opponents in exile, or the majority of the I.A.P.A., say and believe about the Castro regime. In conclusion, I want to make it very clear that neither I, nor *The New York Times*, can accept accusations that we favor the Castro regime or that we favor Communism." The association's directors would not submit the censure motion to a vote, but it was clear that Matthews's continued presence would be disruptive. Within a short time he was no longer a member of the executive committee, and his place on the board of directors was taken by Marian Sulzberger, Dryfoos's widow and one of Punch Sulzberger's three sisters.

By 1962, the Soviet Union's intention of using Cuba as a Cold War wedge in the Western Hemisphere was as clear as Washington's determination to prevent that from happening. A confrontation between the two superpowers seemed unavoidable. The Soviets, emboldened by Kennedy's very public failure at the Bay of Pigs, had aggressively moved forward with plans to turn Cuba into a strategic outpost, one that matched U.S. posts perched within striking range of the Soviet Union. Castro welcomed the Soviet troops and armaments. He was certain that Kennedy would try to make up for his blunders at the Bay of Pigs with another attempt to invade Cuba. A military buildup had been underway in Cuba for some time when a spy plane took startling photographs of several remote missile-launch sites. The ante had been upped considerably; the waiting game was on. Khrushchev had planned to have the medium- and intermediate-range missiles with nuclear warheads capable of reaching the United States installed and armed before Washington knew anything about them. The spy photos exposed his dangerous gambit. Castro called on the Cuban people to prepare to fight off another invasion. On October 22, a pensive President Kennedy announced a naval blockade and ordered troops to amass in Florida. Everyone was watching Cuba, including Matthews.

Despite all the criticism from outside, and the admonitions from inside the *Times*, Matthews had been intent on returning to Cuba. He had not been back since 1960. It was a dangerous lapse, he felt, during which the *Times*'s substantial advantage over other media had dissipated because it had no correspondent there but Ruby Phillips, and she had been forced to leave after the Bay of Pigs. In the fall of 1962, Matthews took Nancie on a ten-nation Latin American tour, part vacation, part research trip. Although writing news articles about Cuba was off limits to him, he was still editorializing about it, and he had the publisher's permission to go there to gather background information. Cuba was to have been the last stop on the tour, and he had arranged the necessary visas before leaving New York. He had mentioned his itinerary to President Kennedy during his chat in the oval office, and the president had asked him to stop by the White House again after the trip for a debriefing. Matthews was in Mexico City, ready to leave for Havana, when the missile crisis erupted. He had already made reservations for what turned out to be the last Cubana de Aviación flight allowed into Cuba before the blockade.

Matthews realized he had again managed to be in the right place at the right time. He believed he was on the verge of another sensational scoop, one to match the Sierra interview, if he could only get to Havana and witness, firsthand, how Castro was handling the developing crisis. He also felt he might once more be able to play a role in history by ensuring that Kennedy and his advisers had an accurate account of events from inside Cuba, one only he could provide. He stopped by the American embassy in Mexico City to see Ambassador Thomas E. Mann and to personally deliver a note he had written to Mann, detailing the arrangements he had made to be in Cuba at that critical moment. He was also mindful of how his own reputation had been battered, and he wanted to ensure that neither he nor the paper would be accused of abetting Castro again:

> I am writing you because it is our intention to go through with this trip to Cuba despite developments of the last twenty-four hours. I do not want my motives to be misunderstood by you or anyone in the Government.

Matthews told Mann that by getting in to speak to Castro and other Cuban leaders, he could flesh out a unique perspective on the enemy, an argument that would be used thirty years later by CNN correspondent Peter Arnett when he remained in Baghdad during Operation Desert Storm. Matthews also offered Mann a special deal, perhaps in the hope of improving his chances of getting in, or simply because he was eager to take on a new role—not just explaining the world but attempting to change it.

> I want to go on record in advance to say that the circumstances being what they are between us and Cuba, I will break a normal rule and keep nothing confidential that may be said to me or that I see in Cuba. If the trip goes through as planned, I will be at the disposal of any U.S. Government authority that wants to know what I saw and heard.

Mann reacted favorably; he even offered to have the embassy's resident CIA agent brief Matthews before he left. Everything seemed to be set, but then the day before he was scheduled to depart for Cuba, Matthews heard from his boss, John Oakes. It was a distressing call. Oakes said he was conveying orders that had come directly from the publisher and managing editor. Under no circumstances was he to board the plane. Regardless of whatever special arrangements he had made, Cuba was absolutely off limits. Matthews was furious, but he followed orders. He allowed the historic opportunity to slip through his fingers, though he did not conceal his bitterness about the decision to keep him shackled. In memos to New York, he argued that he had gained the trust of the State Department, the White House, and even the president himself. But he apparently did not have the trust of his own newspaper.

"*The Times* would have had it as a matter of record that we were cooperating with the White House, State Department and CIA, even though this could not be divulged quickly," he said in a memo to the editors after he returned to New York. "And this would have been aside from a journalistic scoop for *The Times* that no other correspondent in the United States—or anywhere for that matter—could have got." Matthews knew that he, and the newspaper, would have come in for criticism if he had flown to

Havana that day. And there would have been hell to pay had word of his deal to share his notebooks with the government been revealed. But he believed the criticism would have blown over quickly and that his presence there during the crisis would have added invaluable information that had both diplomatic and historic significance, even though Castro later told him that, had he been working in Cuba when the crisis reached its climax, and fears of a military strike were greatest, he would probably have been arrested and held in custody.

Matthews wrote to his brother during the missile crisis and expressed grave concerns about the way it was being handled. The seriousness of the situation temporarily overtook his anger at the way his editors had treated him. "You can imagine how I feel about Cuba," he told John. "I agree that in the circumstances there was nothing else—or less—that Kennedy could do, although the timing is a bit suspicious. I cannot understand why either the Russians or Fidel did this." He was most concerned about the harshness of Kennedy's demand that the missile bases be dismantled, a demand that, based on his perception of Castro's character, he feared would cause the Cuban to obstinately dig in his heels and fight to the bitter end. "I do not believe that Fidel would ever accept this. Therefore, I am convinced that the end of it all will be a military attack by the United States. I can see no other action, although I would not predict when."

Matthews was right about Castro but wrong about an attack. Years after the missile crisis, Castro acknowledged that he had encouraged Khrushchev not to back down, and he was prepared to provoke a shooting war with the United States that would undoubtedly have sacrificed untold numbers of Cubans. It was Khrushchev who backed down, fully realizing that the United States would never accept the continued presence of the missiles in Cuba. Maintaining the missiles there would push the two superpowers into full conflict, a conflict Khrushchev decided he was not prepared to fight. An assurance from Kennedy that the United States would not try to invade Cuba gave Khrushchev the cover he needed to retreat while saving face. After a tense week at the edge of the abyss, the world breathed a sigh of relief. Castro, who had been spoiling for a fight, was one of the few people disappointed that the standoff had ended. He pouted, feeling that the Soviets had marginalized him and betrayed the revolution. Khrushchev, he told University of Havana students a few days after the crisis ended, had no *cojones* (balls).

Matthews was determined to complete the last leg of his Latin America trip. He and Nancie again applied for visas to enter Cuba, then had to postpone the trip several times because of Nancie's ill health. But finally they did get into Cuba a year later, in 1963. Matthews had agreed that it was to be strictly a fact-finding trip for the editorial board. Castro's intransigence during the missile crisis, and Cuba's alliance with the Soviet Union, raised many questions that Matthews would have to analyze for the editorial page, though not for the news columns. That much had been made clear, and he knew that the publisher and the paper's top editors would be watching what he did in Cuba. He was not aware that the FBI and CIA would be watching, too.

The FBI had been keeping tabs on Matthews's travels since shortly after the missile crisis ended. The bureau had recorded how Matthews had advised the Passport Office that he had been forced to scuttle his planned trip to Cuba in 1962 but that he still intended to travel there, perhaps as early as January or February of the following year. It turned out to be October 1963 before he was able to go. The CIA man at the embassy in Mexico had received a tip about Matthews's planned departure date, but it did not take much detective work to know what Matthews was up to. *Prensa Latina*, the Cuban government-run news service, covered the visit in detail from beginning to end. Matthews was given a hero's welcome. The Cubans met Matthews and Nancie at the airport at 1:30 in the morning. Instead of taking them to the Habana Libre Hotel, where they had reservations, the Cubans whisked the bewildered couple to a confiscated Havana mansion. Thinking it was too late to argue, Matthews and Nancie stayed the night, though they insisted on being transferred to the hotel the following day. Matthews felt it was important to notify Catledge about the switch and about other perks provided by the Cubans. They put at his disposal a car and chauffeur, a trip aboard an army helicopter to survey areas flooded by a recent storm, and Castro's own Soviet-made Ilyushin plane.

Faustino Pérez, one of the young rebels who had led Matthews to the Sierra in 1957, was by now director of the National Institute for Hydraulic Resources. He again took the American visitor to Oriente Province, this time to survey damage done by Hurricane Flora. They visited a new school that was being built in the Sierra Maestra. The Cuban press quoted Matthews sounding very much like a visiting Soviet official: "It is a great work," he said in praise of the school project.

While Matthews was in Cuba he received a query from Lester Markel, the powerful Sunday editor of the *Times,* asking him to consider putting together an article for the Sunday magazine. Markel realized that Matthews was in a unique position. He was one of the few foreign correspondents in Cuba, and the only one with reliable access to Castro. Matthews had interviewed Castro again during the trip and had asked him a crucial question: Whose idea had it been to install Soviet missiles in Cuba? His or Khrushchev's? After the interview, Matthews believed that he had a story so important that it would override the restrictions that the publisher had placed on him. He stopped in Mexico City on the way back and there wrote another long memo describing his conversation with Castro and other exclusive news he had gathered. He sent copies to the editors, and a long note to Markel in which he outlined a piece he thought he could write for the magazine, as Markel had requested. When Markel wired back a response from New York, Matthews was surprised and annoyed. "Situation as you must realize is delicate," Markel said in the note. They would discuss it further when Matthews got back to New York.

Matthews was suspicious. "I know better than anybody the 'delicate,' as you put it, nature of the problem of writing on Cuba, although I think it is exaggerated and beneath the dignity of *The Times,*" he responded in a note to Markel. "I was not expecting to write anything, but now I think we should have something, and I will be glad to do it. I just don't like being treated as an untouchable." Only later would Matthews find out that Markel became uneasy about the proposed article after learning that Castro, in a speech at the Presidential Palace, had briefly mentioned Matthews by name. "We spoke recently with a newspaperman who has been an objective and honest newspaperman," Castro told the crowd that had gathered to hear his address. "I do not mean a Marxist-Leninist newspaperman, but a man with liberal ideas, who is the journalist Herbert Matthews."

Castro was toying with Matthews's name, throwing it into his speech in order to underscore the achievements of his revolution. But his casual reference to Matthews exaggerated fears among the editors that Matthews was too close to the revolution.

Matthews returned to New York prepared for more newsroom battles. Regardless of any previous agreement, he argued that he should be cleared to write a comprehensive news analysis for the Sunday paper, or simply present the material as an interview with Castro. He had plenty of material, and plenty of ambition. But after he had submitted the lengthy pieces to Markel, he got back a curt reply: "I have read the piece and I do not think it adds much in the way of light on Cuba, and so I feel we should not print it." Likewise, foreign editor Manny Freedman rejected Matthews's offers to write news articles. "Inasmuch as it was clearly understood before Mr. Matthews went to Cuba that he was not doing any work for the news department, I do not see that we are involved in this matter," he wrote in a memo to Turner Catledge, "nor are we responsible for any difficulties he encountered with Mr. Markel over a magaziner."

Rejecting Matthews put the editors into a difficult position because they knew they had missed the opportunity to report on one of the most important issues of the day out of their fear of Matthews's reputation. Their attempt to undo the damage only made things worse. President Kennedy had just been assassinated, and many fingers were pointed in the direction of Castro and Cuba. Any glimpse of Castro's inner circle was news, and Matthews had ventured deeper into it than any American correspondent. But the editors decided instead to run an article that had already been published in the *New Republic* magazine, written by the French journalist Jean Daniel, foreign editor of *L'Express*. The paper rarely used a freelance writer to cover a story so important, but in this case they published Daniel's article—weeks later than they could have run Matthews's piece.

Daniel had interviewed Kennedy in late October, just after the first anniversary of the missile crisis. Then, three weeks later, he interviewed Castro, and happened to be with him on November 22 to record his initial reaction to news of the president's death. "*Es una mala noticia*" (This is bad news) Castro repeated three times, according to Daniel's report. But the principal focus of Daniel's interview with Castro had been the missile crisis. He reported that Castro told him the primary reason for installing the missiles had been to protect Cuba from an imminent U.S. invasion. "He asked us what we wanted," Castro said in the interview with Daniel, referring to Khrushchev. "We answered him: Arrange that the U.S. understand that to attack Cuba is to attack the Soviet Union," and the result was that Khrushchev decided to bring in the nuclear-tipped missiles. When Matthews had talked to Castro, the Cuban leader claimed that the idea of placing nuclear missiles in Cuba to deter an invasion was his alone, and not the Russians'.

The editors had simply not trusted Matthews and had therefore withheld this important information for weeks. Freedman's reason for selecting Daniel's work over Matthews's was simple: "I would sum it up in one word: Credibility. Mr. Daniel has no reputation in this country as a partisan in the Cuba story."

But the day after this show of faith in the Daniel article, the *Times* backed away from it. In a dispatch from Washington, Max Frankel debunked Daniel's version of the origins of the missile crisis, writing that the comments by Castro in the Daniel account "fascinated many here but persuaded few." Frankel said that most Washington insiders felt Khrushchev hoped that by installing offensive missiles in Cuba he could overcome the Soviets' handicap in the nuclear arms race, giving them a strategic advantage the United States could not match. There seemed to be no logic to the argument that the missiles were defensive because they were capable of reaching New York, Chicago, and Washington. (Documents in Soviet archives later undercut both Matthews and Daniel and showed clearly that sending missiles to Cuba was very much Khrushchev's idea.)

The timidity of his editors infuriated Matthews and made him more determined than ever to publish what he knew. "What I want to get on the record now, although I feel a bit humiliated that I should have to do so, is that I sat on this news and other interesting and important news on Cuba for five weeks in order to protect *The Times*," he wrote Catledge the day Daniel's article appeared. Matthews did not openly object to the story being used instead of his, but he did feel wounded. "[T]he least *The Times* could have done was to cut out the passage in Daniel's account in which he has Fidel say, 'There is one point on which I wish immediately to give you some fresh information,'" Matthews complained, referring to the revelation about the missiles. "As you know, from reading my report, Fidel had given me the same information five weeks before."

Shut out from his newspaper and humiliated by his editors, Matthews again turned to Stanford's *Hispanic American Report,* which agreed to publish his lengthy piece as a separate pamphlet and distributed it widely. I. F. Stone, the iconoclastic editor and news columnist, referred to it as the "Report on Cuba the New York Times Was Afraid to Print." "Considering the paucity of news from Cuba, the sensational character of one story Mr. Matthews brought back and the weight attached to his opinion, it is striking that they were not published by *The New York Times* itself," wrote Stone in his *I.F. Stone's Weekly.*

Much more was at play than a simple scoop. The credibility of the paper, that gossamer-thread link to readers that converts a few ounces of newsprint and ink into a trusted source of information, had been threatened. Both the newspaper's hierarchy and Matthews believed they were defending that trust with their actions. In a note to Oakes, his loyal supporter, Matthews expressed his shock at the paper's efforts to muzzle him. "It surely ought to be clear that I cannot go through the rest of my life

saying and writing nothing about Cuba and what I learned there."
He explained that he had decided to publish the article outside
the newspaper only after he had exhausted every possible avenue
to convince the *Times* to take it. He believed that not publishing
it in *The Report* would have "suppressed information of considerable historic and scholarly interest and value," as well as setting
"an astonishing and unprecedented example of *New York Times*
censorship and suppression of the news."

Oakes forwarded a copy of the memo to the publisher.
Sulzberger showed the calm resolve that was to confound his
detractors time and again during his long tenure at the paper. "I
think I owe you a clear explanation as to why there is some hesi-
tancy on the fourteenth floor," he wrote to Matthews, referring to
the area of the Times Building that housed the publisher's office.
Sulzberger reiterated his confidence in Matthews, and he
expressed support for the idea of editorial writers traveling freely
to the countries they write about. "I was perfectly aware that you
were bound to run into some news stories," Sulzberger said. "The
purpose of the trip, however, was—and to my mind remains—for
background information, and there was a clear understanding
that you were not going to write news articles about it for *The
Times*." He felt it was unfair of Matthews to hold the *Times* to the
standard rule that articles rejected by the paper can be offered to
other publications. Publishing the article under his byline in *The
Report* simply fueled the criticism of the paper and gave the
appearance that Matthews had been censored, rather than that
he had agreed, in advance of his trip, not to write anything for the
news columns. "I understand the Stanford material is gone,"
Sulzberger ruefully noted, "but for future guidance I wish you
would bear in mind that the entire trip was of an unusual nature
and it would be far better for *The Times* if it were kept for the purpose that it was intended—gathering background information."

The spat did not end there. In 1964, Matthews also published a
long essay on Cuba and Latin America in the British magazine
Encounter. "The role of the dissenter is not an easy one in the
United States," he began, going on to describe his personal histo-

ry of difficulties with the Cuba story and the role he felt he was playing as a lone voice of reason in a howling reactionary storm. Just as he had been unwilling to abide Batista's censorship during the insurrection in Cuba, so too did Matthews fight against the censorship he felt had been unjustifiably imposed on him by the *Times*, and, collectively, by American society. In this instance he was appealing to what he believed would be *Encounter*'s neutral audience—composed of British scholars and intellectuals—and that allowed him to be more frank than usual. In the article, he portrayed himself as a martyr for the truth who was misunderstood by an American public grown paranoid about communism and obsessed by the Cold War.

Addressing readers he believed were not as hurt over Cuba as were Americans, Matthews defended his actions, offered no apologies, and lashed out at the performance of his colleagues in the American press. He berated the historian Theodore Draper and others who dared to present themselves as knowing Castro without ever having met him. Matthews claimed that only he could say with any degree of certainty what the bearded one was thinking. And he presented that special relationship with Castro as both the source of his understanding and the cause of his troubles. "To anyone knowing Fidel Castro it was almost ludicrous to see an unsophisticated American public swallow the picture of him as a calculating, trained, subservient Communist applying the rules of scientific Marxism," Matthews wrote. He was convinced that Castro and those closest to him had not been Communists at first but that they led Cuba and their revolution into the Communist camp "long after it began."

It was an academic approach to the issue, Matthews acknowledged, and not one that went down well with an American public thirsting for black-and-white answers. And he was the leading voice explaining, over and over, that "the true picture is black, grey and white." This persistence, he believed, was what made him a dissenter, not simply having "committed the crime of inventing Fidel Castro." He was aware that other newspapermen who had once been infatuated with Castro were now attacking him. Jules Dubois of the *Chicago Tribune* was one of the last major newspapermen to embrace the Castro myth laid out initially by Matthews. By the time Dubois became the first North American to interview Castro on his Pied Piper march across Cuba in the days after Batista fled, he was fully in the grip of Castro's personality. But soon after the executions began, Dubois sensed that he had been mistaken and his instant biography, *Fidel Castro: Rebel-Liberator or Dictator*, which the New Bobbs-Merrill Company published in 1959, raised the possibility that Castro could turn out to be worse for Cuba than Batista. By 1960, Dubois and most other American reporters were convinced that Castro had secretly been a Communist for a long time and had deliberately deceived everyone in those early days. However, Matthews remained steadfast. His adherence to a more complicated explanation of Castro's revolution continued to perturb the Cuban exile community, raise the suspicions of the FBI, and cause trouble for him within the *Times*.

The *Encounter* article, along with an exchange of letters that followed, turned into another conflict with the *Times*. Sulzberger was annoyed when he found out that Matthews had published another article on Cuba. "Herbert, while I sympathize with your determination to defend your ideas, it is obviously impossible to separate yourself from *The Times*. Prolonging the Cuban debate, as reflected in the July and August issues of *Encounter*, is harmful," Sulzberger wrote in the summer of 1964. "The irritations of this situation have long since been healed to the good of you and our newspaper. I do wish you would give this matter the serious consideration I do, and quietly give time a chance to work." In his calm but firm way, Sulzberger was admonishing Matthews, and telling him to please pipe down. In Sulzberger's mind, the whole episode involving Matthews's aborted 1962 trip to Cuba, the rescheduled journey in late 1963, the conditions under which he was not to publish anything, the tussle with Markel over the aborted magazine piece and with the news desk over articles not accepted, the *Hispanic American Report* issue that contained the material that the *Times* had rejected, and the criticism the paper received because of that controversy had become a huge irritation, capped by the article in *Encounter*.

Matthews refused to back down or let the issue rest. He

responded to the publisher's note a few days later, dealing with him in a more confrontational way than he had ever dealt with Sulzberger's father. His response was five times longer than the note he had received from Sulzberger, and it addressed point by point what he said were serious misconceptions. He had not written the *Encounter* article to prolong the Cuban debate as Sulzberger had charged. Rather, Matthews said he had put it together in early 1963 for a book of essays on Latin America to which he had been asked to contribute. When that project fell apart, Matthews sought another outlet and in early 1964 chose *Encounter.* The British editors held on to the piece for six months, but once it became known that the *Times* had refused to print Matthews's Cuba material, *Encounter* decided it was time to publish his piece on dissent, and Matthews agreed.

"*The Times* has nothing to be ashamed of and nothing to be afraid of on the Cuban Revolution," he wrote Sulzberger. "I have played a very special journalistic role in that revolution and what I write is eagerly read by every Latin Americanist in the country and it becomes part of the historic record." He took exception to the publisher's belief that he had gone outside the newspaper in order to defend himself and his ideas, which Matthews said did not need to be defended. In the end, he said, the newspaper's reputation would be more damaged by the publisher's actions to silence him than by anything Matthews had written. "*The Times* is really hurt when it refuses to print important news from a staff member, and *The Times* would really be harmed if it muzzled a staff member who has something important to say and who chooses the most dignified and non-commercial way of saying it."

Matthews later showed Oakes the exchange of memos. "When Punch wrote me after the Stanford piece came out I was shocked at his misunderstanding of the situation but decided not to get into an argument," Matthews wrote. "This time I am much more shocked because he has a complete misconception of the situation—100% complete—and I therefore felt it must be answered and straightened out."

Oakes diplomatically sat out this round. "Very interesting," he scribbled on Matthews's note. "Thanx for letting me see."

* * *

Matthews was certain that his telephone was being tapped, and he believed FBI agents were casing the apartment building where he lived on the Upper East Side of Manhattan. He routinely received death threats in the mail and ignored them. But one afternoon in September 1964, Oakes called him into his office. He introduced Matthews to a young FBI agent named James Kenny who told him he had some disturbing information. The bureau had received word from its sources that an exile group in Miami had put out a contract on Matthews's life. FBI files show that the plot was in a very early stage and was basically the result of a single meeting in which the exiles determined that something had to be done about Matthews. Oakes called Sulzberger, who offered to arrange a security guard and escort. Matthews declined the offer, preferring to wait until the New York City police were notified. Security guards at the Times Building were put on alert and police briefed the doorman at his apartment house. This went on for about three months. By the end of the year, there were no further indications that the exiles were serious about pursuing their threat. Matthews called the FBI agent one last time to ask where the investigation stood.

"The imminence of anything is rather remote," Agent Kenny said.

"Does that mean they've called it off?" Matthews asked.

"I can hardly say that no one is ever going to do anything in the future," Kenny warned him. "But you should put it out of your mind."

Doing so would not be difficult. Matthews had lots of other things to worry about, particularly the effects of the verbal attacks and attempts at character assassination that had come from the Senate hearing rooms in Washington for years. The investigation of Matthews and his involvement with the Cuban story had continued into 1962, but the consequences would last long after that.

naming names

Even after Senator Joseph McCarthy's frenzied quest to expose
the Communist threat to the United States was discredited in the
early 1950s, a number of right-wing senators who shared his paranoia were willing to take up where he had left off. They pushed
the investigations ever further, and prolonged the hunt for Reds
well into the next decade. Herbert Matthews had become one of
their most visible targets, a *piñata* of potential Communist mis-
chief. And indirectly through him, the senators believed they
could get at their ultimate target, the *Times* itself.

It would not be the first instance of the Communist bounty
hunters in the Senate trying to ensnare the newspaper and its editors. In the early 1950s, Senator James O. Eastland of Mississippi,
a conservative Democrat upset by the *Times*'s strong stance in support of school desegregation, held a series of hearings that turned
into newsroom witch hunts. He was looking for, and finding
sketchy evidence of, Communist influence inside American newspapers. Thirty-eight newspaper employees were called to testify.
Of those, twenty-five worked for the *Times*.

The accusations were based on flimsy evidence, but that was

enough to cause great distress within the *Times*. Most of the claims were made by one man, Harvey Matusow, who admitted that he had joined the American Communist Party as a youth. Matusow, an eccentric former GI who later became a paid government agent, worked as a telephone operator at Communist Party headquarters on East 12th Street in Manhattan until he became disillusioned with communism. When he was called to testify before Eastland's subcommittee, he accused the newspaper guild of harboring hundreds of Communists. Matusow singled out the *Times*, claiming there were "well over one hundred dues-paying members" of the Communist Party within its ranks. At a lecture in Montana two weeks later he repeated the charge, but this time he claimed the Sunday *Times* alone had "126 dues-paying Communists." The paper claimed the entire Sunday staff did not exceed 100.

To make matters worse, in 1954, Walter Winchell's television program revealed that a *Times* reporter who had once belonged to the Communist Party was still working at the paper's Washington bureau and, of all things, covering Senator McCarthy's hearings. When called to explain, the reporter, Clayton Knowles, told the publisher that he had indeed joined the party in 1937, when he worked at the *Long Island Daily Press*. But he said he had left the party six years later when he was hired by the *Times*. Knowles apologized to Sulzberger for not having disclosed his affiliation earlier, and he agreed to go before the Eastland subcommittee to reveal the names of others who also belonged to the party.

When Matusow was called to testify again in 1955, he was allowed to repeat his accusations against the newspaper's employees. Sulzberger had the *Times*'s general counsel, Louis Loeb, conduct an internal investigation. Convinced that Eastland had targeted the *Times*, Sulzberger fought back with an in-your-face editorial written by Matthews's boss on the editorial page at that time, Charles Merz, attacking the smear tactics and defending the newspaper's honor.

And our faith is strong that long after Senator Eastland and his present subcommittee are forgotten, long after segregation has lost its final battle in the South, long after all that was known as McCarthyism is a dim, unwelcome memory, long after the last Congressional committee has learned that it cannot tamper successfully with a free press, *The New York Times* will still be speaking for the men who make it, and only for the men who make it, and speaking, without fear or favor, the truth as it sees it.

When, a few years later, it was Herbert Matthews who was being attacked by the Eastland subcommittee, and about whom witness after witness was making accusations, the *Times* published no strident editorial. Nor did it make any bold, defiant statement in his defense. His editors kept silent, although they would later ask themselves whether they had done right by Matthews and given him all the support that he, as a representative of the newspaper's tradition of independence, ought to have had while being attacked. Matthews himself did not think they had stood up to the plate squarely enough for him, but he did not say so publicly until many years later.

The Eastland subcommittee's first attempt to go after Matthews came in 1959, just six months after Castro's triumph. One of Senator Eastland's principal aims was to investigate whether, as he suspected, the U.S. government had helped Castro and the Communists seize power in Cuba. The subcommittee called Spruille Braden, U.S. ambassador to Cuba in the 1940s and a former assistant secretary of state. He declared that "a communist reign of terror" now overwhelmed Cuba. "I am not 100 percent positive that Fidel himself is a Communist," he testified. "That his brother is and that Fidel is surrounded by them, yes."

Braden gave the subcommittee a world-weary account of the Communist threat in the Caribbean and wasted little time in narrowing his attack.

"I was talking about Herbert Matthews and *The New York Times*," Braden said. "I think it is a most disturbing thing; you undoubtedly read his article yesterday in which he was defending this Cuban situation. I think that article shows the degree of infiltration we have in this country; when *The New York Times* publishes on the front page an article declaring that Castro is not a Communist and it is all 'lovey-dovey' and everything is fine down there, and moreover *The New York Times* radio in New York, while I was getting dressed yesterday morning, twice I heard it booming out, 'Read *The New York Times* today. Matthews tells you all about Cuba and that Castro is not a communist.'"

Julien G. Sourwine, the subcommittee's chief counsel and its most vicious inquisitor, a former newspaperman whose dislike of Castro, and Matthews, was unmistakable, then got to the heart of the matter. He asked Braden if he believed the American people had been misled.

"No question in my mind about it," Braden testified in response. "I had an experience yesterday morning. As a trustee of the Dry Dock Savings Bank, I attended a real estate committee meeting. The senior vice president of the bank turned to me and said, 'Good Lord, this Matthews article that came out the day before yesterday, it is perfectly terrible.' I said, 'What about it; what makes you think it is so terrible?' He said, 'I had some friends in the night before last and they were all for Castro, and I was telling them that they shouldn't be, that he was a Communist and I was repeating what you had told me.' He said, 'Now they pick up the morning *Times* and read this. They are going to think either I was lying or a fool.'"

Over the next six years, the Senate held more than ten separate hearings on communism in the Caribbean, and Matthews's name came up in all of them. He held his tongue at the outset and with a great deal of restraint simply let the charges go unanswered. But his patience ran out when the subcommittee's star witness was the one American diplomat with whom Matthews had the stormiest relationship, former ambassador Arthur Gardner. Both Cubans and Americans thought Gardner had been uncomfortably close to Batista before the revolution. It was Matthews's series of articles from the mountains that Gardner felt had made it impossible for him to be reappointed.

At the time of the hearings, Gardner was too ill to travel to Washington. Members of the subcommittee, including Senator Thomas J. Dodd of Connecticut, went to Gardner's home in Watch Hill, Rhode Island, to take his testimony. Dodd had reason to believe that Gardner's version of what had happened in Cuba would make the long trip up the East Coast well worth while. Although the proceedings were secret, it didn't take long for Gardner's testimony to be revealed. He represented a faded era in U.S.-Cuba relations, a figure from a time when Americans were almost as comfortable in Cuba as they were in the United States. In his opinion, Cubans had a special bond with Americans and were grateful to Uncle Sam for having won for them their independence from Spain, a not at all popular point of view in Cuba except in the ranks of the wealthy and powerful, with whom Gardner had socialized. "I never heard anybody use the word 'gringo,' or say 'get out of . . . ,' 'Yanqui get out,' or anything like that," he testified. The United States never "had a better friend," than Batista, he said, but we sold him down the river. He blamed flunkies at the State Department and misguided public reaction for Batista's ouster. But he held no individual or group more directly responsible for what had happened in Cuba than Herbert Matthews and the *Times*.

"Herbert Matthews is one of these people, the do-gooder type, who the minute you mention the word—anybody as a dictator— is out to try to break him," Gardner said scornfully. To his mind, Matthews was directly responsible for the downfall of a friendly regime and for the introduction of a shifty band of rabble-rousers who were causing the United States more trouble than they were worth.

"You have been quoted, Mr. Gardner, as referring to 'Castro worship' in the State Department in 1957. What did you mean by this?" asked Senator Dodd.

"Well, did you read the article that Matthews wrote, after he went up in the hills and saw him?" Gardner responded.

"Yes," said Dodd.

"He wrote a Richard Harding Davis type of article, and he made Castro appear to be a Robin Hood, a savior for the country."

"Yes, but Mr. Herbert Matthews wasn't in the State Department."

"No but he was actually—he briefed Earl Smith—"

"Your successor as Ambassador to Cuba was briefed by Herbert Matthews?"

"Yes, that is right."

Three days later, Smith took the witness stand to describe his meeting with Matthews. He rejected Gardner's insinuation that Matthews had dazzled him during the briefing. But Gardner was not yet finished with Matthews. Senator Dodd provided him with ample opportunity to disparage Matthews's writing and his sympathies.

"What part, if any, do you think Herbert L. Matthews played in bringing Castro to power?"

"I don't think he did anything physically," Gardner testified. "But his articles were such that he created a biased situation against Batista."

"And pro-Castro?"

"Pro-Castro, very strongly."

"Did Herbert Matthews ever contact you while you were the Ambassador in Cuba about—"

"I made every effort, and saw him a good many times, tried to get his friendship, because he and a man named Dubois, who worked for a Chicago paper—both of them were considered by us to be radicals. And I even arranged meetings for him. And I made it possible actually for Herbert Matthews to go down and have this interview, because he asked me."

Gardner then wove a tale that the senators accepted even though it had no apparent basis in either truth or logic. He claimed that he had run interference with Batista so Matthews could interview Castro in 1957. (Years later, Richard Cushing, who was Gardner's press officer, claimed that it was he who had helped get Matthews into the mountains.)

Gardner boasted of how close he had been to Batista, and how leery the Cuban president had been of allowing Matthews to make the trip. He even claimed that Batista knew with certainty that Castro was alive, and where to find him, contrary to what the dictator said in his memoirs. Gardner said Batista had been afraid to make a martyr of him by dragging him out dead or alive. He claimed to have convinced Batista that allowing Matthews to make the trip would not do any harm because Matthews had agreed that on his return he would again stop by the embassy and reveal what he had learned.

"He promised he would come back and tell you about his conversation with Castro?" asked Dodd.

"That is right," Gardner said. "And to this day I never have seen him."

Gardner took one more roundhouse shot at Matthews before winding up his hourlong testimony. Dodd asked him point blank if he felt that Matthews's articles had influenced the way the American people originally felt about Castro.

"I don't think there is any question about it," he said. "I think almost all the newspapers in this country became sort of hypnotized by the thing."

Within six months, a version of Gardner's testimony was published. Matthews was distressed to read that a man who had been the highest representative of the United States in a country so critical to the nation's strategic interest as Cuba had deliberately lied to a Senate subcommittee. He had directly attacked Matthews's reputation as a journalist and had undermined the very basis of his historic interview with Castro.

"It was the most extraordinary thing of its kind that happened to me in my long career—and in its way it was the worst," Matthews wrote years later. "Arthur Gardner had reason to congratulate himself gleefully; he had had his revenge."

Matthews could not let Gardner's account go unanswered. He wrote a column in which he called Gardner a liar, but he did not publish it in the *Times*. Instead, he sent it to the Washington *Daily News*, and Representative William F. Ryan of New York, who knew Matthews, read the article into the *Congressional Record*. Matthews wanted to be called before the subcommittee himself so he would have the chance to directly rebut Gardner's charges. Congressman Ryan was willing to ask the Eastland subcommittee to call him to testify. Matthews first checked with the *Times*'s chief counsel, Louis Loeb, who cautioned against it. Had Matthews been called, he would have refuted Gardner's testimony, which had been given under oath, as Matthews's would also have been. With competing versions of the same incident, the subcommittee would have to assume that one was untrue and that one witness had perjured himself. Matthews believed the subcommittee never called him because doing so would have demolished Gardner's testimony and sent the whole investigation off track—proving perjury instead of flushing out Communists. Gardner never attempted to sue Matthews for calling him a liar in print. But the damage to Matthews's reputation had already been done.

Former ambassador Earl Smith also called Matthews's motives into question. The subcommittee was determined to portray Smith's two and a half hour briefing by Matthews as a breach of protocol, an attempt by anti-Batista forces within the State Department to indoctrinate the new ambassador before he had taken up his post. Julien Sourwine once more controlled the questioning, asking Smith to give the highlights of his conversation with Matthews.

"He did not believe the Batista government could last, and that the fall of the Batista government would come relatively soon," Smith said.

"Specifically what did he say about Castro?" asked Sourwine.

"In February 1957 Herbert L. Matthews wrote three articles on Fidel Castro, which appeared on the front page of *The New York Times*, in which he eulogized Fidel Castro and portrayed him as a political Robin Hood, and I would say that he repeated those views to me in our conversation." (Only two of the three articles ran on page one, and Robin Hood was not mentioned.)

Smith had taken over his post in Havana just after Matthews's series appeared, and he told the subcommittee that he had witnessed firsthand the impact the articles had on Cuba. They "served to inflate Castro to world stature and world recognition," Smith said. "Until that time, Castro had been just another bandit in the Oriente Mountains of Cuba, with a handful of followers who had terrorized the campesinos, that is the peasants, throughout the countryside." Smith testified that Matthews's reports were pure hagiography: "After the Matthews articles which followed an exclusive interview by the *Times* editorial writer in Castro's mountain hideout and which likened him to Abraham Lincoln, he was able to get followers and funds in Cuba and in the United States," Smith testified. "From that time on arms, money and soldiers of fortune abounded. Much of the American press began to picture Castro as a political Robin Hood."

Matthews's writing had greatly influenced the course of events in Cuba, Smith said. "The crusader role which the press and radio bestowed on the bearded rebel blinded the people to the leftwing political philosophy with which even at that time he was already on record," he said. And what was worse, in Smith's view, was that "the official U.S. attitude toward Castro could not help but be influenced by the pro-Castro press and radio; certain members of Congress picked up the torch for him."

Smith's criticism of Matthews was just as virulent as Gardner's. "Without the United States, Castro would not be in power today," Smith stated. "I will put it as straight as that to you, sir." Smith, obviously angry over what had happened in Cuba, tried to draw a strong link between the State Department and Matthews, distributing blame equally among them. "I do not believe that he was ever a consultant or ever employed by the State Department," Smith said, speaking of Matthews. "I believe there was a close connection though, between the Latin American desk and Herbert Matthews."

The subcommittee expected William Wieland, the director of the Caribbean desk who had instructed Smith to meet Matthews, to support Smith's position that Matthews's writing had influenced the State Department. But when Wieland was called to testify he said he had met with Matthews only a few times and they often disagreed about U.S. policy. "In every conversation I can remember having with Mr. Matthews," Wieland said, "he was critical of our attitude toward Cuban matters. I know of no basis for the remark by Ambassador Smith that Mr. Matthews was more familiar with the department's thinking regarding Cuba than our ambassador was."

Matthews had little respect for Smith. It was an enmity dating back to their hectic days in Cuba. They had met twice before the failed general strike in 1958. Smith wrote about one of their encounters: "He [Matthews] said the embassy had intervened in Cuban affairs by trying to be helpful in obtaining free and open elections. I was amused at Matthews' statement because I could not help but think how much he had been intervening in the affairs of Cuba." Matthews considered Smith to be as amateurish as Gardner had been, and just as poor a diplomat. "Smith never appreciated a simple diplomatic axiom," Matthews said, "that one does not ostentatiously back a losing side."

Although Matthews and the *Times* were among the Eastland subcommittee's favorite targets, other journalists eventually came under their crosshairs as well. Over several months in 1960 and 1961, the Senate investigated the Fair Play for Cuba Committee, which Robert Taber, the CBS documentary filmmaker who had made the trip up to Pico Turquino, had helped found. Taber, like Matthews, had been deeply impressed with Castro after coming face to face with him in the mountains. He wrote a book about the revolution and got so personally involved that he was not allowed to continue to work for CBS. He believed that the American press was distorting the Cuban Revolution and that the narrow focus on whether Castro was a Communist in 1959 had blinded most reporters to a truly significant moment in the history of the Western Hemisphere. "We have witnessed a virulent press campaign, concocted of ignorance, half truths, name calling, connotative misdirection and outright fabrication, all tending to erode the first light image of the revolution and to discredit its leadership," Taber had written in a 1960 article in the *Nation*.

Taber was too infatuated with the Cuban situation to realize how deep a hole he was digging for himself. The Fair Play for Cuba Committee was supported by left-leaning authors such as James Baldwin, Norman Mailer, Truman Capote, and Jean-Paul Sartre, and in ads placed in newspapers around the country it encouraged sympathy and understanding for what Castro was attempting in Cuba. The Eastland subcommittee forced Taber to admit that he had gone to Cuba several times since the revolution on flights arranged by and paid for by the Cuban government, implying that he had abandoned his role as a journalist and was acting as a partisan.

But Taber was just a small fry compared to Matthews. Witness after witness was called to testify about the ways in which the United States had mishandled the Castro insurrection, and time after time Matthews's name was raised. In June 1961, it was the turn of Robert C. Hill, the former U.S. ambassador to Mexico, to bash Matthews. "Herbert Matthews has always been an enthusiastic supporter of Fidel Castro," Hill testified. "He believes the movement is not Communist-motivated." By July 1962, a year after the Bay of Pigs and a few months before the missile crisis, the former U.S. Ambassador to Costa Rica, Whiting Willauer, crystallized Washington's problems with Castro and Matthews. He read into the record a paper he had written, titled "The Crisis in United States Interests in the Caribbean." It provided a historical perspective that revealed the intense paranoia of the time.

"The Edgar Snows of Chinese communism are replaced today by the Herbert Matthews [sic] of Caribbean Communists," Willauer had written. Snow was the magazine correspondent who had visited Mao Tse-tung when his rebel army was still struggling to survive in northeastern China. Mao befriended Snow and gave him extraordinary access to the Chinese Communist hierarchy, access Snow used to paint a sympathetic picture of the revolution. The similarities to Castro and Matthews could not be missed. "Neither the Snows nor the Matthews [sic] are Communists, and both can be fairly credited with abhorring it—if and when they recognize it. The trouble with this type of journalism is that it is carrying a banner for a cause, and, in its hate of the dictators, it is blind to the nature of the forces of communism, which are infiltrating the legitimate revolutionary forces."

Senator Dodd, one of Matthews's chief accusers, made it obvious that he had accepted as truth the accounts of Ambassadors Gardner, Smith, and Hill. "Unfortunately, there were those in the State Department who were prone to accept as gospel the evaluation of the Castro movement which found its way into the staid columns of *The New York Times* through the pen of Mr. Herbert Matthews," he said in 1962. "Mr. Matthews assured the American public that Castro was not a Communist and that the Castro movement was not Communist-dominated," Dodd said. Then he compressed into a single thought the misperceptions of several of the witnesses who had appeared before him over the years, each with his own mistaken idea of what Matthews had written about Castro. By then, the actual words Matthews had published were forgotten, but the mistaken interpretation they created lived on. "Matthews built up a hero image of Castro," Dodd said, "in which all the virtues of Robin Hood and Thomas Jefferson, of George Washington and Abraham Lincoln, were contained in a single man."

In a time of misconceptions and lies, the truth itself became malleable. Both the accusers and the accused were willing to believe that image mattered more than reality. Policy was being misshaped by perception, while perceptions were distorted by emotions. Both government and journalism were under tremendous pressures at this critical moment, and both would be forced to change in significant ways in their relationship to each other.

For the rest of his life, Matthews would be accused of sympathizing with Castro and helping the Communists infiltrate the Western Hemisphere. The constant criticism tested his adherence to the Stoics' dictum "Bear and forbear," which he had long before adopted as his moral guide. But things would get immeasurably more difficult after he visited Cuba again in 1966 and returned to face down his editors one last time.

faithful adherence

By the time Matthews stopped at the White House in the early months of 1964 to see McGeorge Bundy, he had been under attack for almost five years because of his positions on Cuba. The assault on his reputation was relentless, but he rarely admitted mistakes. Matthews conceded that he had miscalculated the number of troops and weapons that Castro had with him at the outset of the war, and he eventually acknowledged that Castro had, indeed, gone over to the Soviet camp. But he remained steadfast in his belief that Castro had not owed allegiance to the Soviets before 1960, and he maintained his view that for Castro, communism was not a bedrock political belief but an expedient way of tightening his grip on Cuba. Beyond everything else, he believed that the United States had failed to see the Cuban Revolution as a complex social upheaval, as radical in its own way as the French Revolution. Castro had done far more than simply sweep away the old regime. He was redesigning the social order in Cuba. Not realizing the magnitude of the change Castro had wrought was Washington's costliest mistake. And Matthews was convinced that if Washington continued down this same path, it would lead to disaster.

"[A]n American policy so stupid as to seek to restore the pre-

Revolutionary situation, as we tried to do with the invasion of April, 1961, is no answer," he had written right after the Bay of Pigs revealed how little Washington understood Castro's mystique, what Matthews and others called *"Fidelismo."* The most powerful doctrine on the island had not been imported from the Soviet Union, nor taken from the writings of Karl Marx. Rather, it was the homegrown belief in Fidel and the willingness of Cubans to embrace Castro, with all his flaws, and to stand behind him as he stood up to the United States. Matthews was sure that Cubans would never abandon *Fidelismo* and that the United States would simply have to accept the fact that the revolution was irreversible.

"The hope surely must be that the Cuban Revolution will run a course that brings social and economic benefits to Cuba and that meanwhile can be isolated," he wrote. "Cuba is a small, weak, poor country which could be allowed to work out its own destiny, even if its government is socialistic or communistic. It will not subvert the hemisphere or any countries in it if American policies are wise and sensible."

It was those policies that Matthews wanted to discuss when he called on Bundy, who then was special assistant to President Lyndon B. Johnson, just as he had been assistant to President Kennedy the last time Matthews had been invited to the White House. Now it was a few months after Kennedy's death, and Matthews had just returned from another trip to Havana. He was still fighting with the publisher and his editors about the material he had brought back. Although he was not writing news articles about Cuba, he continued to editorialize about Latin America, Vietnam, and other U.S. strategic interests.

Bundy had a poor opinion of Matthews and the *Times* that went back many years. He had been especially critical of editorials that took a negative view of the recent coup that had deposed Brazil's leftist president João Goulart. Even though the editorials were unsigned, Bundy felt it was obvious that Matthews had written them. They suggested that the American rush to recognize the new regime made it appear that Washington had been involved in the revolt.

Bundy was angry again when Matthews called on him. He began the interview by criticizing the *Times*'s editorial position on Latin American issues. Matthews countered that Bundy might not see eye to eye with the positions taken by the paper because the editorial board's point of view was decidedly sympathetic toward the goals of Latin America.

No, Bundy insisted, it wasn't because the editorials were pro-Latin. He did not like them, he said, because they were based on false information and came to incorrect conclusions that were causing a lot of trouble. The interview turned into a debate, with Matthews vigorously defending his positions. At one point, Bundy had had enough.

"Look," he said, "you have been here an hour and ten minutes during which you talked for one hour and I talked for ten minutes. I thought you had come here to interview me."

Bundy was not alone in feeling that Matthews was more interested in his own views than in those of the people he interviewed. Throughout the Cuban controversy, he maintained absolute faith in his abilities, his self-confidence sometimes bordering on hubris. Even in the face of his harshest critics, he retained a serene sense of control. He had developed this independence of mind as a youth in New York and had become more obstinate as he got older. Self-reliance and ingenuity were qualities possessed by the soldiers of fortune in Richard Harding Davis's books. These were the traits that Matthews hoped to find in the national leaders, including those in the United States, about whom he wrote. In Castro, he had finally come face to face with someone who possessed not only those characteristics but had self-confidence greater than his own. That much had been evident during the interview in the Sierra, and it had not diminished since then. Castro never admitted he was wrong, not even when he made mistakes that put his people at risk. That was something Matthews could relate to.

Matthews's battles with Ruby Phillips had ended only when she was abruptly forced to leave Cuba after the Bay of Pigs invasion.

After a brief rest, she was shifted to the national desk and assigned to the Miami office to cover southern Florida. She was allowed to make occasional trips to the Caribbean, but the editors felt that "in the present circumstances Cuba should probably be considered out of bounds for her."

Working as a reporter outside Cuba for the first time in her life, Phillips struggled. By 1963, she tried to return to what she knew best, but her pieces about Cuba were routinely killed. The Cuban story had grown far too complex for her to handle, and working in Miami cut her off from most of her sources. Manny Freedman, the foreign editor, rejected several of her articles because they seemed "too weak." Freedman killed one of her last stories about Cuba's diplomatic relations with the United States without any more comment than the words he scrawled on the top of her copy: "[J]ust did not seem to come off." Before 1963 ended, Phillips had quit the *Times* and had taken a position with *Newsday*, whose publisher, Harry Guggenheim, had known Phillips since he had been U.S. ambassador to Cuba in the 1930s. The last entry in her file at the *Times* is a note from the national news desk dated October 24, 1963: "Please remove RHP from all of our books." At *Newsday* she went back to covering Latin America, but she was already sixty-three, and she was unable to produce the kind of stories that *Newsday* expected. She soon retired.

With Phillips out of the picture, Matthews redirected his criticism of the *Times*'s Cuba coverage, sparing no one. Tad Szulc, by this time one of the paper's stars, more than once was the subject of a hectoring Matthews note. Matthews and Szulc both were dogged reporters and prodigious writers, but their styles were as different as north and south. Matthews seemed at ease in pinstripes; Szulc rarely wore a tie. In 1964, Matthews wrote a long note to the foreign desk criticizing Szulc's work. "What we are doing is to fall for the *way* Tad writes a story and not for *what* he writes," he said. Matthews was suggesting that Szulc's sources in Cuba were no match for his own, which—he didn't mind reminding the foreign desk—had produced valuable, even historic, information that the *Times* refused to publish. "[I]t seems to me," Matthews wrote, "that it ought to be obvious that Tad was manufacturing a story out of little more than thin air." Freedman acknowledged receipt of Matthews's note, but it changed nothing. Szulc's articles on Cuba continued to appear in the newspaper; Matthews's did not. Szulc got his revenge when, in his 1986 Castro biography, he retold the story of how Castro had bamboozled Matthews in 1957. "Today Matthews is a forgotten man in Cuba," Szulc wrote, inaccurately it turned out. But he felt he had evened the score.

For most of the twentieth century, the *Times*'s headquarters building was located on a side street just off Times Square, which is named after the newspaper. Tourists often have trouble finding it, but protesters always seem to know exactly where it is. They sometimes even manage to find out when national or foreign leaders are scheduled to meet with the editorial board so they can array themselves outside in protest. Occasionally, their target is the paper itself.

Matthews remembered how about 400 Cubans had been able to locate the building without difficulty in 1957. They had demonstrated outside the newspaper on a sunny afternoon in June with signs of praise for him and the *Times*: "WHO CARE [*sic*] WHAT THE DICTATOR SAYS? WE TRUST YOU. WE LIKE MR. MATTHEWS." But on a wintry February day in 1964, another group of protesters carried a far less friendly message. About forty angry Cubans with signs, organized by the Cuban Workers Revolutionary Front, an anti-Castro group in New York, decried the paper's coverage of the revolution.

"MATTHEWS NUMBER ONE ENEMY OF CUBA'S FREEDOM," read one sign. By this time, Matthews's name was invariably linked with Castro's. The Senate hearings had left the impression that Matthews felt there was nothing wrong with the Communist system, and much about it that was right. "DOWN [*sic*] MATTHEWS AND ALL THE COMMUNISTS OF THE NEW YORK TIMES," read another placard. Some of the same people who had invited Matthews to speak at their anti-Batista rallies or who had praised Matthews for his courage in breaking Batista's censorship were now demanding his head. The exile community in the United States held Matthews and the *Times* responsible for the troubles in Cuba. The words "ever since Matthews" had become a catchphrase that Castro's enemies in Cuba and the United States would use for decades. The phrase stood for a complex set of assumptions about Matthews and the *Times*, many derived from faulty conclusions or misdirected rage. "Ever since Matthews made Castro a hero," or "Ever since Matthews got fooled by Castro," or some other version of the phrase has started countless arguments in Miami and Union City, New Jersey, and anywhere else Cubans gather to lament the tragedy of their nation. The phrase has turned out to be as enduring as Castro himself.

From his office on the tenth floor, Matthews wouldn't have heard the protesters on the sidewalk below. But he undoubtedly would have known they were there.

And the FBI knew where Matthews was and what he was doing. The bureau's file on him was growing as his critics provided a steady stream of salacious tips. J. Edgar Hoover took them all seriously, especially when they came from such sources as the publisher William Randolph Hearst, Jr. In one note to Hoover, Hearst passed along an allegation that Matthews belonged to the Communist Party. The bureau investigated and though it found nothing, the accusation fit what it believed about Matthews. When Castro invited two dozen American newspapers to send reporters to attend the 26th of July celebrations courtesy of the Cuban government, the bureau's interest was again piqued, even though the *Times* did not receive an invitation. "I bet Matthews had his finger in this one," Hoover scrawled across the bottom of the file, just as he had set off the bureau's investigation in 1957 when he scribbled a note asking what the bureau knew of Herbert Matthews. By 1965, the answer was: plenty.

In order to make sure that its Reserve Index, the master list of people considered security risks, was current, the bureau annually reviewed each name. In 1965, the FBI was convinced that the plot to kill Matthews hadn't changed his attitude toward Cuba at all. Even though repeated contacts with informants produced "no pertinent derogatory information" about Matthews, the bureau had no reservations about keeping him on the index. Agents had notified Matthews of the death threat against him, but they had not brought him in for a security interview as they did with other people on the index, fearing he might write something that would embarrass the bureau. Besides, there seemed to be no question about where his sympathies lay. "There were no changes in the subject's pro-Castro attitudes," the bureau concluded. Matthews's name remained on the index because "of the subject's persistent and faithful adherence to the Castro regime in Cuba and because of his continued writings in behalf of the Cuban Revolution."

But none of that writing had appeared in the news columns of the *Times* for several years, despite Matthews's persistence and his repeated attempts to drift back to the story. In 1966, he arranged another visit to Cuba and tried once more to write for the news pages about the revolution. He flew to Havana in mid-April and remained there for three weeks, making the rounds of officials and getting in to see Castro, the first correspondent from the *Times,* or any other newspaper, to interview him in nearly six months. But Castro had not made it easy for him. He kept Matthews waiting for several days. Finally, when Matthews was about to leave, Castro agreed to see him. Afterward Matthews typed out pages of notes. By the time he was done, he had over 25,000 words, which he sent off to Oakes's assistant, former labor reporter Abe Raskin, with instructions to copy them and pass them on to other members of the editorial board and to the news department.

Buoyed by the excitement of being back in Cuba, where he was a distinguished visitor instead of an outcast, Matthews optimistically called in an editorial about conditions there. He felt it was balanced, critical where it needed to be but generally favorable about the impressive conditions that he had witnessed. "The facts of the case here in Cuba—and they are facts not opinions—are that the Castro regime and the Cuban revolution have never been stronger, more unified or from their point of view more hopeful," he wrote.

But once Sulzberger saw the editorial, he killed it.

Matthews did not know that when he called Raskin the following day. He had heard nothing from New York about the editorial or about his notes. It soon became clear to him that his optimism had been misplaced, that his ability to persuade New York to consider the historic value of his reporting on Cuba or the validity of his opinions on the revolution had ended. There was no interest in running the editorial, or any news article. The double failure made him realize he had come to the end of the line with the *Times* over Cuba. As disturbing as such feelings were, they were not entirely new. He had gone through a similar disappointment three decades before. When Matthews sent a personal note to Oakes he included a copy of a page from "The Education of a Correspondent." In it, he described what it had felt like to send his last dispatch from Spain, realizing that he had supported a lost cause.

"But the lessons I had learned"—he had written of Spain— "They seemed worth a great deal. Even then, heartsick and discouraged as I was, something sang inside of me. I, like the Spaniards, had fought my war and lost, but I could not be persuaded that I had set too bad an example . . . ."

Then, in the note to Oakes, Matthews wrote, "When I called Abe from Havana the day after sending a hopeful Monday column and realized from the way he talked that it was all going to happen again, my mind went back to this page and I gathered some wry comfort." In his mind, fear had won out over courage; propriety had bested integrity, and there was nothing more to do about it but accept it for what it was. "I am signing off on Cuba for *The Times* except, of course, for any required editorials, although my last one was so mutilated that I wished I hadn't written it. I am sending this simply as a way of saying: 'the incident is closed.'"

But as he was writing that note, Matthews already had other

plans for a project that he knew could trigger a final showdown with Sulzberger. Matthews had been approached by the editorial director of Penguin Books to write a biography of Castro for a series the publisher was doing on famous contemporary figures. Penguin did a good job of buttering him up, telling Matthews, "You are uniquely suited to write the biography. I doubt if there exists anywhere anyone else so uniquely suited by your combination of gifts and experience, as well as by the fact of your presence in Cuba and personal acquaintanceship with Castro and his colleagues during their guerrilla days."

Matthews happened to agree with that assessment. And, as always, he took into account the project's financial considerations. A popular biography of Castro might bring in some badly needed cash to help pay off mounting debts he and Nancie had incurred since returning to New York. But there was more at stake here than a few thousand dollars. "I am sure you will believe me when I say I am not only thinking of the professional and financial angle," he wrote Oakes, "but of the historic record about which I have always had a strong feeling in my life on all contemporary subjects."

He told Oakes that even though his deadline for delivering the manuscript was a few years off, he was eager to get started, beginning with the 1966 trip. He ended the letter on a falsely hopeful note. "I presume," he wrote, "there will be no objection on the part of *The Times.*"

These were difficult days for Matthews—feeling shut out, ostracized by his colleagues, prohibited from attaching his name to anything having to do with Cuba, feeling his age, feeling the insults pile up. Walking near Times Square one day with his old friend the photographer Bernard Diederich, Matthews pointed to one of the exclusive clubs where he was a member and told Diederich, "I'm no longer welcomed there." It disturbed him to think he had become an object of pity. Gay Talese, who had started his reporting on the *Times* for the book that would become *The Kingdom and the Power,* saw Matthews's trials as a clear example of the newspaper's hypocrisy. Quick to condemn censorship whenever and wherever it took place, the newspaper had nevertheless turned its back on Matthews and refused to publish what he wrote about Cuba. Talese pictured Matthews sitting "rather quietly in Room 1048" among other editorial writers who were busy making their learned pronouncements on a world of issues, while Matthews, having been spurned by the news department several times, was left with little to do but write "anonymously for *The Times* editorial page on Latin American affairs, including those on Cuba—about which he has often been critical; other than that, he devotes himself to his books and his belief that history will finally absolve him. But at the age of sixty-six, he is not counting on a clearance during his lifetime."

After he published that account, Talese worried that he might have made Matthews's life even more difficult, and he wrote to apologize. Matthews responded by dismissing the notion that anything Talese had written could have hurt him; after more than forty-four years on staff, he felt he was as permanent a part of the newspaper as the presses themselves. He chastised Talese in the same tone he had used to upbraid Punch Sulzberger after *Encounter* had published his article on Cuba. "Your letter still shows a complete misunderstanding of my position on the paper," he told Talese. He was not being punished, he insisted, and he was not bitter, although his actions and words suggested otherwise. "In the case of the Cuban problem," he wrote, "I disagreed strongly and openly with the attitude that *The Times* has taken about it and will continue to do so, but this does not mean that either my attitude toward *The Times,* nor theirs to me, could change because of Cuba."

In early January 1967, just over six months after his final confrontation with the paper over Cuba, and one day shy of his sixty-seventh birthday, Matthews submitted his resignation. In a note to Oakes, he gave his declining health as one reason. The recurrent tuberculosis had taken its toll, and he had had to be careful about himself since his heart attack in 1949. Other illnesses and debilities all combined to slow him down considerably. What he did not say in the letter was how tired he had grown of his new role as untouchable, how much it bothered him to realize that the newspaper had shown weakness. Not weakness in its unwillingness to defend him—that he could deal with and soldier on. But he believed the paper had failed to stand up for the truth, and the historic record. He knew that no other newspaper in the United States would have put up with so much and still have kept someone like him on its staff. At the same time, he felt the paper had let down not only him but, more important, its readers. "It would have been inexcusable for *The Times* to have done anything else," he wrote. "I believe it should have done more."

But he would not dredge up any of those issues in his letter of resignation. Rather, it was as straightforward and businesslike as it would have been had he remained a secretary in the newspaper's business office where he got his start nearly forty-five years before. "This is a regretful notification that I must resign," he wrote. "If it is all right for you, I would stop work on May 1." Matthews planned to dive full time into the Castro book. And he had other books that he wanted to write, but he felt he was "no longer strong enough to do a day's work and write books on the side. I am quite tired nowadays when I finish a day at the office." The only nod to sentimentality was a brief and subtle one. "It has been a long run—six weeks short of 45 years by the time I leave—and there has to be an end to everything." He had but one request, totally in keeping with his character, which John Oakes would describe as "stubborn individualist, gloomy prophet, and dour observer." When it came time for him to end his last day as an employee of the only newspaper where he had ever worked, Matthews asked to be allowed to simply "steal silently away, by which I mean no fuss, no farewell party, no silver trays with everybody's name on it, no nothing. Let nature take its course."

Oakes asked Matthews to reconsider his resignation, assuring him that he had a place on the editorial board for as long as he wanted it. Matthews refused to change his mind. "Enuf is enuf," he would say in a handwritten note to his boss. But Oakes did manage to convince him to delay his departure until September. And he made it possible for the *Times* to fulfill Matthews's request for a low-key departure and still mark his resignation in some formal way. The editorial page carried four articles in which Matthews summed up his career. It was a tour-de-force of concise writing and potent, edgy opinion. Each piece focused on a different part of the world, ending with Latin America and, of course, Cuba. "For the United States, Fidel Castro and the Cuban Revolution brought Latin America to life after a long period of indifference and neglect," he began the last essay. "When Cuba's *Jefe Maximo* and his Government turned Communist and later almost brought on a nuclear war, somebody had to be blamed. I was." He still had not surrendered his admiration for Castro, who had "the most fantastic career of any leader in the whole course of Latin America's independent history." He bragged that his 1957 interview had indeed launched the most critical phase of that career. Then he tipped readers off to his thinking in a way he hadn't done before. Harking back to the fabulous stories in *Real Soldiers of Fortune* and the life of Richard Harding Davis, Matthews put journalists like himself in the dubious company of rebels and rogues.

"Guerrilla fighter, political agitator, journalist—something is risked, whether it be life, freedom or the respect of the Establishment and of the majority."

Then, in a final summing up of his controversial life at the *Times*, Matthews referred to himself simply as a newspaperman, the term he favored. He concluded with words that could have been his own eulogy: "A newspaperman walks with the great of many lands," he wrote, "but he must go on his own way—right to the end of the road."

But the way to that end of the road would not be tranquil, any more than any part of his life had been. When readers saw that Matthews had resigned, some refused to allow him to forget the controversies he had caused.

"Dear Sir," Murray Gladstone of Greenwich Village wrote to Matthews on the back of a four-cent postcard on August 31, 1967.

I note with satisfaction the close of your disastrous career. Quite contrary to the windy opinions of your colleagues of

the New York Times, you will be remembered for your support of the bloody Spanish Republic of 1937 to [*sic*] human-
itarian Fidel Castro in 1957, only as:

    Herbert L. Matthews

    A Fool who was Believed by Fools

Matthews saved that postcard, along with other denunciations
he had received over the years. They were, he believed, part of the
story and belonged in the historical record. They also were proof,
if any additional proof were needed, that as a newspaperman he
had done his job, and done it well.

"One of the most useful functions of a newspaperman," he
would write years later, "is to disturb the peace, to speed humanity on its endless road of conflict and contradiction, to challenge
accepted ideas and principles if they seem outworn or unsuited."

On September 30, 1967, Matthews walked through the doors of
the Times Building for the last time as an employee. With Nancie,
he headed to a rented villa on the French Riviera, where he would
work on his biography of Castro. And, for the remainder of his
life, he continued to disturb the peace.

a cordial witness

April 23, 1968
Antibes
Dear John,

   . . . there was only one reason for us staying here—the book. Otherwise, we were certainly sold a bill, and it has been one of the strangest experiences of our lives—six months of complete isolation in an uncomfortable house without a comfortable chair or bed, consistently cold or chilly weather until now, nothing to do and nowhere to go except Cannes for lunch once or twice a week. And expensive! Aside from the high rent and cost of heating, France is the costliest country in Europe to live in. We have managed because *The Times* paid a three-month salary bonus and because the auctions of our belongings were successful.

Love to you both,

HLM

Writing weekly to his older brother John, and John's wife, Jeanette, had been a touchstone of Herbert Matthews's life, and never more so than after he left the *Times* with a blend of excitement and worry—about money, about his health, and about reviving his reputation. He often told John that writing Castro's biography felt like waving a red flag in front of his critics. But he plunged ahead, convinced that he possessed a history and authority that no one else could match.

Old Antibes, on the French Riviera, was a strange place to be writing about Cuba. It was the off-season—they had arrived in November 1967, just a few weeks after he left the *Times*—and the resort had shut down for the winter. They hoped the Riviera would remind them of the enjoyable times they had in Europe in the 1930s and 1940s, despite the monstrous trouble that was brewing then. There was also a degree of snobbishness to being on the Riviera, a bit of faded glory that resembled in certain ways their own lives. Instead of being near the beach as he had hoped, the villa Matthews rented was several blocks inland, on a busy street far from everything, including the store he walked to every morning to buy a newspaper. Even in the off-season, the rates were barely sufferable, and most of the time they were left without friends, support, or access to files beyond those they had brought with them. When he needed help looking up references or quotations, he wrote John. A few years older than Herbert, John was also retired and eager to help.

Matthews may have sneered at Antibes and called it "dowdy and provincial," but its stillness and quiet provided the right conditions for him to work.

Sunday, March 17
Antibes
Dear John,
    . . . It was because of our seclusion here with nothing to do gave me the possibility of working 6 or 7 hours a day seven days a week—with Nancie nobly keeping up on the really dull chore of typing what will be nearly 500 pages. Within a week I'll send you a list of books on which I will need the names of the publishers and the year of publication of the books I cited—for a bibliography at the end.

                                                    Love to you both,
                                                    HLM

Far from his critics, and the constraining yoke of the *Times*, Matthews fell into a scholarly routine, his life finally achieving the kind of predictability that he always believed he might have had at a university. He reveled in the simplicity and reliability of his daily schedule: He went out in the morning for the newspaper and freshly baked bread, then he would work on the manuscript, writing the first draft in longhand on yellow legal pads while Nancie typed out the previous day's work. They would break for lunch at a local restaurant, their one big meal of the day and about their only extravagance. "When we go into our restaurants in Antibes or Cannes we shake hands with the proprietor, his wife, the waiter and the chef—and when we leave we go through the same performance to say good bye," Matthews wrote John. "Everyone considers himself just as good as the next man—there is no class feeling. Maybe it is the heritage of the French Revolution." They would return to work after lunch, and continue as long as they had the stamina. Nancie, battling a host of her own health issues, did not cook at all. It was Matthews who took over the kitchen to prepare their evening meal, such as it was: usually a salad, cheese and toast, and a glass of wine. After dinner they played dominoes or watched French TV until the day ended.

The biography was Matthews's first book since 1964, when he had agreed to write one on Cuba for a Macmillan young readers' series. Perhaps remembering how much he had been influenced by Harding Davis's writing when he was a child, Matthews had taken pains to portray Castro in a clear and simple light in that book. Unable to obfuscate Castro's true character with layers of explanation, Matthews had been forced to strip down his writing. Doing so, he fashioned some of his sharpest descriptions of the Cuban Revolution and revealed an admirable frankness about Castro's character. "Castro is by no means a model to be blindly admired or copied; he is not a good person by normal moral standards," he wrote. "If he has done some good, he has also done much harm. He is the most dangerous enemy that the United States has ever had in the Western Hemisphere. And to invite the Russians to install nuclear missiles in Cuba in the summer of

1962, risking the horrors of a world destroying war, was inexcusable. Yet, having said this, it is still a fact that Fidel Castro is a most extraordinary creature who believes that he is doing good. He is a very mixed up person, but he is not evil."

In the full-scale biography that Matthews was working on in 1968, he fleshed out many of the same themes, revisiting many of the most controversial moments of the first years of the revolution. As he trolled through his papers and personal archives, he stumbled across the signature that Castro had given him in the mountains. Even then, before he had written a word about Castro or his dreams of revolution, he had known there would be doubters. The scrap of paper with the elaborate autograph was supposed to overcome the complaints of the censors and the objections of the cynics, but it hadn't. That was just the beginning of the doubts about his work in Cuba, and now, more than a decade later, those doubts were haunting him still. Matthews conceded his own failure to convince his American critics that he had not deliberately tried to mislead anyone. And he knew that he had been just as unsuccessful in getting his supporters in Cuba to believe that he was neither a participant in the revolution, nor one of its supporters—merely a newspaperman reporting the truth as best he could render it. The project in Antibes was simply one more attempt to do the same thing.

By late March, with little else to do but work, Matthews had completed the manuscript, not more than six months after he retired. He and Nancie celebrated with half a bottle of champagne and sent the book off.

April 10, 1968
Antibes
Dear John,
    . . . Personally, the big news is that I received a most heartening letter from the editor of Penguin a few days ago—
"read with relish and delight, sustained interest and quality, a magnificent achievement, congratulations . . . ." Naturally I was delighted, myself, and Nancie too—one never knows

about one's own writing, at least not until it has cooled off and you can step back and look at it. . . .

Love to you both,
HLM

In 1969, *Fidel Castro* was published in the United States by Simon and Schuster. A dozen years had passed since Matthews had crouched next to Castro in the forested edge of the Sierra, but none of his passion for the rebel or his revolution had faded. Nor had the constant criticism of the previous decade dampened his enthusiasm for the Cuban story. Matthews did not compare Castro to Robin Hood in the book, but he did liken him to Oliver Cromwell and John Brown, calling Castro the type of "romantic revolutionary" who crops up in history time and again. "Fidel is one of the most extraordinary men of our times," Matthews wrote, "but he is neither saint nor devil. Take him for what he really is." On the central question of Castro's Communist history, Matthews gave no ground, insisting once again that his revolution had not been directed by Moscow, nor did it necessarily acquire a Communist tint until that was the only option left. "Fidel, as I have said, uses Communism; he finds it valuable but that is different from believing in the Communist ideology."

He expected the reviews to be scathing, and they were. Rather than an objective biography, reviewers considered the book a prolonged fan letter, or a tortured exercise in logic. *Newsweek,* no fan of Matthews, said he "resolutely tries to explain Fidel by his actions rather than his rhetoric." But the primary focus of the reviews, and the most damaging comments, were about Matthews himself. Critics felt that his infatuation with Cuba and Castro bled through every page. Matthews wasn't entirely unprepared for such criticism. After leaving Antibes, he and Nancie flew to London, and there awaited additional reviews that John forwarded to them. "Don't be afraid to send me unfavorable reviews," Matthews wrote. "There are bound to be lots of critics violently disagreeing with me and attacking the subject—Fidel and the Revolution—and by indirection the book. The one type of criticism that would upset me is if I have made any bad mistakes *of fact*. I know I made several minor ones and there must be more in a book with thousands of facts."

Not even the most negative reviews could point to any serious mistakes. Rather, it was the old battles that had to be fought all over again, and Matthews knew he was bound to lose. But what he did not suspect was a direct attack from the *Times* itself. "*Fidel Castro* is his second book on a subject that possesses him," John Leonard wrote in the *Times* review. "We have only begun to accustom ourselves to the idea that, like Niels Bohr poking among the quanta in his Copenhagen laboratory, media can alter the phenomenon they describe by the very act of looking at it. Now we must cope with a possible corollary to that notion: the phenomenon may alter (or hypnotize) the observer, however neutral he presumes himself."

By the time John sent him a copy of Leonard's review, Matthews was in Canberra, Australia, visiting his entomologist son, Eric, who now lived there. The newspaper clipping John had sent there made Matthews's first stay in Australia a nightmare and planted in his mind the idea that the reviewer "for some reason I don't know seems to have it in for me."

Monday, May 19, 1969
Embassy Hotel, Canberra
Dear John,
    . . . The clipping of *The Times* daily review arrived yesterday and it certainly was a shocker. No one else—and I've now seen about ten reviews—remotely takes such a line. The bad thing about it is his wild, really vicious, attack on me and the book. He goes to such extremes that, among knowledgeable people, he defeats his purpose, but only a handful are knowledgeable. I could pick out any number of crazy things, like that I refuse "to leave his story alone," as if the Cuban Revolution is over, Fidel isn't there and we can forget all about it. This is aside from the fact that he might have thought that perhaps I was asked to write the book. Isn't it

ironical that this one (so far) devastating review should be in my own newspaper?

> Love to you both,
> HLM

Self-confident as always, Matthews refused to give his critics an inch. He felt the Castro biography had been a literary success, if not a popular or financial one, and he retained that feeling years later when he reread it while researching a book of memoirs. "I agree that it is overly enthusiastic and pro-Castro—quite unnecessarily so in places. There are some mistakes which are inexcusable, but minor ones." He thought it would hold up in the long run better than books on Castro written by historian Theodore Draper and other authors. "I think it will be read when theirs and the others are gathering dust on the shelves, but whoever reads it will have to make allowances for my bias."

Matthews had established a workable pattern for dealing with retirement. He would establish a temporary base somewhere that was comparatively inexpensive yet alluring. There he would produce a massive handwritten manuscript while Nancie kept up with the typing. Matthews thought of his books as ways to set the historic record straight, but from the start of his career he had always hoped they would also bring in extra money. But as quickly as the money came in, it also went out. He and Nancie bounced from France to London to Rome to Australia and back, renting apartments for a few months at a time, searching for accommodations that would allow them to maintain at least a semblance of a standard of living beyond what they could afford on a meager pension and the newspaper's severance of thirty-six shares of New York Times Company stock per year for ten years after he retired. Eventually, he would have to sell the Goya prints he had bought in Spain in 1938 for $225. They were auctioned at Sotheby's in London in 1974 and brought £4,100, netting them a profit of $7,700.

Each bad book review pricked his ego and started him worrying again about money. But the negative reactions did not keep him from writing. As the years passed, Matthews kept up his ambitious pace, preparing the first drafts of his manuscripts in longhand, consistently reading a wide range of classic and contemporary literature despite recurring migraines and mounting ailments. He made two more research trips to Cuba. The first was for his 1971 memoirs, *A World in Revolution*. Reviews were brutal. It was as if Matthews had once again been hauled before the Inter-American Press Association and attacked by his enemies or—and this hurt even more—undermined by those he considered to be friends. "Always a romantic, Herbert Matthews has never been able to subordinate the partisan in him to the reporter," wrote John Chamberlain in the *National Review*. Chamberlain claimed to have special insight into Matthews's character, having worked at the *Times* when Matthews was starting out there. "The story went around in the City Room that Matthews wanted to get abroad and become a Lawrence of Arabia," Chamberlain wrote about their formative years in the late 1920s and early 1930s. Now, in 1972, Chamberlain wrote that Matthews had not changed much since those early days. "He speaks of himself as a 19th century liberal, a devotee of John Stuart Mill, but his addiction to causes and his propensity for being dazzled by men of power have frequently put blinders on him." Other reviewers took a similar approach. Matthews was particularly annoyed by the *Chicago Tribune*, which he felt had treated the book as his "war with *The Times*."

Matthews then embarked on an updated version of his book on the Spanish Civil War, *Half of Spain Died*. The *Times* ignored it, and he wrote John from Rome that total sales of the book were fewer than 1,900 copies, "which reflects no review in *The Times*—but, of course, had it been reviewed, it might have been one of the truly devastating reviews and that would have been worse than nothing." To Matthews, it seemed the newspaper had deliberately attempted to sabotage the book. And he felt it did not help that John Leonard, who had panned his Castro biography, was now editor of the *Book Review*.

In 1972, Matthews signed a contract with Charles Scribner's Sons to revisit the whole Cuba question. He received a $5,000 advance for the book, which he originally called "Sunrise in Cuba: An Essay in Understanding." The publisher, however, insisted on a title that was more pointed and less hopeful. When the book was published in 1975, it was called *Revolution in Cuba*, and the cover carried the tag line "A New Look at Castro's Cuba by America's Foremost Authority." Only on the title page did "An Essay in Understanding" survive.

To prepare for what he expected to be his last chance to set the record straight about Cuba, and about himself, Matthews took a final flight there in 1972. It was his tenth trip to the island since 1959. He anticipated finding that much of the unrealistic early promise had gone out of Castro's revolution, especially after the failure of his fanatical campaign for a 10-million-ton sugar harvest in 1970. The revolution was maturing, but into what Matthews wasn't sure. Nor did he know how he would be received there by Castro or the Cuban people. So much time had passed, and there had been so much bad blood between the United States and Cuba. As he waited for his visa to be approved, he shared some of his concerns with his brother.

April 30, 1972
Dear John,
. . . I doubt it will be possible to be optimistic any longer about the Revolution. The economic situation is awful. Fidel has made so many mistakes, and goes on making them, along with impossible promises. It is a real mess. I just hope I feel better when, or if, I can see it for myself.

Love to all,
HLM

As always, Matthews understood the importance of being an eyewitness, of seeing the truth for himself. He was seventy-two years old and frail when he arrived in Havana in blistering summer heat. Mortality weighed heavily on him. It must have been evident to those he saw, because he was treated with a level of

respect that had been absent during recent visits. This time, everyone was willing to see him, even Raúl Castro, who showed up with
his wife and their oldest child, whose birthday, Matthews noted,
was February 17, "the day of the year I saw him, Fidel, et al., in the
Sierra."

Now, in September 1972, he held a long interview with Castro
in the Presidential Palace. Both men were certain it would be
their last meeting. They sat in rocking chairs during the talk,
Castro rocking energetically at times, reaching over to make a
point by putting his hand on Matthews's knee or getting close
enough so that, if he wanted to, he could have whispered as he
had during their first meeting. They were so close that Matthews
could observe that Castro, by now forty-six, had a few gray hairs in
his famous beard. "Oh yes, a few," Castro said. As always, Matthews
made the most of his access to Castro, as well as his own participa-
tion in the important events of the revolution. "I feel that I have
lived with the Cuban Revolution since its birth to its present
robust adolescence," he wrote in the book. "Fidel, his brother
Raúl, and virtually all the revolutionary leaders do not look upon
me as an outsider. I fully realize both the handicaps and the
advantages that this relationship entails. To me, the Cuban
Revolution is not object; it is subject."

This last visit seemed to bring life back into him in a swirl, as if
he had relived all the moments of conflict and triumph from 1957
onward. He constantly compared his life before Cuba with what
happened afterward. In letters to Nancie he was joyous, declaring
Cuba to be "the friendliest spot on earth for me," and also a place
haunted by myths. As he left Havana on a flight to Mexico, he
struck up a conversation with a young Englishman he had run
into briefly at the Mexican consulate in Havana. The man, much
his junior, was taken with the romance of the Cuban Revolution,
as many still were, and he knew vaguely about Matthews's role in
its origins. But the line between history and myth is flexible, and
Matthews was astonished by one of the young man's questions: "Is
it true," he asked as they crossed the Caribbean, "that Errol Flynn
went up there with you?" Flynn had not been there for the inter-

view in the Sierra, but he had been captivated by Matthews's swashbuckling depiction of Castro and sympathized openly with the revolution. Years after the interview had been published, Flynn traveled to the Sierra to make a pseudo-documentary movie about the rebels called *Cuban Story*, and he was in Castro's camp on the night Batista fled.

The young passenger's fractured history represented a light note in what otherwise was a somber letter from Matthews to Nancie (who was too ill to accompany him to Cuba) about a significant turning point in their lives. Matthews was coming to the end of the road on Cuba. During the toughest period of criticism he had clung to the belief that history would eventually be on his side. Castro had famously declared, "History will absolve me," and Matthews felt the same way about himself. When the hysteria and maliciousness had faded away, he believed people would recognize that he had reported the twists and turns of the revolution more thoroughly, and more perceptively, than anyone else. And, in the end, he believed that history would conclude that he been right all along.

> Sept. 16, 1972
> Mexico City
> Dear Nancie,
>   . . . It is a simple fact, and not a swelled head, that I know more about the Cuban revolution than anybody else could possibly know—but who is going to believe me, or be interested? Of course, I can and will get it all into the book, and I could ask the same questions . . .

The trip ended up restoring Matthews's belief that the revolution would benefit the Cuban people. Achievements in health and education were already apparent, and despite the absence of democracy, Matthews detected promising advances in racial equality and economic justice. His serious character flaws notwithstanding, Castro had changed the course of history. Matthews confessed to Nancie that there had been days when he felt he had indeed created a monster, but what he saw on this last trip put his mind at ease.

I had my long years of anxiety, and thoughts that perhaps I had done something very harmful, and many black doubts about the Revolution. But I am convinced now that they have struggled through to something good for Cuba, and something that is at last beginning to succeed. I almost feel like a Boy Scout who, instead of doing one good deed in a day, has done one good deed in his life. All of which may prove to be one more Walter Mitty dream, to be sure, but from the way things look now, I don't think so.

Love to Priscilla,

HLM

Revolution in Cuba was published by Charles Scribner's Sons in 1975. This time, Matthews was willing to overlook the negative reviews because he felt he finally had some luck in the draw for what he considered to be the most important one. The *Times*'s *Sunday Book Review* had selected Professor Kalman H. Silvert. Silvert was one of the foremost scholars on Latin America and a political scientist who had corresponded with Matthews years earlier. Matthews was ecstatic about Silvert's review and felt it compensated for the *Times*'s slights on previous books. The review was as much about him as the book. He felt that someone finally understood what he had been trying to say, and did so in powerful terms. "It is not communism that Matthews favors," Silvert wrote. "Rather it is the activity of people he sees as essentially decent, trying to create a truly sovereign and culturally integrated society, master of its own fate."

By the following March, Matthews was complaining to John about the sluggish sales of *Revolution in Cuba*. "When my book came out in August, the heat was off Fidel, hopes of a rapprochement with the United States, recognition of his economic success and the political stability, some acknowledgment that I had, after all, been right—and now we are back where we started with Fidel, I don't doubt, again Public Enemy No. 1 and I, as his apologist, once again in the doghouse." Castro had sent some 37,000 Cuban troops to help the Popular Movement for the Liberation of

Angola (MPLA) seize control of most of the newly independent West African nation. Even Matthews had trouble understanding what Castro was trying to do. "How can Fidel treat them like children and think he can get away with it?" he wrote his brother. "For the first time I am developing serious doubts, or asking myself questions. Is Fidel, in his way, doing what Mussolini did in Abyssinia and Spain? Is he developing a touch of megalomania?"

Without realizing it, Matthews was discovering an essential truth about Castro—he was capable of constantly reinventing himself and creating myths about his persona and his beliefs. He had become a political chameleon who could bedevil both friends and enemies. Matthews had an inkling of this; after all, he had seen Castro nearly clueless in the mountains about his economic and political plans, and through the years he had reported on his inconsistent attitudes about governing. Yet Matthews was incapable of seeing that this was not just an aspect of Fidel's volcanic character: The very instability of it was the nature of Castro, it was who he was, and that would always make dealing with him unpredictable. Driven by his own ego to claim that he, and only he among American writers, knew the real Castro, Matthews was unable to acknowledge the inescapable fact that Castro was unknowable because he was always shedding one skin and growing another to suit the times. To have done so would have diminished his own importance, and Matthews had been through too much to be willing to do that.

Although the Cold War no longer raised the same level of suspicion as it had during the missile crisis, it continued to generate anxiety. Matthews realized that he was overly enthusiastic about Castro and Cuba, but he knew that critics of the revolution were far more emotional about it than he was. Each of his attempts to portray Castro as the most extraordinary leader in Latin American history was countered by a charge that Castro was a deceitful megalomaniac intent on spreading communism around the world. For many Americans, the standoff in the Caribbean was a tangible imprint of the Cold War, bringing home the delicate nature of the balance between world powers and the ease with which normal life could be turned into a nightmare. Cuba receded as an issue only when Vietnam overtook it. But then Castro would seize another opportunity to create havoc elsewhere in the world, as in Angola, or Grenada, and attention would be riveted once more on the Communist beachhead ninety miles from the United States. Then the same questions would be asked again: Who let this happen? What would be the next place to fall? And Matthews's name would pop up once more.

He and Nancie continued to try to live like well-to-do sophisticates on their declining fortunes. Each letter to John, or to his sister Rosalie, who lived in Mexico, described the worrisome state of their finances. He complained about the fitful performance of their New York Times Company stock, and the high cost of just about everything. They searched for the cheapest place to live, and that search led them to the end of the world, literally, when they decided to settle in South Australia, near their son. Eric Matthews had focused his research on a single creature, the dung beetle, and had become expert on its peculiar habits. He had been recruited to South Australia, where his expertise was warmly received. It was believed that the dung beetle could be used to reduce the number of flies, something about which Matthews was particularly sensitive; he had often said and written that the worst thing about being a war correspondent was putting up with the flies.

Matthews first visited Australia in 1969 and was not thrilled by it. But in later years, as his money dwindled and his health declined, he realized it made sense to live there. Doing so put them close to grandchildren Christopher and Leslie, but Matthews always felt he was marooned in a backwater. Although he had never been particularly close to his own children, Matthews doted on his grandchildren. And he looked forward to a future in which he would be exonerated. He understood that by writing as he had about Cuba, and Spain, and Ethiopia before that, he had presented images and information that went against what many people at the time wanted to believe, and he had caught hell for it. He felt he was doing what a reporter was supposed to do—to disturb the peace and help readers understand the world around them. The bias that he openly acknowledged did not interfere with the truth, and history would eventually see it that way.

Matthews foresaw a time, half a century or more in the future, when his role in the origins of the Cuban Revolution would be reassessed and portrayed for what it really was—the honest work of a veteran newspaperman who had witnessed great things. His words had influenced the policymakers in Washington at a time when they were clueless about what was happening ninety miles from U.S. shores. After all the hysteria had died down, and all the accusations had been shunted aside, he believed it would be clear that he had told the truth just as it had happened.

That was the reason he treasured an inscription Che Guevara wrote in one of his books, *Pasajes de la Guerra Revolucionaria:*

For H. Matthews, ideological enemy at all times and our friend since the Luminous days of the Sierra Maestra, as a cordial witness to the Understanding between men who speak different tongues.

che
Havana, November 3, 1963

Matthews included that inscription on the penultimate page of *Revolution in Cuba.* He did not object to Che's description of him as a "cordial witness." Even when he criticized Castro for taking unacceptable risks, as he had during the missile crisis, or for making costly blunders, as he had in attempting an unrealistic 10-million-ton sugar harvest in 1970, Matthews chided him gently. He always tried to balance criticism with praise that left the final balance in Castro's favor. Che understood the value of Matthews's bias from the outset, as had Castro, because both men were masters of propaganda and manipulators of image. They were far more perceptive in this regard than Matthews. They exploited Matthews's bias while he never accepted the notion that his writing had created a skewed picture of reality that, for a time, had become reality itself. In retirement, he looked back over the earliest days of the revolution and more honestly assessed his role.

But by then Castro had already come to be widely seen as a villain. So had Matthews. And that is what they both would continue to be, going their own way, right to the end of the road.

a good fight

Writing *Revolution in Cuba* had purged a great deal of the anger and frustration that Matthews carried with him to Australia. He was in his mid-seventies, with uncertain health. But his mind and will were as strong as ever. He and Nancie found a place to live in the resort community of Glenelg, close to the beach, though they rarely ventured into the water. They went practically nowhere except occasionally to dinner, when their battered budget allowed, or to visit Eric and his young family, who lived nearby. Matthews and his son had never been close, but now they forged a fragile bond. They were in fact quite similar—both were driven, focused on their work and for the most part more comfortable around books or beetles than people. Eric had little interest in journalism, which had kept his father away from his family for so many years. And to Matthews, his son's intense study of the dung beetle was an eccentricity made estimable only because it offered the possibility of relief from the plague of black flies that were one more reason for him to dislike living in Australia.

But while neither man had any great interest in the other's expertise, they found common ground in science. Even as his eyes dimmed, Matthews was aware of the great advances being made around him, particularly in the biological sciences, and he thought that unraveling the mysteries of the physical world could provide an entrée into the human soul. Under his son's influence, Matthews abandoned his lifelong enjoyment of reading whodunits and immersed himself in studying the worlds of science and religion, hoping to find a way to tie up the loose ends of his life. The two fields complemented each other the way Matthews complemented his son, and vice versa. Religion was a search for the meaning of life, whereas science explained the processes of living. Together they could make existence manageable. But Matthews approached the fields with an emotional detachment, as though he were undertaking scholarly research. He studied religion, but he did not become religious. He read scientific works that Eric recommended, but he did not put his full faith in the scientific method.

Rather, he continued to be an observer, vehement as ever about his own conclusions. He put his musings together in one final manuscript, handwritten on legal pads that he left for Nancie to type. The book was not about Castro or Cuba, though it revealed some of what Matthews had felt about the controversy. He originally planned to call it "The Education of an Editor," echoing his own 1946 book, *The Education of a Correspondent,* which he had always considered his best. But he crossed out that title and gloomily penciled in "Valediction: Random Thoughts on an Approaching End." The possibility that no publisher was likely to accept such a book did not dampen his enthusiasm for the project. He went on writing furiously in a multitude of voices, offering folksy advice on retirement and the most intellectually challenging observations about the nature of existence.

Mostly though, Matthews seemed intent on finding a way to validate his most controversial writing. He was on a crusade, as he had been since 1957, and he was intent on showing that there was no way for a writer to filter biases completely out of his writing. He believed it was a process as predictable as any in biology, and an argument as logical as any in philosophy. "Physicists tell us that the particles within an individual's body are never static," Matthews wrote in the unpublished manuscript, drawing on his study of modern science to look in the mirror. "The man who began to write this paragraph is literally, in a physical sense, a different man from the one who is now ending it. One must accept Kant's assertion that 'it is altogether beyond our powers to explain that I, the thinking subject, can be the object of perception to myself, able to distinguish myself from myself.' In unphilosophical language, one cannot get away from oneself, and I do not try to. On the contrary, this is *my* pilgrim's progress—a final lap."

This period of reading and reflection was as liberating to Matthews as a postgraduate education. He marked the date—November 11, 1975—on which he finished rereading Dante's *Divine Comedy*, using the same edition of the book that he had read for the first time as a Columbia undergraduate in 1921. The intervening fifty-four years had only intensified his satisfaction with the poet's work, from the first lines, with their clear suggestion of the course of his own life—"Midway through the path of life that men pursue I found me in a darkling wood astray"—to the last, with its ecstatic vision of God: "The love that moves the sun and the other stars." He reexamined his early embrace of stoicism as a philosophy by which to lead his life. And it was clear that he had followed the example of the Stoics, who "aimed to live virtuously, relying on themselves, without hope for escape from this wicked world, nor for a reward in the hereafter. They believed that intention was everything and achievement of little or no importance." Matthews had long considered the very model of stoicism to be Farinata degli Uberti, a character from the *Divine Comedy*. Farinata was a Florentine leader who in the poem was assigned for all eternity to the Sixth Circle of Hell, the one reserved for heretics, because he told an unpopular truth and was accused of heresy. Matthews saw himself as Farinata, whose only sin had been to be an honest messenger.

Matthews read the New English Version of the Bible from beginning to end. And to counter the dull oversimplifications he had found there, he reread the Authorized Version. He reopened Trollope, Dostoyevsky, and Jane Austen, savoring their subtleties. But he refused to pick up anything by Saul Bellow, Patrick White, Anthony Burgess, or other contemporary writers. He took to rereading the romantic poetry of his youth—Robert Burns, Byron, Shelley, Keats, Browning, and Tennyson. He conceded that he had in some ways built his life on illusions of childhood that were mistaken. He once was fascinated by the Crusades, he wrote, without realizing the cruelty of the pogroms the Crusaders unleashed in the name of religion; he once worshipped Richard the Lionhearted, but now came to think of him as a "stupid, callous swashbuckler." His forty-five years as a working newspaperman and war correspondent had convinced him that man's nature was essentially violent and there would never be an era of peace outside "the peace of a nuclear grave." He admitted that even in the moment of his darkest and most pessimistic thoughts, he found no solace in formal religion, which he had abandoned long before.

Although his family had been nominally Jewish, Matthews seems to have spent no time inside a synagogue as an adult, and his children knew almost nothing of their heritage. Nancie was Protestant, and Eric and Priscilla had been confirmed in the Anglican Church. In the 1950s, when Priscilla told her father that she was engaged to marry a Jewish man, she worried he might object. That was the first time she heard him say, "We are Jewish, too." But Matthews thought of himself as a "religious unbeliever," like Einstein. He did not have faith in God or a life after death, but he felt that ethics and morality were important and that, ultimately, it is the way one leads one's life that counts most. His experiences as a correspondent had not given him much faith in the ability of governments to act morally. But he did not deny the possibility that men could strive for a better future within the boundaries of a political system, though which system worked best wasn't exactly clear to him.

His own views on politics had remained constant. He felt most comfortable with a liberal political philosophy and had seen the world that way for most of his adult life. "I always was, and still am, a liberal," he wrote in the "Valediction" manuscript, "but everyone has to recognize the enormous historic and economic importance of Marxism in all its forms and respect the power wielded by socialist governments and leaders throughout the world." After reappraising the strengths and weaknesses of Marxism and the tremendous turmoil it had caused, he concluded that as a political system it still offered advantages for many people in the world. "Economically, capitalism works rather better but (writing as I do in mid-1977) the capitalist world with its years of high inflation, high unemployment and recurrent crises, is in no position to throw stones at the socialist world."

Although he professed to being agnostic in politics as well as in religion, Matthews had always supported liberal ideas and he accepted the possibility that communism could, if controlled, be a force for good. He said he was "never remotely tempted to become a convert to Communism," but he saw what he believed to be "genuinely democratic features in a generally authoritarian system" and concluded that for many people, communism represented an opportunity to better their conditions considerably. "It is certainly arguable that the Russian, Chinese and Cuban peoples are better off under Communism than under their previous regimes," he wrote. This was a decided shift from his earlier position on communism, during the height of the Cold War. He had publicly opposed the most doctrinaire aspects of communism, undoubtedly an attempt to counter charges that he was a sympathizer. In *The Cuban Story*, Matthews had felt compelled to give a McCarthy-era-style declaration about his views: "I never belonged to any Communist group or party. I have considered myself a liberal, and liberalism—not fascism, McCarthyism, John Birchism or what Senator Fulbright calls "Right-wing radicalism"—is the real opposite and enemy of Communism."

He never considered himself the enemy of Cuba or of Castro. The two men had traveled down similar paths since their first meeting, transformed first into heroes, then into villains. They long shared the sense of being right when everyone else is wrong.

Like Castro, Matthews was much concerned about the verdict of history, and in the last months of his life he continued to try to set the record straight. He made no startling revelations in the final manuscript; that would have been out of keeping with his vision of himself as a truthful observer who throughout his career had withheld nothing. He mentioned a few mistakes that he had never publicly recognized before. He was worried that he hadn't given sufficient attention to the possibility that Mussolini had used poison gas in Abyssinia. And he thought he might have downplayed somewhat the mischievous actions of the Spanish and Russian Communists in Spain during the civil war there. But, he said, "the important thing is not making errors but in persisting in them." Then he added a note: "also not correcting them."

Now that fifty years have passed since Matthews met Castro in the mountains, the accuracy of his reporting can be more fairly assessed. On the most important questions, the ones about Castro's communism, the implosion of the Soviet Union and the end of the Cold War suggested that Castro has always been driven by power rather than ideology. He has shown himself willing to exploit any situation in order to preserve his grasp on that power. He proved to be an even less doctrinaire Communist than Matthews had foreseen. When the Soviet Union dissolved, Castro's Cuba did not disappear. Driven by necessity, he grudgingly permitted tepid forays into free enterprise and welcomed the investment dollars of capitalists from Canada, Italy, and Spain, who built resort hotels grander and more exclusive than anything Batista had attempted. Castro even swallowed hard and, for a number of years, permitted Cubans to use the American dollars he claimed to find so vile. Cuba became an aberration, a tilted, crazy-quilt version of communism, taking no orders from any international committee.

That willingness to capitalize on events for his own gain was an aspect of Castro's character that Matthews had attempted to convey in his post-revolution articles, but his message was too complicated for a time when the world clamored for simple answers. Whereas Che Guevara's socialist ideals were fixed early on, and Raúl Castro's dalliance with the Communist Party dated back to his teen years, the ideological roots of Fidel Castro's evolution were always harder to trace. But having seized total control more easily than anticipated after Batista fled, Castro had to grow a political system to support his hold on power. There were many confounding signals along the way that neither Matthews nor any government official, university scholar, or competing journalist had predicted. "Communism was not a cause of the Cuban Revolution; it was a result," Matthews wrote in his Castro biography. "It was the presence of problems and events, not the inept, small and bungling Cuban Partido Socialista Popular, nor the cautious, diffident but generally contented Soviet Union, that brought Castroite Cuba into the communist camp."

Questions about Castro and his ideology have tortured at last count ten U.S. presidents and legions of diplomats and State Department professionals. "I doubt that historians will ever be able to agree on whether the Castro regime embraced Communism willingly or was forced into a shotgun wedding," Matthews wrote as far back as 1961 in his first book on Cuba. Castro biographies continue to be written, and the final assessment remains the same. "Castro really never became a 'Communist' at all," the American foreign affairs columnist Georgie Anne Geyer wrote in her 1991 biography. "The new thing in history that Castro did was to destroy the Communist Party and create his own Fidelista party, which he called Communist in order to stand up against the United States and gain backing and to borrow power from the Soviet Union. For the first time in history, a national leader converted the Communist party to himself." In 2003, fifty years after the attack on the Moncada barracks, Leycester Coltman, a former British ambassador to Cuba, reached essentially the same conclusion in his biography of Castro. For decades, all but the most radical works about Castro have essentially balanced his idealism and uncanny ability to survive against the ruthlessness of his dictatorship. To people everywhere in the world he is a fiery symbol of defiance, eliciting admiration from the coffee shops of Canada to the crumbling cities of Africa for standing up to the American bully. For five decades, American officials have failed to guess what Castro was going to do next, or even come to a general consensus about who he is or what he wants.

Any writer who dares to try to explain the Cuban Revolution risks a barrage of criticism. Exiles who hate Castro are sure to attack, as are the Cubans themselves and their liberal supporters in the United States. Matthews's most egregious error was not misidentifying Castro. Everyone did that. Rather, it was in persisting in his perception of Castro as an idealist long after he had transformed himself into a demagogue. Matthews was not being subversive, nor was he deliberately distorting the truth. He simply continued to report what he saw and what he honestly believed to be the truth, without taking into account the prism of his own bias. In doing so, Matthews was the forerunner of a breed of journalist that has become increasingly powerful in the early years of the twenty-first century. Bias is now a badge of honor in radio broadcasting, television news, and the slant of some newspapers. Conservative commentators on talk radio believe, as Matthews did, that bias is unavoidable, as integral to journalism as is asking questions. They believe, as he did, that it is futile to deny that bias exists. Driven by ideology, they can claim to deliver the news in a fair and balanced way because their bias is not hidden. They do not accept the notion, and neither did Matthews, that reporting can be dispassionate and biases subjugated to rigid demands of fairness.

The real danger of bias—openly professed or insufficiently policed—is the way it limits the truth. "I make only one boast in all my career of 23 years in journalism," Matthews wrote in *The Education of a Correspondent*, "I have never written anything I did not believe to be true." But much that he wrote turned out to be untrue, going back as far as his description of Fascist motives in Africa. When he and Ruby Phillips were filing contradictory reports on Cuba before and after the triumph of the revolution, neither had a lock on the historical truth. Both were blinded by their own biases without acknowledging how those limited perspectives shaped the way they reported their stories. "I have tried to serve no cause but that of the truth," Matthews wrote, "and in so far as possible—human nature being what it is—I have followed my reasoning and not my emotions to where it led, regardless of the conclusion." By the time he met Castro in the Sierra he was clearly overcome by emotion, not an uncommon reaction when interviewers come face to face with historical figures like Castro. But Matthews had not been driven by ideology when he flew to Cuba on his secret mission. He bore his skepticism about Castro's chances of success through the long round of interviews in Havana before he headed into the mountains. He did not trudge through the deep forest with the intention of building up Castro, whom he had never met and did not know. His own biases, prejudices, and personal history laid the groundwork for what happened during the three hours of the interview. But then Matthews was not sufficiently vigilant to prevent his fascination with Castro from seeping into his writing. His rigid self-confidence deluded him about the words he wrote, and the impact they had. "Many of my stories harmed a cause in which my heart lay," he wrote, "but I have no remorse and no regrets."

But Matthews did harbor resentment. He believed that he had been treated badly by closed-minded editors at the *Times* who refused to accept uncomfortable truths. And it hurt to think that some of his colleagues had gloated over his misfortunes. He thought he should have won a Pulitzer Prize, certainly for the Castro interview, or for his editorials on Cuba, or for those on Vietnam later in his career. He attributed his failure to win the award to the unwillingness of the paper to support him. For almost as long as he had worked for the *Times,* he harbored a professional paranoia and felt that certain people there were against him.

But if any editors did keep Matthews's name off the Pulitzer list, they may have done him a favor. Had Matthews won for his reporting on Cuba, there would have been a ferocious campaign in later years to strip the prize from him. The existence of the prize would itself have become a target, especially for the Cuban-American exiles in Florida and New Jersey who have continued to blame Matthews and the *Times* for helping Castro come to power. Mere mention of Matthews's name is enough to set them off, just as Walter Duranty's name is a red flag for Ukrainian nationalists. For over fifty years, they have tried to discredit the Pulitzer Prize that Duranty won in 1932 for his work in the Soviet Union.

In 2004, the *Times*, under pressure from the Ukrainians, had a Columbia professor, Mark von Hagen, an expert in Russian history, examine Duranty's work. If the editors hoped for an exoneration, they were disappointed. After reviewing the series of articles that won Duranty the Pulitzer and researching the man's deeply flawed character, von Hagen came to several conclusions, all of them quite damning. Duranty relied on inaccurate statistics but rarely warned readers they might be less than the truth. His goal was to see the United States establish formal relations with the Soviet Union, and to help that happen he emphasized Stalin's positive achievements while downplaying the often brutal manner in which they were accomplished. In the end, von Hagen determined that Duranty's prize should be rescinded. Bill Keller, the executive editor and a former correspondent in the Soviet Union, refused, saying that to take away the prize smacked of old-fashioned Soviet revisionism.

Although critics try to link Matthews with Duranty, the comparison is, at almost every level, unfair. Von Hagen concluded that Duranty had willfully tried to mislead his readers about Stalin. Matthews made mistakes but did not deliberately distort the news. Duranty's unsavory character and sordid personal life also affected his writing. Von Hagen discovered that he had a lover who worked for the Soviet secret police, and he probably maintained a close working relationship with the KGB. Nothing in Matthews's personal life suggests anything similar. Duranty lived in the Soviet Union for years. Critical reporting would have gotten him expelled; buttering up Stalin protected his special access to the Kremlin. Matthews never lived in Cuba, and he did not need to worry about pulling his punches in order to stay there. His good fortune to have been first into the Sierra guaranteed him a special place in the hearts of the revolutionaries that would have been hard to lose. But he would have lost it, had he stopped taking Castro's side, the only parallel to Duranty's situation.

Both of these controversial correspondents attempted to influence U.S. foreign policy. Seldom has the work of journalists shaped so completely the way broad social movements, and the flawed men who led them, were perceived by the majority of Americans and the U.S. government. When Matthews was writing about Cuba, there was still a lingering sentiment among foreign correspondents, especially at the *Times,* that they could play a dual role as journalists and envoys. Just as Duranty did what he could to help Washington normalize relations with Stalin, Matthews clearly felt it was in the best interest of the United States to maintain close ties with Cuba. Even when relations between the two countries soured, he urged caution. He blamed Washington for misinterpreting the radical nature of the revolution and ignoring the nationalistic feelings Castro had awakened in the Cuban people.

The lesson, of course, is that in dealing with charismatic leaders who rise up in other countries, whether close to us or distant, image can be as important as reality, or it can skew reality, as we determine who are our friends, and who are our enemies. Correspondents are always going to be used by those who seek power. And the more positive the portrayal, the more welcome they will be. But a good correspondent does not rely solely on sources for information. A good correspondent digs, confirms, challenges, and ultimately weighs information from a number of sources. It is asking the impossible to expect a correspondent to be able to see the future, to know when what is the truth at one point will no longer be the truth in the future. The only safeguard is to tell the story honestly and without bias.

But Matthews's work was defined by his bias and the open way in which he acknowledged that he was taking sides. He was not alone in believing that passion and soul can breathe life into reporting. As Vietnam eclipsed Cuba in the late 1960s, the most effective war reporting was clearly driven by biases as pronounced as Matthews's. Reporters such as Neil Sheehan and David Halberstam wrote passionately about what they believed was the wrongness of the war when the U.S. government, and some of their editors back in New York, sorely wished they would stick to the facts. But many Americans were willing to believe what they wrote. The writers with the greatest power to influence policy have always been the most passionate—Richard Harding Davis on the Spanish-American War, John Reed on the Russian Revolution, Edgar Snow on Mao's Long March, Ernest Hemingway on the Spanish Civil War, Norman Mailer on Vietnam—though not necessarily those most anchored to the truth.

The same passion that can bring a correspondent's work to life also poses dangers, and has the potential to undermine both trust and credibility. With the Cuban story, there was a national sense of outrage when the Castro that had originally appeared on the scene, with his youthful confidence and his Jeffersonian ideals, revealed his dark soul. It was seen as a betrayal of national interests, the hoodwinking of hundreds of millions of people and the governments of both Cuba and the United States, and Matthews played a central role in that drama. Arthur Hays Sulzberger's idea of creating superjournalists who were both foreign correspondents and editorial writers undoubtedly helped provide Matthews with a unique stage on which to act. But the experiment led to such regrets that the paper never attempted it again.

In the end, the hero that Matthews invented for the American public turned out to be a myth, and the story of that invention itself was transformed into myth, a malicious blame-seeking tale of naïveté, hubris, and arrogance. The heart of the myth became the interview itself, a dramatic moment of awakening perceptions filled with symbols—the forested wilderness, the doomed dictator, and above all, the image of the resurrection of the slain hero by a faithful apostle who spends the rest of his life defending his action, and his hero. Cuba still commemorates the anniversary of the interview, showing old films of Castro and Matthews on television each February. A bronze plaque with his name is prominently placed on a memorial to heroes of the revolution near the Havana waterfront. Military strategists study the interview and use it to teach the value of propaganda and a sympathetic press in psychological operations. And sometimes, the whole incident is reduced to farce. In 2001, a rock opera called *Herbert Matthews Goes to the Sierra* was produced in Seattle, with Matthews portrayed as an idealistic reporter too wrapped up in his discovery of Castro to see the truth. The Internet has intensified the Matthews myth, fed by a renewed outpouring of hatred from the exile Cuban community that has refused to forgive him for inventing Fidel, or to forgive themselves for not having carried out their plans to eliminate the correspondent they despised.

Matthews expected the fury of the exiles, and he was not surprised to find out that the FBI was spying on him. The criticism of other journalists got under his skin, but for the most part he was adept at keeping it in perspective. He was flattered by the enduring admiration of the Cuban people and the warm receptions they always extended him when he visited the island. What he had not expected, and what he always found especially difficult to accept, was the *Times*'s refusal to print his reporting from Cuba. To him, the paper had betrayed not only him but its readers. Editors held onto important information that should have been made public simply because it had come from him. The publisher and editors insisted that they trusted him, but they did not stand up for him when critics attacked his reporting.

Years after Matthews wrote his last story, some of those editors conceded that they should have done more for him. Former managing editor Turner Catledge had second thoughts about the way he had treated Matthews, and without coming up with any easy answers, left open the question of whether or not the *Times* had done right by him. He believed that Matthews was overzealous and had sacrificed some of his, and the paper's, credibility by taking sides so publicly with Castro. But he was also dogged by the notion that when the criticism from outside became too heated, the paper had abandoned one of its most loyal writers, a man who had only reported what he had seen.

"I think *The Times* demonstrated, in the Eastland episode and many others, its willingness to stand by its people if it believed they were right. But in Matthews' case, we were concerned that he, and we, had not been entirely right," Catledge wrote in his memoirs. "It was not an easy decision, or one I was fully satisfied with; in retrospect I have the haunting thought that Matthews was more sinned against than sinning."

Matthews was shocked to read Catledge's raw remarks, but he remained gracious. "I hope that he meant the *readers* would not believe my Cuban stories because of my undisguised sympathies," he wrote in 1976. "So far as *The Times* is concerned, they had to absorb a great deal of criticism for my work, and let it run longer than any other paper would have, since they trusted my ability and integrity. I think they were wrong to close the news columns to me, from the *news* point of view, but they could have been right from the angles of readership and administration. I do know that for years they missed out on unique and otherwise unobtainable news from Cuba on my trips."

Matthews argued this point right up to his last days. Even as he mused on what would happen after his death, he remained grounded in his faith in his own work. He sent John Oakes a photograph of himself taken before he retired and asked that when the time came for his obituary to be written, this photograph be used rather than a more recent, and less flattering, one taken by his son that had appeared on the flap of his last two books. He was as concerned as ever about his legacy, about what would be remembered of him after he was gone, even what image of him might be the last to appear in the *Times*. A grainy photograph of him puffing on a cigar next to Castro in 1957 had once proved that he had gotten the biggest scoop of his life. Now, in his final months, he was again worried about giving proof that he had, indeed, been where he said he had been, seen what he said he had seen, and done what he said he had done.

"Some essence, some faint and ghostly distillation from my passage through life will linger, perhaps in Spain, certainly in Cuba, or New York or Rome, or with my children and grandchildren and their children and grandchildren and so on," he wrote in the "Valediction" manuscript. By the time he was finishing work on the book, Matthews was seventy-seven and in failing health. He noted that at the end of *Education of a Correspondent,* he had reflected on old Ulysses' yearning to start over again, and wondered then if he, too, would ever have such a yearning. He was forty-five when he wrote that book and convinced his days as a correspondent were over. But, as he noted in the unpublished manuscript thirty years later, "by a freakish chance, I did 'sail on'—this time to Cuba where, on February 17, 1957, I got through the Batista lines and into the Sierra Maestra where I interviewed the then unknown young rebel, Fidel Castro. That indeed, was to start a politico-journalistic war for me which went on for many years. I was fifty-seven. It was a good fight, and I believe I won it."

That was the truth as he saw it, no more and no less, but it was not what happened. Considering the outcome, and the tattered state of his reputation—fairly earned or unjustifiably hung on him—it would be difficult for anyone else to come to the conclusion that Matthews had won this fight in any sense, except in his own mind.

Herbert Lionel Matthews died of an intracranial hemorrhage on July 30, 1977, in Adelaide. At first his family thought he had been hit by another one of the migraine headaches he had suffered throughout his life, but it turned out to be an uncontrollable bout of bleeding, and it eventually killed him. An agnostic to the end, he had his body cremated and the remains placed beneath a simple plaque near the edge of a rose bed at Centennial Park in Pasadena, South Australia. After the torrent of words by him and about him, all that is written on the small brass plaque in the cemetery is, "Herbert L. Matthews, 30th July 1977, Age 77." But even in death he stirred controversy. The Veterans of the Abraham Lincoln Brigade, often accused of Communist sympathies during the Spanish Civil War, published a paid death notice in the *Times* that unwittingly served to resurrect old accusations: "We Americans who fought in the Spanish Republican Army against the Franco rebellion can never forget his fearlessly honest coverage of the tragic three-year war. He was a great newspaperman and, for 40 years, a staunch friend." The formal obituary in the *Times* described him as being "one of the most criticized newspapermen of his time" and said the criticism had primarily been caused by the fact that "many people saw the truth in a different way." As if to prove the claim about Matthews's being controversial, a few days after the obit appeared, the paper published a letter to the editor from John Oakes. He had been ousted as editor of the editorial page just a few months earlier by Punch Sulzberger, who wanted to steer the *Times*'s editorial stance away from Oakes's liberal politics toward a more centrist line. In his published letter, Oakes objected to the *Times* obituary, and defended Matthews.

To the Editor:

If Herbert L. Matthews was one of the most controversial journalists of his era, that is only because nothing arouses more bitter controversy among a newspaper's readers than honest reporting that contradicts their emotional preconceptions.

It was Herbert Matthews' opportunity—and responsibility—to report at first hand on some of the most wrenching issues of our times, including the Italian invasion of Ethiopia, the Spanish Civil War and the Castro revolution.

And it was Herbert Matthews' distinction that throughout his career he never deviated from the truth as he perceived it, he never pandered to the popular, he never permitted either the threat of abuse or the lure of fame to move him from the highest standards of journalistic integrity.

For the last 18 of his 45 years' service on The Times, which ended with his retirement a decade ago, he was a member of the Editorial Board. His colleagues knew him as a writer of taste and sensitivity, a philosopher of courage and conviction, and a meticulous craftsman who loved the English language and used it well. He was a man of quality, an honor to the profession and to the newspaper he served so long. His death is a loss to us all.

John B. Oakes
New York, Aug. 3, 1977

"Valediction" was never published, despite Nancie Matthews's efforts to get Scribner's to take it. Matthews's daughter, Priscilla, kept the handwritten pages in a worn leather portfolio in her home in England after that, forgotten and unread. Castro, of course, has remained as controversial a figure as ever, surviving conflict after conflict, hanging on to power and the world's attention, confounding all those who await his final hour. He, however, has never forgotten those first days, and the role that myth played in helping launch his revolution. In 1995, he was in New York for five days to attend the fiftieth anniversary commemoration ceremonies of the United Nations. On his last day in the city, he visited *The New York Times,* just as he had in 1959 when the publisher agreed to welcome the famous bearded rebel and offer coffee and cigars but "*no* drinks." Many things had changed since then. Castro no longer smoked, and even if he had, not even the publisher was allowed to light up in his own office. All the editors Castro had met on that first visit to the paper were gone, and in place of the aging Arthur Hays Sulzberger there was his grandson, Arthur Ochs Sulzberger, Jr. Castro was the one constant, and as always he was ready to discuss the stormy course of his revolution and his relationship with the United States.

Strolling down a hallway lined with photographs of the newspaper's Pulitzer Prize winners, Castro coyly asked the publisher, "Where is Matthews?" He had just finished retelling the legend, now reality in his own mind, of how he had ordered his ragtag soldiers to fool Matthews by marching around him in circles. "Marching in circles" had become a symbol of Matthews's frustrated efforts to pursue his truth and his brand of journalism— intensely personal, glistening with bias, ideology, and mythmaking. Castro too was mixing myth with truth, and determining, as he always had, that myth was the more powerful. And being so, it was far more preferable than the dusty truth. Matthews's visit in 1957 had been "really very helpful," Castro said.

Five years later, after another UN ceremony and another walk down the same hallway, Castro repeated the same story.

The truth was put to the same test both days, and every day Castro lives. No one in the hallway but Castro had been there, in the Sierra, at the dawn of that new era, when the leaves of the *guaguasí* trees dripped with morning dew and there was the passion of revolution in the air.

And no one but Castro could say whether it truly had been so.

Behind the glass enclosure of Case 99 in Room 14 of Batista's old
Presidential Palace in Havana, the very place that Castro's regime
has sardonically turned into the National Museum of the
Revolution, there is a copy of the photograph of Herbert
Matthews and Fidel Castro smoking cigars together in the Sierra.
"The first months of 1957 were very important for the guerrillas,"
says the heading over the display. "Transcendental events
occurred, such as the first victorious combat at La Plata, the meeting of the national directorate of the 26th of July Movement and
the interview with the journalist of The New York Times, Herbert
Matthews." Just below the photo is a small portable typewriter, a
battered gray case with kelly green keys that is identified as the
one Matthews used during his famous interview with
Commandante Castro.

It isn't. Matthews, a meticulous note taker, never mentioned
hauling a typewriter to the interview. It would have been unwise
for him to risk being found with a typewriter when he was supposed to be on a fishing trip or inspecting farmland. Nor would
it have made sense to drag the extra weight of the typewriter

through the mud on his midnight rendezvous, sliding down embankments and forging across rivers up to his knees in cold water. He had not even brought a notebook. Instead he used a few pages of lined paper folded in three for his notes—the ones he'd had Castro sign to prove he'd been interviewed—and left the Sierra immediately after the interview ended. Eric Matthews said his father still had his trusty Olivetti with him in Australia, and the family says it has never donated another to the museum in Cuba.

This is just a small example of how even now, half a century after the interview that started it all took place, Castro is still dissembling, freely rearranging history to serve his own myth. He continues to wage the battle of ideas that he was fighting in 1957. He has created a ministry for the "Battle of Ideas" within his government and has plastered the Cuban countryside with propaganda billboards proclaiming the enduring legacy of his intellectual revolution. One bus stop on the road to Bayamo in Granma Province sets the tone for the entire campaign, proclaiming simply, "Our ideas are our strength."

Matthews remains an enduring part of the Castro myth. And in Cuba, he is still a hero. Besides being enshrined in the museum, Matthews is honored in the old hotel Sevilla where he stayed before heading into the Sierra. There is a framed photograph of him in the lobby, alongside the famous actors and politicians who were guests there in the past. Most Cubans who lived through the revolution know his name, and many born after 1959 are taught that while *The New York Times* is today just another tool of the *Yanqui* imperialists controlled by the Miami mafia, Herbert Matthews told the truth about Cuba from the very moment he and Fidel crouched beneath the *guaguasí* trees on the farm of Epifanio Díaz on that cold morning long ago.

After studying what happened during that interview for a long time, I understood that Castro had carefully planned to mislead Matthews. But I also knew that Matthews was not just a conduit for information. He had prepared himself well for the interview, checking with sources in government and in the opposition, and he had expressed a great deal of skepticism about Castro in the editorials he wrote before meeting him. He did not try to assess Castro's character from the comfort of his New York office, but rather he ventured into the Sierra, at great danger and obvious discomfort, to see for himself. It was a textbook example of journalistic due diligence, and it was not easy.

I know it was not easy because to understand more clearly what Matthews went through to get the interview with Castro I undertook a similar journey, relying as he did on local guides who know the mountains well. It was the summer of 2005 and like Matthews, I traveled in a four-wheel-drive vehicle over dirt roads and across shallow rivers into the Sierra, to the farm that was still owned by the family of Epifanio Díaz, just one of what turned out to be many constants in that region. One of Epifanio's Díaz's descendants, a lean, taciturn sixteen-year-old son of the revolution who I will call Ramiro, although that is not his real name, said he knew where the interview took place. When I told him I wanted to go there, he looked puzzled. But he agreed to take me.

Ramiro borrowed a pair of rubber boots and a machete, and he and I set out into the same densely forested foothills that Matthews trudged through fifty years ago. We passed three thatched-roof huts with dirt floors that seemed not to have changed at all in the half century that has elapsed since the interview. Scrawny dogs barked as we hiked past. There are no roads, no electricity, no telephones, and no running water. Sturdy oxen tethered to wooden yokes and plow blades made of trees are still used to plow small fields of corn, beans, and yucca when there is some flat ground. But mostly it is an endless stretch of lanky trees—*guaguasí*, mahogany, *almasigo*—and prickly scrub.

Ramiro led the way, his dark shirtless back covered in sweat. For more than an hour he hacked at the dense undergrowth. At the edge of a ravine he slipped down fifty feet to the Río Tío Lucas, which we had to cross several times. Then, finally, nearly two hours after we left the hut where he lived with his family, when I was seriously considering turning back because he did not seem to know where we were going, and I was not sure I would feel confident that the place he brought me to was the right one, he scampered back up the ravine. "It's here," he shouted triumphantly.

On flat ground at the top of the ravine, deep in the dappled shadow of the *guaguasí* and *almasigo* trees, I was greatly surprised to see a three-foot-high marker made of the porous marble that is quarried in the area. In all the reading and research I had done, all the interviews with Cubans and Americans, with people who worked with Matthews and with his family, I had never seen or heard a mention of any monument. "In this place, Commander in chief Fidel Castro Ruz met with the North American journalist Herbert Matthews on February 17, 1957." The marker stone had been erected in 1997, the fortieth anniversary of the interview. But because it is so remote, visitors obviously have been few. Ramiro was first brought there by his schoolteacher, as part of a history lesson. Others might have called that visit his indoctrination into the battle of ideas.

Matthews is still honored in Cuba for telling the truth, and condemned in the United States for distorting it. Even in the Sierra, at what could be considered ground zero of Castro's revolution, only the calendar year seems to have changed. The hut where Ramiro's family lived consisted of two large rooms. The floor was dirt, packed hard and smooth. There were a few rustic *taburete* chairs, handmade of wood and goatskin. A baby doll wrapped in plastic hung on the wooden walls, the only crude attempt at decoration in the hut. Rain dripped steadily through the thatched roof. When it was dark outside, it was dark inside. There was no electricity. The Camilo Cienfuegos school, about five miles away, represented one recent improvement. But it hadn't opened up many opportunities for Ramiro or provided his family with the kind of new society that Castro promised.

The sheer desperation of the scene stunned me. All the rancor and bloodshed of half a century, for this? How could so little have changed, when so much has changed?

* * *

Even today there are plenty of people who would place the blame for these distressing circumstances on Herbert Matthews. But I need to set something straight, even if doing so reopens old wounds and reignites a bitter war of words. Herbert Matthews and the *Times* did not bring communism to Cuba. The sensational articles that he wrote after sneaking in to see Castro are some of the most provocative news stories ever written—half a century later they are still celebrated in Cuba and damned in Miami and New York and any other city where Cubans of a certain age gather over small cups of sweet coffee—but they were not the reason Castro triumphed.

In the end, Castro was Castro, and being Castro, he possessed such an uncanny ability to survive that he would have managed to stay alive long enough to seize power whether or not Matthews had arrived at the moment when he and his revolution were utterly prostrate. Castro could have triumphed without Matthews, but then history would have been different. What Matthews did was invent the image of Fidel Castro that at first captivated and then infuriated most Americans. It sometimes seems that Castro could only have been invented, that he was not a man but a baffling series of illusions conjured in the Caribbean heat. Before Matthews showed up, Castro was a man, a rebel, a hero. What Matthews did was invent Fidel as an idea, a conception that could remain elusive, always changing, unknowable, unfathomable, and therefore, in the end, undefeatable.

Like any invention, this image making was the work of many men, though just one claimed credit. Matthews played a central role with his articles and editorials, and when it was time for someone to be blamed for the mess in Cuba, he was a convenient target. But many others had a hand in it—the U.S. diplomats in Havana who famously misread the anti-Batista opposition, those in Washington who did not know enough about U.S.-Cuba relations to understand that history ensured that any revolution in Cuba would by its very nature be anti-*Yanqui*, the other news organizations that first embraced Castro, then allowed their antipathy toward him to slant their coverage. No journalist can truly be without personal bias. But a news professional learns how to keep that bias caged so it stays out of the news.

I am convinced that Matthews did not set out to present a distorted picture of Castro. Castro's was a revolution of images and myths. His whole life is now more than reality—it is a myth built on a foundation stone that Matthews laid. For Matthews, Castro was the perfect "solider of fortune," a hero created by ideas, whose most powerful weapon was his mind. I do not think Matthews got the story wrong at the beginning. Over five decades of watching Castro, the world has learned what kind of chameleon he truly is—unpredictable, vengeful, irrational at times but always focused on his primary goal of holding onto his power. The political system that exists in Cuba today bears only a faint resemblance to the Soviet-style communism he imposed in the early 1960s. The beautiful resorts that now shimmy up the powdery beaches of Varadero and the swank hotels in Havana and Santiago are off limits to ordinary Cubans make a mockery of his professed allegiance to an egalitarian socialism. A dual economic system, one with convertible currency and plenty to buy for tourists, and another with practically worthless coins and almost nothing on the shelves for his own people, reveals how corrupted his ideals of equality have become. Dissidents say that Castro acts as though he hates the Cuban people. At Epifanio Díaz's farm, the ordinary Cubans I met and spoke to are optimistic that their conditions will improve because, they say, Castro cannot live much longer.

Most of the classic characteristics of communism have been distorted in Cuba or they have disappeared, except for one. The system controls what people think and what they say. The wrong words can still have disastrous consequences—people are passed over for housing if they are not considered sufficiently patriotic. Dissidents still disappear. Prisons remain full of people convicted of anti-revolutionary activities, like possessing carbon paper, or writing sentences like the ones you just read.

So it is no wonder that at Epifanio Díaz's farm, in the foothills of the Sierra Maestra, where Castro got his legendary start, those who are old enough to understand are reluctant to express themselves until they are certain that there is no danger. Ramiro had not yet reached that point, but for the others, it was my willingness to march into the Sierra behind Ramiro, and my gringo accent, that eventually lifted their suspicions. By the time we had returned to the house where his family waited for him, they were willing to let me know how they felt about Matthews and the revolution.

"Yes, we remember Matthews, and what it was like at the time," said a sixty-five-year-old man whose nearly translucent blue eyes were luminous in the gloom of the leaky hut. He said he had helped the young rebels in 1957 by bringing them blankets and supplies while they tried to elude Batista's men. He watched Castro's forces grow stronger and more numerous. He cheered when he heard that Batista had fled and that the *barbudos* had seized control of Havana.

But now, like many other Cubans who are brave enough or frustrated enough to admit it, he is bitter. "We have nothing," he said, "and what little we can grow we have to watch before someone steals it. We expected more, much more, and we are so very disappointed. I think that when all this is over, we will be able to be friends again," the old man said. He meant Cubans like him and Americans like me. That's the way it used to be, he said, before all this. That's the way it should be again. And it will happen, of that he was sure. He is waiting for the day that the advance obituary I wrote of Castro can be published in *The New York Times*, signifying that the final chapter in the story that began not far from where he stood will finally be underway.

What happens then will be another Cuban story.

ACKNOWLEDGMENTS

In the spring of 2001, Chuck Strum, a friend who was then the editor of the obituaries desk at *The New York Times*, asked me to take on the job of writing the advance obituary of Fidel Castro. I was then the Americas business correspondent for the *Times*, covering North, South, and Central America. I had previously been bureau chief in both Mexico and Canada, which gave me the chance to fly to Cuba several times and write about what was going on there. The obituary was a long-term project—Castro then was seventy-five and in no immediate danger of dying—but Chuck, who now is an associate managing editor at the *Times*, knew I would want to be the one to announce to the world that Castro was dead. That project led directly to this book.

Another seminal event that contributed to the origin of this book goes back even further. While I was working in Mexico, I got to know many terrific journalists. One of the very best is Dudley Althaus, of the *Houston Chronicle*, a hardworking foreign correspondent and a knight of a guy. During one of our many nights together over tequilas and war stories, Dudley mentioned that he had written his master's thesis at the University of Texas on the

Spanish Civil War correspondence of Herbert Matthews, noting the tremendous criticism Matthews had come under from Catholics in the United States and his own editors at the *Times* for what he wrote. He also mentioned that Matthews was a packrat who had saved nearly every scrap of paper he had ever read or written anything on, mostly to leave a permanent record of what he believed was the rightness of his work. As I began to look more deeply into Matthews's life, Dudley was the first person I contacted, and he provided invaluable help, from beginning to end, when he read through part of the manuscript and made important criticisms and suggestions.

Being a *Times* correspondent myself helped me understand some of what Matthews had gone through. I was pleased to find the paper record of his dealings with editors, publishers, and colleagues preserved in the *Times*'s formidable archives, now stored in the old subbasement printing rooms at Times Square. My indefatigable guide there in the caverns of *Times* history, Lora Korbut, diligently answered my questions and pulled the files I needed. After a while, she knew so much about Matthews and Ruby Phillips that she was suggesting files I hadn't thought of looking into, all of them producing valuable insights into Matthews's struggles with his editors, and with the truth.

And I need to acknowledge, as always, *The New York Times* itself for providing so many opportunities, and especially Bill Keller, executive editor, who winced when he heard that I was writing about Matthews and the *Times* after so many unflattering books about the newspaper were being published but encouraged me anyway. Other *Times* colleagues also lent a hand. Susan Edgerley, Metro editor, made it possible for me to do some of the research I needed. Julia Preston, Sam Dillon, and Sam Roberts, authors of their own important and notable books, both agreed to take time to read through parts of my manuscript. So did Tim Padgett, *Time* magazine's knowledgeable Latin America correspondent, a thoughtful critic of contemporary journalism, and a treasured friend. The few *Times* veterans still around who knew Matthews or had worked with him generously offered their reminiscences and thoughts. In particular, Arthur Gelb, Max Frankel, and Mike Leahy shared their insights, and I appreciate the help.

Another serendipitous step came in 2003 when the University of Notre Dame and the Helen Kellogg Institute for International Studies generously provided a research fellowship at the South Bend campus that gave me the chance to shape my growing interest in the way news shapes foreign policy into a book. The institute provided not only space to work and the time to do it but a sublime atmosphere of inquiry and collegiality that fired my imagination. I especially want to thank Scott Mainwaring and Christopher Welna for providing a fantastic opportunity to research the early history of the Cuban Revolution and gave me a platform for testing some of my ideas against an extraordinary set of scholars, including the Reverend Bob Pelton, Marifeli Perez-Stable, and Richard Snyder.

Stuart Krischevsky, my agent, helped shape the project from the beginning and stood by patiently as I insisted on pursuing a particular vision of it. The extraordinary people at PublicAffairs—especially Peter Osnos and my confidante and editor, Lisa Kaufman—were willing to stir up the old controversies about Matthews in a new book. I would like to thank the Butler Library at Columbia University and the conscientious and efficient staff in the Rare Book and Manuscript Library, who helped me through the mountain of material in the Herbert L. Matthews Collection. I especially want to thank Bernie Crystal, who before he retired was willing to poke through material that had not yet been sorted in search of a particular item I suspected was there.

As in other projects I've worked on, I made extensive use of that most incredible resource, the New York Public Library main research branch in Manhattan. It remains a singular marvel of the city, an endlessly giving institution and unbounded source of inspiration.

Although my research primarily focused on Herbert Matthews's life in the United States, I am grateful for the help I received from some generous Cubans, including Mario Llerena, Dr. Humberto Lezcano Ortiz, Juan Vega, and Bernardo Toscano of the

Permanent Mission of Cuba to the United Nations. In Cuba itself, where the *"batalla de ideas"* is still raging, I received no help at all from the Castro regime, despite my repeated requests and their repeated assurances that assistance would be forthcoming. But many Cubans outside of government aided me. I fear that including their full names here could lead to them being punished by the regime for telling the truth. But besides Ramiro there are Alexi, Mayté, Omar, Raidel, and Yamela. They all know how much I appreciated their assistance, even if they will have to wait for the regime to change before they can see this book. And parts of my Cuba research could not have been completed without the faithful assistance of Gladys Boladeras in the Mexico City bureau of the *Times*.

The far-flung family of Herbert Matthews was especially helpful as I continued to ask for material. Dr. Eric Matthews in Australia provided photos, invaluable letters, and memories that filled out my understanding of his father. His sister in England, Priscilla Mills, patiently answered my questions and provided an unexpected opportunity when, in a handwritten letter, she offhandedly mentioned that she had an unpublished manuscript left behind by her father. Also quite interested and eager to help were Jim Michaels and Jim Michaels, Jr., Matthews's relatives and both distinguished journalists themselves, who provided important information and three portfolios of letters that revealed some of Matthews's turmoil. John L. Matthews, Jr., generously gave of his time at the very beginning of my project and provided important direction. Ruby Phillips's daughter, Marta Dean Phillips, could not lead me to any documents because her mother had not left any, but she confirmed important aspects of her mother's professional relationship with Matthews.

Many others helped along the way: Bernard Deiderich, Tim Golden, Professor Ronald Hilton, Don Hewitt, Professor Jerry Knudson, Boris Kozolchyk, Louis Nevaer, Professor Lisandro Perez, Dr. Robert Pastor, Bobby Posada, Henry Raymont, Alan Riding, the American Assembly, the John F. Kennedy Library and Museum, and the Museum of Television and Radio.

Finally, as always, I must thank my family for sacrificing so much to support me while I was spending so much time on this book. My wife, Miriam, was my window into a Cuba that no longer exists, and she never tired of my questions about what it was like for a young girl to live through a revolution. I suppose I would have to thank Fulgencio Batista, Fidel Castro, and Herbert Matthews for providing the circumstances that brought her to New York in 1961 and set in motion the long sequence of events that led to our life together. If not for them, and the revolution that they all played their role in, she might have remained in Guanabacoa, across the harbor from Havana, and we might only have passed each other in the street one warm sunny day, she an emerald-eyed Cuban *dama*, and I just one more curious American tourist wondering what kind of a place Cuba really was.

And I would like to dedicate this book to the memory of my dear mother, Phyllis DePalma, who passed away before I had a chance to finish writing it. She was my earliest inspiration, my first teacher, my life's guide, and though I miss her terribly, I can still feel her gentle hand on my shoulder, and can hear her sweet voice whispering encouragement in my ear.

Introduction

The scrap of paper bearing Fidel Castro's signature is preserved in the Herbert L. Matthews Collection (Box 1, Folder 13) at the Rare Book and Manuscript Library of the Butler Library at Columbia University, along with the seven pages of lined paper that Matthews used as notes during the Sierra interview. In a memo to curator Wade Doares dated April 3, 1968, just after he finished the manuscript of *Fidel Castro*, in Antibes, Matthews describes the history of the lost signature and explains how he found it "recently" among photographs of Cuba.

Chapter 1: Could Anything Be Madder?

The landing of the *Granma* is now such a creation myth in Cuba that descriptions of it are found in many sources. Among those I used to recreate this scene are: *Episodes of the Cuban Revolutionary War, 1956–1958*, by Ernesto Che Guevara; *Diary of the Cuban Revolution*, by Carlos Franqui; *Fidel: A Critical Biography*, by Tad Szulc; *The Cuban Dilemma*, by R. Hart Phillips (Ruby Phillips's pen name). The *Granma* itself is now encased in a protective glass shed and sits in a heavily guarded public park behind the old presidential palace. The word *Granma* is now the name of the official Cuban government newspaper, which has published many of the personal histories of the survivors of the landing. It is also now the name of the province in southeastern Cuba where the landing took place. Matthews's mocking description of the invasion is one sign that he went to Cuba in 1957 with no preconceived notions about Castro or the revolution. Another is found in his book *Revolution in Cuba*, in which Matthews wrote that in January 1957, "I knew nothing about Fidel."

Chapter 2: Message from the Mountains

Cuban history, especially of the Batista era, is covered in great detail in *Cuba: The Pursuit of Freedom*, by Hugh Thomas; *The Cuban Revolution: Origins, Course and Legacy*, by Marifeli Pérez-Stable; and in several books written by Batista himself, including *Cuba Betrayed* and *The Growth and Decline of the Cuban Republic*. The memos written by Ruby Phillips to her editors in New York are preserved in various folders of the archives of the *New York Times* under her name or the name of the editor to whom the memo was sent. The narrow building at 106 Refugio in Old Havana that was Phillips's office for many years still stands and has been painted green. It is now a residence, and no one who lived in the neighborhood in 2005 could recall the *Times* being housed there. The building's facade is marked by four holes that appear to have once held a sign identifying it as the newspaper's office. Felipe Pazos's account of meeting with Phillips and Matthews appears in a long memo he wrote in 1960 recalling the events (now held in the Matthews Collection at Columbia, Box 1).

Chapter 3: Real Soldiers of Fortune

The National Personnel Records Center, Military Personnel Records Division, in St. Louis, Missouri, indicates that Matthews's military service was brief, beginning August 16, 1918, and ending May 16, 1919. He was discharged at Ft. Mead, Maryland, with the rank of private and was given a World War I Victory Medal. The copy of Richard Harding Davis's *Real Soldiers of Fortune* (P. F. Collier and Son, 1906 edition) that was given to him by his mother in 1909 is held at the Columbia University library in a box of material that has not yet been cataloged. The inscription "To Herbert Matthews From Mother" is written in pencil on the first page. The book is otherwise unmarked. The New York Public Library has computerized census records available that include the original handwritten forms from the 1910 census showing that Samuel Matthews was employed in the "blouses and suits" business and that his father, like Frances Matthews's father, had been born in "Poland Russia." Priscilla

Matthews provided the details about her father's reaction to the death of Frances. Matthews's 1926 letter to the publisher is held in Arthur Hays Sulzberger's files at *The New York Times* archives. Martha Gellhorn's relationship with Matthews in Spain is outlined in *Gellhorn: A Twentieth-Century Life*, by Caroline Moorehead.

Chapter 4: Dawn in the Sierra

The seventeen pages of typewritten notes that Matthews prepared while in Havana are contained in the Matthews Collection at Columbia (Box 2). Nancie Matthews wrote her recollections of the trip to the Sierra for an article in *Times Talk*, March 1957. Matthews's original handwritten notes from February 17, 1957, are also in the collection (Box 1). A copy of Matthews's answers to ten detailed questions on the interview asked by Guido García Inclan of *Bohemia*, dated March 13, 1957, is in Box 2 of the collection. And in 1976, Matthews sent Professor Jerry Knudson of Temple University a series of letters responding in detail to questions about the interview. They are contained in Box 36.

Chapter 5: Impenetrable Fastnesses

Contemporary accounts of the conditions at Castro's camp on the day of the interview, and the actions of Castro's men during the three hours Matthews was there, are in *The Twelve*, by Carlos Franqui, as well as in Franqui's *Diary of the Cuban Revolution* and Che's *Episodes*. Hugh Thomas devotes a chapter of his monumental *Cuba: The Pursuit of Freedom* to the interview and writes that it "immediately made of Castro an international figure." For another assessment of its impact, see William Ratliff's *The Selling of Fidel Castro: The Media and the Cuban Revolution*, in which he says, "Seldom has a single writer so influentially set the tone—at least as perceived by a broad cross-section of its interested readership—toward a person, movement or historical phenomenon." The retouched photograph of Matthews and Castro together is in the Columbia Library collection. The figures of the two men have been outlined in black ink to add clarity. Otherwise, the photo appears fuzzy but unaltered.

Chapter 6: A Chapter in a Fantastic Novel

Details of the meeting between Pazos and Llerena are contained in *The Unsuspected Revolution: The Birth and Rise of Castroism*, by Mario Llerena, and were confirmed and supplemented by an interview with him at his tiny apartment in Miami on April 25, 2005. A copy of the teletype message from Santiago Verdeja is in the archives at the *Times*. Franqui's recollections of the immediate aftermath of the Matthews interview are in his *Diary of the Cuban Revolution*. Matthews preserved the congratulatory notes and letters he received after publication of his series, and they are now in the Columbia Library collection.

Chapter 7: The Best Friend of the Cuban People

Che's account of the "most painful days of the war" is contained in his *Episodes* and in Franqui's *Diary*. The "Fast Delivery" truck used by the student radicals remains on display in the park behind the Presidential Palace, bullet holes still piercing its steel sides. Inside the palace, bullet holes in the marble staircase leading to the second floor have never been repaired, and a plaque outside the president's office commemorates the farthest advance of the would-be assassins. The Museum of Television and Radio made available the program "Rebels of the Sierra Madre: The Story of Cuba's Jungle Fighters," along with uncut outtakes from it. Don Hewitt, who is identified in the credits as editor, recalled that he merely supervised Taber, who controlled the project and did most of the editing. Hewitt called him "a strange bird." All that Hewitt knew about Castro at that time was that he was "a guy in the mountains devoted to revolution." The program, sponsored by Prudential, ran on a Sunday night, May 19, 1957, in place of the popular program *You Are There*.

Chapter 8: Decisive Battles

Matthews declared himself to be the man who invented Fidel in a memo to Orvil E. Dryfoos, January 22, 1958, that is now contained in *The New York Times* archives (Matthews biography, Folder 3, dated 1958–1960) and in Box 2 at Columbia. Matthews referred to himself that way in several other documents through the years, using the phrase with a blend of irony and pride. Homer Bigart's personality is depicted in William Prochnau's *Once Upon a Distant War*, though a careful reading of his reports from Cuba shows how mistaken even this great reporter was about Castro. Ruby Phillips outlines some of the disagreements she had with Matthews leading up to Castro's victory in her book *Cuba: Island of Paradox* (written under the name R. Hart Phillips). Castro's "Mi Querido Amigo" letter to Matthews is in the Columbia Library collection (Box 1). The memo that C. Allan Stewart, deputy director of the Office of Middle

American Affairs, wrote to his boss at the State Department is contained in *Foreign Relations of the United States: 1958–1960. Volume VI, Cuba,* as is the gloomy forecast by Ambassador Earl E. T. Smith about the impact of the arms embargo.

Chapter 9: You Can Fool Some of the People

The editors' meeting at "21" is described in Turner Catledge's *My Life and The Times.* The talking points notes are contained in Box 2 of the Matthews Collection at Columbia, but they do not indicate where the talk was given in January 1959. Ruby Phillips's background comes from her personal file at the *Times* and from *Cuba: Island of Paradox.* Several conversations with her daughter, Marta Dean Phillips, who lives in Florida, also added to the portrait. Nicholas O. Berry referred to Phillips as "he" in his *Foreign Policy and the Press: An Analysis of* The New York Times' *Coverage of Foreign Policy* in 1990 (p. 11). Max Frankel's comments on Castro and Matthews come from his *The Times of My Life and My Life with* The Times, and from an exchange of e-mail messages in January 2003.

Chapter 10: All Out of Step but One

Matthews's "Horatio" comment comes from *The Cuban Story,* p. 284. The FBI responded to my Freedom of Information request with a boxload of documents from its file on Herbert Matthews, beginning on March 24, 1957, and continuing through to his retirement in 1967. The files include tips from sources inside the United States and in Cuba, Matthews's Reserve Index file, the alleged "bribe" of Batista, and the death threat against Matthews by Cuban exiles. The exchange of letters with James Reston is contained in the Columbia files. President Kennedy's appointment book, now held at the Kennedy Library and Museum, shows a late afternoon off-the-record meeting between the president and Herbert Matthews on July 3, 1962. Matthews's own notes on the meeting are in Box 27 at Columbia. Although the CIA's response to a Freedom of Information request was slim, the six documents the agency provided show that he was being spied on by his own office in Mexico City.

Chapter 11: Dark Days

Theodore Draper and Herbert Matthews engaged in a running feud over Castro and Cuba that was played out in the pages of academic publications. But on Castro's 1961 speech they were in rare agreement. See Draper's *Castro's Revolution: Myths and Realities*, and especially the exchange of letters with Matthews in the appendix. Castro's recollections of the development of his revolutionary ideas are outlined in *Fidel: My Early Years*, edited by Deborah Shnookal and Pedro Álvarez Tabío, director of the Office of Historic Affairs in the Cuban Council of State. The joke about Castro getting his job through *The New York Times* is often remembered as a cartoon, but William F. Buckley, Jr., used that phrase as the title of an article he wrote for *American Legion* magazine in March 1961. The Hemingway quotes are contained in letters that have been in the possession of Eric Matthews and are used with his permission. In a brief exchange of e-mail messages, Professor Ronald Hilton confirmed some aspects of his relationship with Matthews and vehemently rejected the notion that Matthews had in any way contributed to Castro's rise to power. Matthews's City College addresses are contained in Box 2 of the Columbia archives. "Punch" Sulzberger's memos concerning Matthews are in the *Times*'s archives.

Chapter 12: Naming Names

The bizarre story of Harvey Matusow is related in Catledge's *My Life and The Times*, and in *The Trust: The Private and Powerful Family Behind The New York Times*, by Susan E. Tifft and Alex S. Jones. When Matusow died in 2002, his obituary in the *Times* described him as "a paid informer who named more than 200 people as Communists or Communist sympathizers in the early 1950s, only to recant and say he lied in almost every instance" (February 4, 2002, p. 7). The background of the decision leading to the powerful editorial written by Charles Merz is given in *The Trust*. The testimonies given before the various Senate subcommittees are available through the U.S. Government Printing office.

Chapter 13: Faithful Adherence

Matthews preserved the details of his meeting with McGeorge Bundy (April 24, 1964) in typewritten notes that are now in Box 32 of the Columbia Library collection. William Randolph Hearst's June 21, 1965, letter to J. Edgar Hoover about Matthews and other journalists' being Communists is referred to in a heavily censored document produced by the FBI in response to my Freedom of Information request. The editorial from Cuba killed by Punch Sulzberger is at Columbia (Box 32). Matthews's note to John B. Oakes about the Castro biography is held in the John B. Oakes Collection at Columbia, part of which is not yet cataloged. Matthews's letter of resignation to his boss is also in the unboxed part of the Oakes Collection. Mr. Gladstone's acerbic postcard to Matthews is a priceless part of the Columbia collection (Box 19).

Chapter 14: A Cordial Witness

Jim Michaels, Jr., a *USA Today* foreign correspondent who is part of Herbert Matthews's extended family, provided three portfolios brimming with hundreds of letters from Matthews to his brother, John. Though voluminous, that batch of letters represents just a portion of the correspondence between the two men.

Chapter 15: A Good Fight

Priscilla Mills kept the untyped manuscript for her father's last, unpublished book at her home in London. Her recollections of her father, especially his declaration of their Jewish heritage, were given in an interview in New York on January 7, 2005. Professor Mark von Hagen's comments came from his written report to the *Times* and from an interview in New York on June 23, 2004.

Epilogue

Observations from Cuba are current as of August 2005. Some things might have changed since then. Much will be the same.

BIBLIOGRAPHY

Aparicio Laurencio, Angel. *Es Historia el Libro Que Hugh Thomas Escribio Sobre Cuba?* Madrid: Editorial Catoblepas, 1985.

Arnett, Peter. *Live from the Battlefield: From Vietnam to Baghdad, 35 Years in the World's War Zones.* New York: Touchstone Books/Simon and Schuster, 1994.

Baker, Carlos. *Ernest Hemingway: A Life Story.* New York: Charles Scribner's Sons, 1969.

Batista, Fulgencio. *Cuba Betrayed.* New York: Vantage Press, 1962.

———. *The Growth and Decline of the Cuban Republic.* New York: Devin-Adair Co., 1964.

———. *Paradojismo: Cuba, Victoria de las Contradiciones Internacionales.* Mexico: Ediciones Botas, 1964.

Berry, Nicholas O. *Foreign Policy and the Press: An Analysis of* The New York Times' *Coverage of U.S. Foreign Policy.* New York: Greenwood Press, 1990.

Betto, Frei. *Fidel and Religion: Castro Talks on Revolution and Religion with Frei Betto.* New York: Simon and Schuster, 1987.

Bonsal, Philip W. *Cuba, Castro, and the United States.* Pittsburgh: University of Pittsburgh Press, 1971.

Cabrís, José D. *Batista: Pensamiento y Accion.* Habana: Presna Indoamericana, 1944.

Catledge, Turner. *My Life and* The Times. New York: Harper and Row, 1971.

Desnoes, Edmundo. *La Sierra y el Llano*. Habana: Casa de Las Americas, 1969.

Dubois, Jules. *Fidel Castro: Rebel-Liberator or Dictator?* Indianapolis: New Bobbs-Merrill Co., 1959.

———. *Freedom Is My Beat*. Indianapolis: New Bobbs-Merrill Co., 1959.

———. *Operation America: The Communist Conspiracy in Latin America*. New York: Walden and Co., 1963.

Duranty, Walter. *Babies Without Tails*. New York: Modern Age Books, 1937.

———. *I Write as I Please*. New York: Simon and Schuster, 1935.

Falcoff, Mark. *The Cuban Revolution and the United States: A History in Documents, 1968–1960*. Vienna: U.S. Cuba Institute Press, 2001.

Frankel, Max. *The Times of My Life and My Life with* The Times. New York: Random House, 1999.

Franqui, Carlos. *Diary of the Cuban Revolution*. New York: Viking Press, 1980 edition.

———. *Family Portrait with Fidel*. New York: Random House, 1984.

———. *The Twelve*. New York: Lyle Stuart, 1968.

Fulbright, J. William. *The Arrogance of Power*. New York: Random House, 1966.

Fursenko, Aleksandr, and Timothy Naftali. *One Hell of a Gamble: Khrushchev, Castro, and Kennedy*. New York: W. W. Norton and Co., 1997.

Geyer, Georgie Anne. *Guerrilla Prince: The Untold Story of Fidel Castro*. Kansas City: Andrews and McMeel, 1993 edition.

Glennon, John P., ed. *Foreign Relations of the United States, 1958–1960. Volume VI. Cuba*. Washington, D.C.: United States Government Printing Office, 1991.

Guevara, Ernesto Che. *Episodes of the Cuban Revolutionary War, 1956–1958*. New York: Pathfinder, 1996.

Harding Davis, Richard. *Notes of a War Correspondent*. New York: Charles Scribner's Sons, 1911 edition.

———. *Real Soldiers of Fortune*. New York: Charles Scribner's Sons, 1914 edition.

———. *Soldiers of Fortune*. New York: Charles Scribner's Sons, 1906 edition.

Knudson, Jerry W. "Herbert L. Matthews and the Cuban Story." Pamphlet by the Association for Education in Journalism, 1978.

Lazo, Mario. *Dagger in the Heart: American Policy Failures in Cuba*. New York: Funk and Wagnalls, 1968.

Leante, César. *Hemingway y la Revolucíon Cubana*. Madrid: Editorial Pliegos, 1992.

Llerena, Mario. *The Unsuspected Revolution: The Birth and Rise of Castroism.* Ithaca, N.Y.: Cornell University Press, 1978.

Lockwood, Lee. *Castro's Cuba, Cuba's Fidel.* Boulder: Westview Press, 1990 edition.

Lopez-Fresquet, Rufo. *My Fourteen Months with Castro.* Cleveland: World Publishing Co., 1966.

Marquez Sterling, Carlos. *Historia de Cuba: Desde Colon Hasta Castro.* New York: Las Americas Publishing Co., 1963.

Marton, Kati. *The Polk Conspiracy: Murder and Coverup in the Case of CBS News Correspondent George Polk.* New York: Farrar Strauss and Giroux, 1990.

Matthews, Herbert L. *Cuba.* London: Macmillan Co./Collier-Macmillan Limited, 1964.

————. *The Cuban Story.* New York: George Braziller, 1961.

————. *The Education of a Correspondent.* Westport, Conn.: Greenwood Press Publishers, 1970 edition.

————. *The Fruits of Fascism.* New York: Harcourt, Brace and Co., 1943.

————, ed. *The United States and Latin America.* Englewood Cliffs, N.J.: Prentice-Hall, 1963.

————. *The Yoke and the Arrows: A Report on Spain.* New York: George Braziller, 1961.

Matthews, Herbert L., with Nancie Matthews. *Assignment to Austerity.* Indianapolis: Bobbs-Merrill, 1950.

Matos, Huber. *Cómo Llegó la Noche.* Barcelona: Tusquets Editores S.A., 2002.

Moorehead, Caroline. *Gellhorn: A Twentieth-Century Life.* New York: Henry Holt and Co., 2003.

Paterson, Thomas G. *Contesting Castro: The United States and the Triumph of the Cuban Revolution.* New York: Oxford University Press, 1994.

Pérez-Stable, Marifeli. *The Cuban Revolution: Origins, Course, and Legacy.* New York: Oxford University Press, 1993.

Phillips, R. Hart. *Cuba: Island of Paradox.* New York: McDowell, Obolensky, 1959.

————. *The Cuban Dilemma.* New York: Ivan Obolensky, 1962.

Prochnau, William. *Once Upon a Distant War: Young War Correspondents and the Early Vietnam Battles.* New York: Times Books/Random House, 1995.

Ratliff, William E., ed. *The Selling of Fidel Castro: The Media and the Cuban Revolution.* New Brunswick, N.J.: Transaction Books, 1987.

Reed, John. *Ten Days That Shook the World.* New York: Penguin Books, 1966 edition.

Robinson, Eugene. *Last Dance in Havana: The Final Days of Fidel and the Start of the New Cuban Revolution.* New York: Free Press, 2004.

Salinger, Pierre. *With Kennedy.* Garden City, N.Y.: Doubleday and Co., 1966.

Schlesinger, Arthur M., Jr. *A Thousand Days: John F. Kennedy in the White House.* Boston: Houghton Mifflin Co., 1965.

Seelye, John. *War Games: Richard Harding Davis and the New Imperialism.* Amherst: University of Massachusetts Press, 2003.

Serfaty, Simon, ed. *The Media and Foreign Policy.* New York: St. Martin's Press, 1990.

Shnookal, Deborah, and Pedro Álvarez Tabío, eds. *Fidel: My Early Years.* Melbourne, Australia: Ocean Press, 1998.

Smith, Earl E.T. *The Fourth Floor: An Account of the Castro Communist Revolution.* New York: Random House, 1962.

Suchlicki, Jaime. *Cuba from Columbus to Castro and Beyond.* 5th ed. Washington, D.C.: Brassey's, 2002.

Sweig, Julia E. *Inside the Cuban Revolution: Fidel Castro and the Urban Underground.* Cambridge: Harvard University Press, 2002.

Szulc, Tad. *Fidel: A Critical Portrait.* New York: Avon Books, 1986.

Taber, Robert. *M-26: Biography of a Revolution.* New York: Lyle Stuart, 1961.

Taylor, S. J. *Stalin's Apologist: Walter Duranty, The New York Times's Man in Moscow.* New York: Oxford University Press, 1990.

Thomas, Hugh. *Cuba: The Pursuit of Freedom.* New York: Harper and Row, 1971.

Thomas, Hugh, with George A. Fauriol and Juan Carlos Weiss. *The Cuban Revolution, 25 Years Later.* Boulder: Westview Press, 1984.

Tifft, Susan E., and Alex S. Jones. *The Trust: The Private and Powerful Family Behind* The New York Times. New York: Little, Brown and Co., 1999.

Welch, Richard E., Jr. *Response to Revolution: The United States and the Cuban Revolution, 1959–1961.* Chapel Hill: University of North Carolina Press, 1985.

Weyl, Nathaniel. *Red Star over Cuba: The Russian Assault on the Western Hemisphere.* New York: Hillman/MacFadden, 1961.

PUBLICAFFAIRS is a publishing house founded in 1997. It is a tribute to the standards, values, and flair of three persons who have served as mentors to countless reporters, writers, editors, and book people of all kinds, including me.

I. F. STONE, proprietor of *I. F. Stone's Weekly*, combined a commitment to the First Amendment with entrepreneurial zeal and reporting skill and became one of the great independent journalists in American history. At the age of eighty, Izzy published *The Trial of Socrates*, which was a national bestseller. He wrote the book after he taught himself ancient Greek.

BENJAMIN C. BRADLEE was for nearly thirty years the charismatic editorial leader of *The Washington Post*. It was Ben who gave the *Post* the range and courage to pursue such historic issues as Watergate. He supported his reporters with a tenacity that made them fearless, and it is no accident that so many became authors of influential, best-selling books.

ROBERT L. BERNSTEIN, the chief executive of Random House for more than a quarter century, guided one of the nation's premier publishing houses. Bob was personally responsible for many books of political dissent and argument that challenged tyranny around the globe. He is also the founder and was the longtime chair of Human Rights Watch, one of the most respected human rights organizations in the world.

· · ·

For fifty years, the banner of Public Affairs Press was carried by its owner Morris B. Schnapper, who published Gandhi, Nasser, Toynbee, Truman, and about 1,500 other authors. In 1983 Schnapper was described by *The Washington Post* as "a redoubtable gadfly." His legacy will endure in the books to come.

Peter Osnos, *Founder and Editor-at-Large*